12 TIMES 12

12 TIMES 12

144 Sun/Ascendant Combinations

Joan
McEvers

ACS Publications, Inc.
San Diego, California

International Standard Book Number 0-917086-61-9

Cover Design by Larry Ortiz

Printed in the United States of America

Published by ACS Publications, Inc.
P.O. Box 16430
San Diego, CA 92116-0430

First Printing, May 1984
Second Printing, December 1984

DEDICATION

To Woody... who believes

Also By ACS Publications, Inc.

TABLE OF CONTENTS

FOREWORD

This is a **FUN** astrology book. A cookbook, if you will. I know that other astrologers do not always have very good things to say about the cookbook variety of astrology, but I feel it is a good starting place for the layman.

This book is for the person who has some interest in the art of astrology. And believe me, it is an art, as well as a science. I tell my students that astrology is "the art of observation." And that is what is in this book... my observations of astrological types. It is the accumulation of notes from my observations of friends, students, clients and family members. The charts of prominent people are there so that the reader will have someone to identify with.

There are several people I would like to thank for their invaluable help in putting this together. Lois Rodden, who supplied many birth data and with whom I agree, that all data should be listed and the source given. The sources in this book are, to my knowledge, valid and many times there were other data given for various people, but I chose the chart that I felt was the most fitting. Robert Jansky, who after looking at a rough draft, encouraged me to finish. And Marilyn Smith, who spent many long hours proofreading and correcting. I would like to express my appreciation to Maritha Pottenger for her expertise and dedication in editing this edition — also for her unstinting help and inspiration.

And above all, all those people whose astrological charts I have drawn my observations from.

I hope this book gives enjoyment to the seasoned astrologer, food for thought to the astrological student and that it will pique the curiosity of the casual reader.

INTRODUCTION

The average person usually knows his or her Sun sign which is based on the day of birth. But most people are unaware of the Moon, the eight planets and the **"Ascendant"** or rising sign which are so important in indicating how people express their personalities. This rising sign is based on the **time** of birth and must be taken from a properly calculated birth chart.

The Sun represents the soul (inner essence); the Ascendant is the chief expression of the personality (conduct, character and outer appearance). It is this distinction, more than any other, which separates **you** from all the other members of your particular Sun sign. Often people say that they do not believe in astrology because they can't see how all humans can be lumped into twelve groups, corresponding to the twelve Sun signs. And of course, they're right. ... people cannot be categorized into twelve stereotyped groups.

Since the Sun and Ascendant may appear in any of the twelve signs of the zodiac, there are one hundred and forty-four possible combinations. These can be likened to one hundred and forty-four windows through which the personality is expressed. The Ascendant colors the manifestation of the Sun sign. These combinations indicate a delicate shading to the character and individuality.

Of course, the Moon and planets, especially those which rule the Sun and Ascendant signs, give additional keys to the personality. A complete horoscope is very complicated, reflecting the complexities of the unique individual whom it mirrors. This combination of the Sun and Ascendant though, more than any other, shows your basic identity, what your physical appearance is like, what particular traits of character are stressed in your personality and your way of being and becoming in the world.

In this book each of the one hundred and forty-four combinations is examined and explored as to personality traits and vocational aptitudes with example charts of prominent people for illustration. In the beginning of each chapter, there is a brief summary of the usual traits, characteristics and appearance of each sign. Then each combination of the Sun expressing through that sign is discussed and illustrated. Combinations are further defined by the decanate of the Sun and Ascendant plus the house placement of the Sun. Decanates refer to which third of the sign is occupied by the Sun or Ascendant. There is a Decanate Table and a fuller discussion of the meaning of decanates in the Appendix at the back of this book. The Appendix also contains more detailed information about houses, the relationship of time of day to rising sign, and ruling planets.

CHAPTER ONE

ARIES ASCENDANT

You are a leader in thought and action and you desire and need to be at the head of whatever is going on. Most Aries are restless, impatient, generally aggressive and outgoing. You are at your best when actively engaged in some new enterprise. You act in a very direct and dynamic way. At some time in your life, you may engage in rash behavior which results in injuries to your head or face. This can be avoided by learning to temper your urgency to act. At times you appear hasty and headlong in your zest to throw yourself into things. You are really happiest when in a position to guide, control and govern yourself and others, as you have the ability to act decisively, map out the future and lay out methods of action.

Extroverted and headstrong, diplomacy is not generally one of your virtues. You can, in fact, turn others off with your often blunt and tactless approach. You are a self starter but may have trouble seeing your many starts through to a productive end. However, you are not easily discouraged and possess very strong will power, generally doing well in vocations requiring quick decisions, executive or mechanical ability, responsibility and physical activity.

Forcefully optimistic, expressive in speech, determined in effort, you are intense when interested and passionate when excited. Fearless, fiery, quick-tempered, resentful of abuse and imposition, you are liable to go to extremes of indignation; yet you do not hold a grudge for any length of time. You admire scientific and mechanical concepts and are often quite philosophical. You have no time for gossip, are rarely malicious or cruel and tend to lump all people into two groups: your friends or your enemies.

You have a strong constitution and can survive high fevers but are susceptible to headaches which could be related to kidney infections or feeling unable to freely express yourself. Impatient, waiting frustrates you and illness could result if you don't deal with your anger. Medication is not your thing and you will rarely have to worry about drug addiction as you usually won't even take aspirin or a sleeping pill. Until you develop patience and a more placid approach to life, you will tend to handle any health problems in the way you handle all problems... head-on.

Since Aries is the first sign of the zodiac, you want to be first in everything and this even carries over into your appearance. You seem to lean forward when you walk, as though you are in a hurry, as you often are. Your nose juts forward and your chin may recede a bit, adding to your anxious-to-get-going attitude. You are usually slim, but wiry, have sharp features, are somewhat muscular and average to tall in height. Your hair is plentiful, but men tend to have a bald spot in the front, or it could be referred to as a "high forehead." You have small eyes and are often farsighted, seeming to be peering into the distance. Your eyebrows are thick and bushy and unless you pluck them, they may grow together over the bridge of your nose. Because of your farsightedness, you may have two vertical lines between your eyes and as you get older there is a tendency to develop lines or ditches on either side of your mouth. Grace is usually not apparent and your movements are frequently quick and jerky.

Many of these characteristics apply to persons with the Sun in the 1st house, regardless of what sign the Sun is in or what sign is rising. When you channel your driving energy into positive action, you achieve your goals in short order and develop into a proven leader.

ARIES ASCENDANT — ARIES SUN

If you were born between March 21st and April 20th between approximately 5 AM and 7 AM, you may have this combination.

Always active and on the go, your extreme enthusiasm needs a constructive outlet or you can feel as trapped as a rat in a cage. With a 12th house Sun, it is especially important that you feel able to communicate your energy into the active creation of beauty: gymnastics, dance, skating, swimming... anything that relates to grace in movement. Your drive should be directed into a positive channel to avoid mental strain. You are emotionally intense because of the push/pull between the fire need to go **out** and the water need to turn **inward**. With the Sun in the 1st house, your vulnerability could be physical rather than mental. Don't overdo your desire for energetic, risky activities. If the first decanate is occupied by the Sun or Ascendant, your tendency to rush headlong into activity can cause you to be accident prone and you would be wise to look before your leap. Courage is your watchword. With the third or Sagittarian decanate rising or occupied by the Sun, you may adopt quite a philosophical outlook or be enamored of sports: the kind that require self-projection rather than the team variety.

Cale Yarborough
March 27, 1939
7:00 AM EST
Timmonsville, SC
34N08 79W57

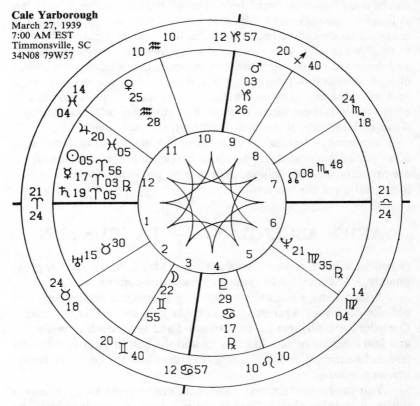

Source: Gauquelin (A)

Egotism is your biggest pitfall and you need an active outlet such as sports or some kind of creative challenge if you are to handle this positively. When the Leo decanate is occupied by either the Sun or Ascendant, you may find self-expression through acting, gambling, playing the stock market or in some kind of risk-taking sport such as motorcycle or car racing. Cale Yarborough, the race car driver, is a good example of the energy constructively channeled. He has a 12th house Aries Sun, Mercury and Saturn as well as Aries rising. Mercury rules his 3rd house of transportation and Mars, the ruler of all that Aries, squares the Sun indicating the drive to be daring and adventurous.

Energy is the keyword here. The position of Mars, the ruler of Aries, will denote how you expend your tremendous, dynamic, driving force. If Mars is in one of the fire signs (Aries, Leo, Sagittarius), you can be one of the most impulsive and competitive of people. When Mars is in an air sign (Gemini, Libra, Aquarius) your energy manifests in a mental mode and verbal communication of some kind will be your thing. "Me first" is your motto and you plunge headlong into schemes and dreams as you honestly believe you can do things better than anyone else. If Mars is in a passive sign (earth or water), your drive is subtle and less apparent to others, but it is still there. When it surfaces, it often astounds those who are unaware of your ability for quick action. Your endurance is also emphasized by these placements.

You **need** to feel that you are the leader in all your undertakings. Since you are very capable, when your boundless energy and enthusiasm are properly focused, this should cause no problems. Others are willing to follow a proven leader.

ARIES ASCENDANT — TAURUS SUN

If you were born between April 20th and May 20th between approximately 3 AM and 5 AM, you may have this combination.

Aries activity is somewhat tethered by Taurus practicality and given definite direction. Aggressive practicality epitomizes this placement. Consider actress/singer Barbra Streisand and her show business savvy and know-how. She has Aries rising and the Sun in Taurus in the 1st house. Leadership ability is strongly evident and she certainly knows her own mind.

You can be hesitant and undecided, drawn one way by Aries enthusiasm and the other by Taurus caution. But once you've pulled the two together, achievement is your keynote. If the Sagittarian decanate is on the Ascendant, you are farseeing yet practical; philosophical but down to earth and you accomplish your not inconsiderable goals with Aries directness and Taurus stick-to-itiveness. With the Leo decanate rising, you have great flair and this combined with a good voice can push you into the performing spotlight. The Aries decanate on your

Ascendant emphasizes a need for action.

Barbra Streisand
April 24, 1942
5:15 AM EWT
Brooklyn, NY
40N45 73W55

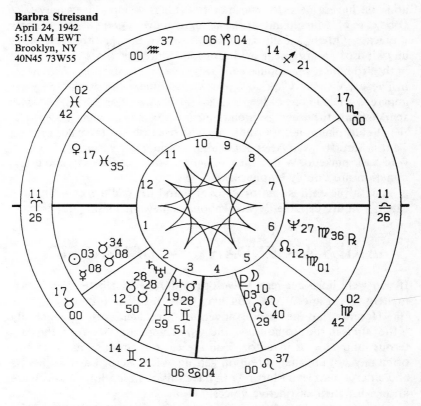

Source: Church of Light quotes "Predictions" August 1967 (B)

You are quite materially oriented, especially with the Sun in the Taurean decanate. This combination can symbolize the capable businessperson, the creative adaptor, the dependable boss or manager. Business success is emphasized as a potential with the Sun in the Capricorn decanate. The Sun in the Virgo decanate suggests a strong streak of practical realism. You are persistent, enthusiastic and determined, especially with the Aries decanate rising. Once you establish your goals, you are unstoppable. With the Sun in the 2nd house, you are very creative, often poetic or musical and you could be a composer as well as a fine instrumentalist. Taurus is very rhythmic and usually has a pleasant voice, so singing is often your avocation if it isn't your business. A 1st house Sun accentuates the theme of leadership and the pursuit of the good things in life.

With Mars in Cancer, Scorpio or Pisces, security is emphasized and you have a need to own material things which you usually take good care of. Mars in any of the air signs shows a good ability to communicate. Others usually don't want to take Barbra Streisand on in any kind of an argument or discussion. Since her Mars is in Gemini in the 3rd house, she applies her energy to communication. With Mars in Taurus, Virgo or Capricorn (earth), steadiness and productivity are apparent. Mars in one of the fire signs (Aries, Leo, Sagittarius) indicates sparks within the otherwise stolid Sun and you may be quite a go-getter.

Venus plays an important role here because it is the ruler of your Taurus Sun. If it is in Aries or Gemini, considerable versatility is within your basic makeup. With Venus in Taurus, your steadfastness and determination are doubly emphasized.

With the enthusiasm of Aries fire and the endurance of Taurus earth, you are capable of tremendous achievements on your terms.

ARIES ASCENDANT — GEMINI SUN

If you were born between May 20th and June 21st between approximately 1 AM and 3 AM, you may have this combination.

Here we find the dashing adventurer or adventuress — especially if the Sun is in the 3rd house — the witty entertainer or writer, the dexterous innovator or inventor. You are curious, mobile, aspiring and often have an unusual, attention getting voice. Actor Basil Rathbone and entertainer Dean Martin both have this combination and both are known for their distinctive voices.

Nervous energy seems to accompany this placement; the fiery Aries drive is dissipated somewhat by Gemini's versatility. Fidgety, restless, one foot always out the door, when someone says, "Let's go," you say, "Where?" and without even waiting for an answer, you're off. The pitfall here is having too many irons in the fire (especially with the Aries or Sagittarius decanate on the Ascendant) allowing none of them long enough time to heat up and leave a lasting impression. With the Leo decanate rising, you have an aristocratic air, sometimes appearing to border on hauteur, but beneath your somewhat arrogant exterior, you have insatiable intellectual curiosity. You need to know something about everything but do not necessarily want to spend too much time learning it.

Naturally, the position of Mercury is an important key to this combination since it rules your Gemini Sun. If it is in Taurus or Cancer, there is a counterbalance to some of the extreme restlessness of the

Aries/Gemini union within you. But if Mercury, or Mars (your Ascendant ruler) is also in Gemini, changeability and scatteredness are more noticeable. You are likely to jump from one activity to another and may have trouble seeing things through.

Dean Martin
June 17, 1917
11:55 PM CST
Steubenville, OH
40N22 80W37

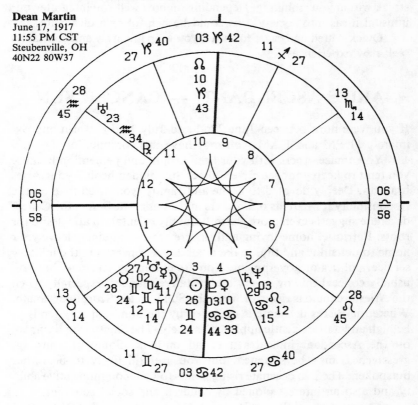

Source: Gauquelin (A)

With the Sun in the 3rd house, writing and acting may appeal to you, also any field that demands physical dexterity and constant motion... auto racing, dancing, mechanics, sports. The Sun in the 2nd house symbolizes ability with mathematics and money management and handling, so you would be an excellent auditor, bookkeeper, receptionist or bank teller. This combination is one of the best in the zodiac for direct sales ability. But no matter which house the Sun is in, you need a field in which you are not tied down to routine hours and boring details.

Insatiable curiosity is likely to be even more central in your nature when the Sun occupies the first (Gemini) decanate. The second (Libra) decanate symbolizes tremendous sociability; you are likely to know almost everyone and have something to say to all of them. The third (Aquarian) decanate for the Sun suggests an original and inventive streak within your thinking. Depending on how well you integrate your unusual ideas into society, this could be helpful or a disadvantage.

Quick-witted and eager to travel, you keep life lively and constantly seek new experiences.

ARIES ASCENDANT — CANCER SUN

If you were born between June 22nd and July 23rd between approximately 11 PM and 1 AM, you may have this combination.

You amaze others with your keen insight and perception because you tend to keep your sensitive Cancer Sun hidden behind your Aries bravado. Deeply devoted to home and family, you often take on the responsibility for parents or brothers and sisters. The Sun in the Cancer decanate suggests even more warmth, family orientation and desire for roots. Patriotic, home-loving and sincere, you will quickly leave your home to defend it and thus make a good career person in the military service, politics or government. You are extremely sensitive, but you usually conceal this by a very authoritative manner, especially when the Aries decanate is rising or when the Sun is in the Scorpio decanate. Where the Pisces decanate is occupied by the Sun, empathy tends to be high and a more gentle approach is likely. The Sagittarian decanate on the Ascendant indicates a broad outlook. Some of your aggressiveness may be softened, but you are still likely to be rather outspoken. The Leo decanate rising points to your communicative ability and also an interest piqued by children and social activities.

You are potentially the businessperson *extraordinaire* with a sure touch for money making. Mining, geology and related earth sciences could appeal to you if your Sun is in the 4th house. With the Sun in the 3rd house, you could be the outgoing salesperson with your finger on the public's pulse, the careful auto mechanic, the bus or taxicab driver who is a folksy and entertaining conversationalist. The Sun in the Scorpio decanate suggests a penetrating approach and understanding of people's deeper motivations. Where the Pisces decanate is occupied by the Sun, sensitivity and empathy is highly apparent.

Industrialist and philanthropist, John D. Rockefeller had this combination of Cancer Sun with Aries rising and he used his organizational skills to build an empire.

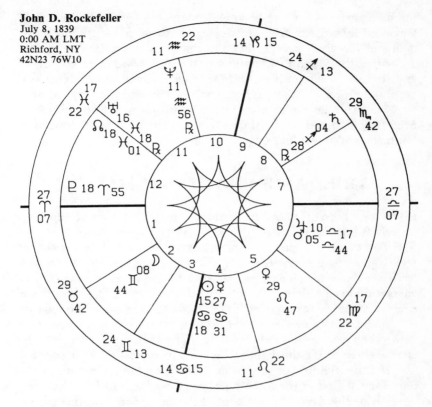

John D. Rockefeller
July 8, 1839
0:00 AM LMT
Richford, NY
42N23 76W10

Source: *Sabian Symbols* #799 (DD)

You tend to think in terms of "I" or "me" and you can, if you allow this habit to go unchecked, be the extreme egotist. Conflict between the freedom needs of Aries and the homey needs of Cancer may cause you as a child to cling closely to your parental home, but when you reach adolescence, you astonish your family by your eagerness to get out into the world. Once you establish yourself in business, the arts or a profession, success seems to come readily to you and you bask in its reflected glory.

If the Moon (ruler of Cancer) or Mars (your Ascendant ruler) is in an earth sign (Taurus, Virgo, Capricorn) you are shrewd with your money and a good investor and moneymaker in sales, particularly real estate, commodities and home furnishings. When the Moon or Mars is in a fire sign (Aries, Leo or Sagittarius), you may come across as bold, daring and venturesome and it is only those who know you intimately who are aware of your tenderness. With either planet in Gemini, Libra or Aquarius (air signs) your social consciousness is evident and you are friendly, witty and charming. With the Cancer Sun and either the Moon or Mars in a water sign, you are very intuitive and you have a sure instinct for business and financial investing. You are usually very attached to home and family and are very caring.

Once you have integrated your need for independence with your need for emotional ties, you devote great energy to both close commitments and individual self-expression.

ARIES ASCENDANT — LEO SUN

If you were born between July 23rd and August 23rd between approximately 9 PM and 11 PM, you may have this combination.

You often have an aristocratic bearing and are at times, almost regal. Aggressive, optimistic and outgoing, you radiate charm and leadership. Given a choice, you always lead and never follow. Active, energetic and ambitious, you are often interested in sports, though not necessarily of the team variety unless you can be captain. You are an individualist and prefer to achieve on your own rather than be involved with group activities. Golf, bowling and swimming afford you the chance to be in the limelight while you are expressing your talents.

If either the first or second decanate is on the Ascendant or the Sun is in the first or third decanate, you have the principle of double Aries or double Leo, which is a lot of dynamic energy for one person to handle. All your enthusiasm and drive must be constructively directed. A client with this combination has been undergoing psychiatric counseling for child abuse. It was difficult for him to restrain himself when his children acted normally boisterous. He expected his children to be paragons of virtue. When they acted like normal children, he became abusive. He needed more realistic attitudes about children and a positive channel (sports, competitive games, business) for his fiery aggression.

The Sagittarius decanate rising or occupied by the Sun suggests a sense of adventure and often indicates a devil-may-care attitude. Princess Margaret Rose of England epitomizes this dynamic combination. Her Sun in the 6th house shows her sense of duty, but with the Aries Ascendant and Uranus, the planet of independence in the 1st house, she finds the duty trip a difficult one.

If Mars is in a fire sign (Aries, Leo, Sagittarius) you may need to curb a tendency to lord it over others. Usually kindhearted and very creative, you must avoid pomposity and an overbearing manner.

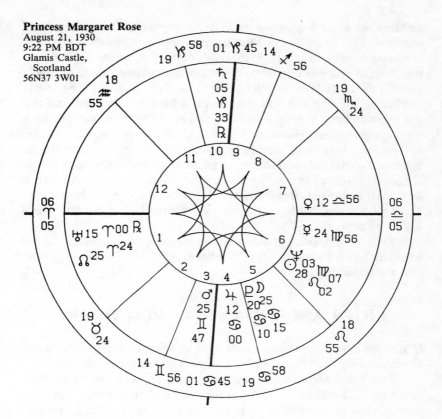

Princess Margaret Rose
August 21, 1930
9:22 PM BDT
Glamis Castle,
  Scotland
56N37 3W01

Source: R.H. Oliver quotes *NAJ* July-Augusty 1958 (B)

Because you are very capable yourself, especially with Mars in an earth sign (Taurus, Virgo, Capricorn), you expect others to perform as well as you do. This can lead to a demanding, competitive attitude. When others do not or cannot live up to your expectations, you may arrogantly turn away from them, leaving them bewildered at your sudden cold shoulder. This is a strong potential when Mars in in Cancer, Scorpio or Pisces — sensitive, self-protective placements. Your feelings are deep and you instinctively resist revealing too much vulnerability. With Mars in air signs (Gemini, Libra, Aquarius), you have been known to rush in where angels fear to tread, but because of your fearless spirit, things usually work out well for you. Your quick wits also help extricate you from sticky situations.

With a 5th house Sun, you could pioneer in the creative art and music fields. With Mercury in Leo coaching, teaching and counseling children are good areas once you learn compassion and understanding. With a 4th house Sun or Mercury in Cancer, you express well socially and could achieve success in the fields of home decorating and building. With Mercury in Virgo, you might consider architecture or drafting.

If the Sun falls in the 6th house, some Virgo qualities are present in your personality and you may find it a bit easier to handle all the fire in your chart. You may do well in an area where you can perform a service for others. However, this should be a service where you can rely on your own individuality and initiative, rather than bowing to another's commands and desires. Knuckling under to someone else is almost impossible for you. You, of all Aries Ascendants would rather boss than be bossed. Regardless of the house your Sun is in or what decanate is rising, with your sunny, outgoing disposition, you are a joy to be around.

Vivacious, charming, active and expressive, you sometimes overwhelm others with your energy, but they usually adore your dynamism and excitement.

ARIES ASCENDANT — VIRGO SUN

If you were born between August 23rd and September 23rd between approximately 7 PM and 9 PM, you may have this combination.

This combination can work well together, with the Virgo particularity toning down Aries' usual headlong rush into things. Together they achieve thoroughness in action. You like to get things accomplished, but will take the time to give attention to details which is not generally an Aries trait. Sometimes though, this pairing of signs does not work so well and you may find yourself pulled between practicality and exuberance. Always interested in new ideas, you want to know how and why they work, especially if you have the Sagittarius decanate on the Ascendant. You are willing to spend time and effort seeking new methods and avenues of self-expression.

Though at times you seem careless and offhanded, especially with the first decanate rising, your Aries Ascendant is masking a very fastidious Sun and you are, in reality, very discriminating and conscientious. Energetic, ambitious and painstaking, this combination works well when you are in a position to render some unique service to mankind. Jack Valenti renders a unique service to the movie industry with his 6th house Virgo Sun. Mars, ruler of his Ascendant, is in Leo in the 5th house which relates to drama and acting. He acts as a watchdog for the film industry.

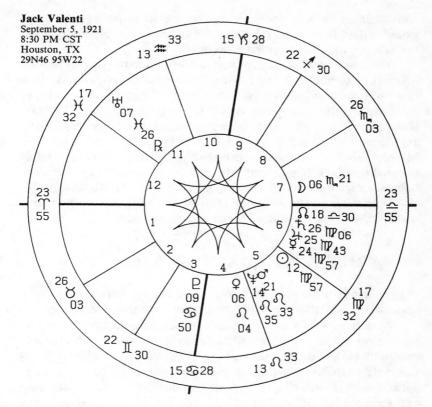

Jack Valenti
September 5, 1921
8:30 PM CST
Houston, TX
29N46 95W22

Source: Gauquelin (A)

A 5th house Sun often indicates musical ability and the patience to learn to play an instrument well; and the Aries inventiveness can symbolize a composer, orchestrator or arranger. This is also true with the Leo decanate rising which indicates a need to perform or the Sun in the Taurus decanate which symbolizes potential musical ability or other artistic talent. The Sun in the 6th house suggests an interest in diet, hygiene and nursing and can be the position of the doctor, surgeon or veterinarian. This is also an excellent potential for those with the Sun in the first (Virgo) decanate. These placements may show ability in food and commodity marketing. With typical Virgo attention to detail and Aries drive, you are a very good businessperson. Proper care should be given to your diet with this house placement as you could be prone to ulcers and bilious headaches. You need to take time with your meals and not rush through them or eat on the run if you would avoid this.

Satisfaction with your work will also contribute to good health. You would rather own the business than be an employee, especially when the Sun occupies the Capricorn decanate.

The position of Mercury, as well as Mars, is very important because Mercury rules your Sun sign. When Mercury is in Leo, or if Mars is in a fire sign, it indicates a dramatic flair that Virgo does not always have and certainly can make use of. If Mercury is in Libra, or Mars is in an air sign, you are more socially oriented than the average Virgo and with your Aries drive you can be a social leader or arbiter. When Mercury is in Virgo, or Mars is in an earth sign, your ability to be selective and tasteful is highlighted. Mercury or Mars in a water sign symbolizes a caring approach which can help to get the job done well.

With the great energy of Aries firing the careful, predictable engine of Virgo, you are capable of much accomplishment.

ARIES ASCENDANT — LIBRA SUN

If you were born between September 23rd and October 24th between approximately 5 PM and 7 PM, you may have this combination.

Argument is your **piece de resistance**. The polished argument and persuasion of the politician and tactician shows strongly here, especially with the Sun occupying its own (Libra) decanate. The Leo or Sagittarian decanate rising highlights your charm and you come across as sociable and entertaining on the positive side, with much to say on a variety of subjects. If used negatively, you may try to monopolize any conversation and others may find you a crashing bore. The Gemini decanate for your Sun also can indicate a very talkative individual — as well as versatile and multi-talented. There might be an element of risk involved with your career as with Eddie Rickenbacker. He was a race car driver before he became a World War I flying ace and he demonstrated his Aries vitality by surviving for three weeks on a raft in the Pacific Ocean after his plane was downed in the second World War.

If Mars is in a fire sign or if the first decanate is rising, you may tend to be a bit foolhardy and need to learn to think before you take off in several directions at once. But your courage is unquestioned. Mars in an earth sign indicates more direction for your energy and you are capable of prodigious feats. Mars in an air sign underlines your verbal facility. You are likely to be quite articulate, using words skillfully, a good devil's advocate. Where Mars occupies a water sign, you are likely to be more subtle in your approach to life, a good diplomat, able

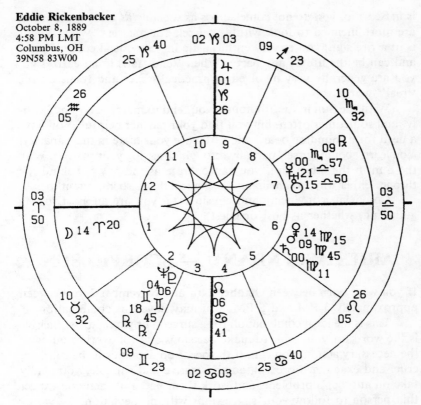

Eddie Rickenbacker
October 8, 1889
4:58 PM LMT
Columbus, OH
39N58 83W00

Source: Colonel Frank Noyes quotes his mother, given in *AA* April 1968 (DD)

to go around obstacles rather than meeting them head-on.

You are well able to present your rather original views in an acceptable and agreeable way, especially with the Sun in the Aquarian decanate. Thus often you are an outstanding lawyer, judge or wise leader in government circles. Influential, forceful and cultured, you generally manage to have your own way, frequently overriding objections with sheer charm and persuasiveness. You deal well with others on a face-to-face basis and usually are found in a position of authority. Somehow on an inner level, there is conflict between the loner side symbolized by Aries and the partner side symbolized by Libra and you may be at odds with yourself though you rarely, if ever, let others know of this inner unrest.

Venus, the planet that rules your Sun assumes importance in this pairing. If Venus is in Libra, you are very socially oriented; if Venus is in Scorpio, you do not come across as sociably as most Librans but are more inclined to look within yourself for answers. When Venus is in a fire sign, you're very enthusiastic in your social commitments and can be the life of any party. When Venus falls in an earth sign, you are generally very involved in practical issues and focus on the "real" world.

With the Sun in the 7th house, you tend to marry early and hastily, and sometimes often, but you find your partner helpful. You have a need for a sounding board and often use your mate in this capacity. You learn about yourself partially through observing your partner. With the Sun in the 6th house, you can operate as the power behind the throne. Either way, you maintain the control that is so important to you.

Convivial, convincing and considerate, you are an asset to any gathering, whether as host or guest.

ARIES ASCENDANT — SCORPIO SUN

If you were born between October 24th and November 23rd between approximately 3 PM and 5 PM, you may have this combination.

This is the ideal combination for a surgeon or psychiatrist. Incisive is the word for you. Able to make decisions and follow through with the necessary action, you can, if the occasion demands it, be ruthless, cruel and exacting. Forceful, administrative and capable, you gladly take on another's problems and work them out. But then you expect that person to follow your suggestions with no deviation.

You are very perceptive, supportive and creative, but your emotions tend to be violent and need constant and watchful monitoring. The more control you exercise, the more likely there will be periodic explosions. You need to learn to express easily and comfortably before issues build up inside. With the Moon, the planet that symbolizes the emotions, in an expressive fire (Aries, Leo or Sagittarius) or air sign (Gemini, Libra, Aquarius), more spontaneity is likely. Where the Moon is in a water (Cancer, Scorpio, Pisces) or an earth sign (Taurus, Virgo, Capricorn), your feelings are still deep, but less easily shared. You do become emotionally involved in everything you do and burn with the intense fire of the zealot. Nothing is too difficult for you to attempt. The harder the challenge, the more daring you are. Indeed, you are capable of moving mountains.

You are quite materially oriented especially with the Sun in the Cancer or Scorpio decanates. This combination can symbolize the capable businessperson, the creative adaptor, the dependable boss or manager. You are persistent, enthusiastic and determined, especially with the Aries decanate rising. Once you establish your goals, you are unstoppable. With the Sun in the 2nd house, you are very creative, often poetic or musical and you could be a composer as well as a fine instrumentalist. Taurus is very rhythmic and usually has a pleasant voice, so singing is often your avocation if it isn't your business. Musical or other artistic talent is even more likely with the Sun in the second (Pisces) decanate. A 1st house Sun accentuates the theme of leadership and the pursuit of the good things in life.

Joseph McCarthy
November 14, 1908
3:00 PM CST
Grand Chute, WI
44N22 88W24

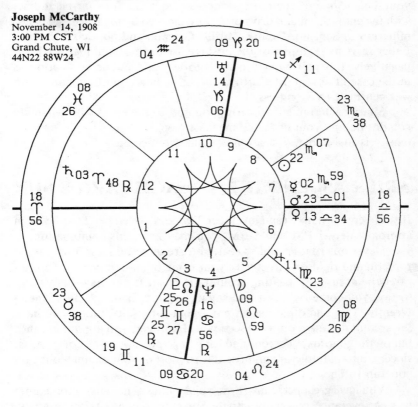

Source: R.H. Oliver (B)

If Mars and Pluto, your rulers, are in earth or air signs, it may be easier for you to find a constructive outlet for all your drive and energy. You need to channel your energy into productive accomplishments or mental keenness and intellectual pursuits. Mars or Pluto in fire or water signs symbolizes even more intense emotionality which needs an arena for exciting, vital activity. If you do not handle the issues of these planets in an affirmative way, much of your attention will have to be given to dealing with a tendency to violence and uncontrollable passions.

The first or third decanate rising or the Sun in the 7th house could denote a position in politics, law enforcement or counseling. The Sun in the 8th house, especially with the Aries decanate rising, indicates ability in finance as well as the medical fields. When the second (Leo) decanate is on the Ascendant, the stock market or sports may attract you. This is one of the most pioneering combinations in the zodiac, with the enthusiasm and drive of Aries enhanced by the force and determination of Scorpio. Evangelist Billy Graham and politician Howard Baker serve as examples of the positive use of this combination. Used negatively, this pairing can bring notoriety and public vilification as in the case of Joseph McCarthy, the communist hunting senator who was censured by Congress.

Sharp, determined, forceful, you go "to the end" with whatever you do; be sure your ends and means are positive. Your emotional intensity is incredible; you are not a halfway person.

ARIES ASCENDANT — SAGITTARIUS SUN

If you were born between November 23rd and December 22nd between approximately 1 PM and 3 PM, you may have this combination.

Never one to take a back seat, you are direct, honest, outspoken, forceful and right on target with your often blunt comments. You can rarely be accused of beating around the bush. If you have something to say, you come right out and say it... good, bad, but never indifferently. Tact and diplomacy are not your long suits, unless you have the second decanate on the Ascendant. However, you are not unkind, but on the contrary, generous and forgiving. You are naive, courageous, sincere, intrepid, tolerant and friendly so most of your companions find you fun to be with.

You have great personal warmth and enthusiasm but you sometimes lack perseverance, especially with the Sun in the second (Aries) decanate. Fond of travel, if you are unable to actually get on a plane or train, you console yourself with the armchair variety, imagining yourself leading the "Charge of the Light Brigade" or climbing the Alps with Hannibal. Your interests are greatly diversified; you are an entertaining speaker on a wide variety of subjects. With the first (Aries) or third (Sagittarius) decanate on the Ascendant, you could be attracted to the sports field. If the Leo decanate is involved with either the Sun or Ascendant, you may find yourself in the entertainment field ala Bette Midler or Sammy Davis, Jr. Midler has the Sun in the 8th house and exudes a certain sexuality — not uncommon with an eighth house focus. Mars, her Ascendant ruler, is in Leo symbolizing her dramatic flair.

Bette Midler
December 1, 1945
2:19 PM HST Zone 10.5
Honolulu, Hawaii
21N19 157W52

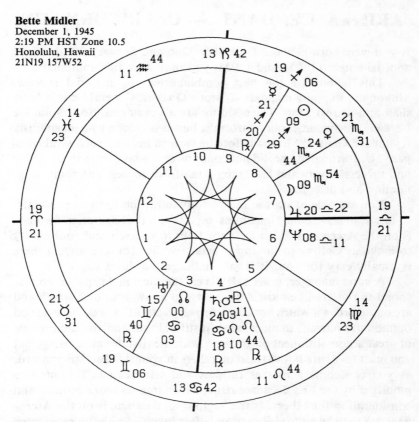

Source: *Contemporary Sidereal Horoscopes* (A)

With a 9th house Sun, you are usually generous with funds and advice, philosophical and very often religiously oriented. This is also likely when the Sun occupies the first (Sagittarius) decanate. You sometimes have a tendency to rush blindly into things and can get quite carried away with causes and crusades without investigating them thoroughly and thus you can be quite gullible and on occasion, deceived by supposedly well meaning friends and acquaintances.

Teaching, writing and lecturing all have appeal and you have a great regard for the law, often functioning in some type of law enforcement field, especially when the Sun is in the 8th house.

Vibrant, exciting, living life fully, your zest and enthusiasm easily rub off on others.

ARIES ASCENDANT — CAPRICORN SUN

If you were born between December 22nd and January 21st between approximately 11 AM and 1 PM, you may have this combination.

This is one of the best combinations for material success. Millionaire shipping magnate Aristotle Onassis, General George Marshall and actress Mary Tyler Moore are all examples. So is John De Lorean, the dynamic, nonconformist business tycoon who ingeniously revitalized General Motors before he formed his own successful company. Unfortunately, he did not continue to use his energy in a positive and successful way and has taken a fall from success and fame to ignominy and disgrace.

You are able to start at the bottom and climb to the top, usually so fast as to leave others breathless, especially if the Sagittarian decanate is on the Ascendant, denoting your faith in yourself and your ability to make it. Getting to the top is what you live for and staying there is usually easy for you. It is the challenge that lures you.

A good manager, practical, clever, skeptical and capable, you respond to flattery like most Aries, but you know your own worth and are out to prove it which are Capricorn characteristics. You have a good opinion of yourself, in most cases, justifiably so, and you are capable of great accomplishment particularly with the first decanate rising. But you must take care not to tread on others in your steady climb upward, as you can come across as ruthless and self-seeking. This may be modified by the Leo decanate rising which implies more warmth and consideration for others. If the Sagittarian decanate is on the Ascendant, you can be quite visionary and often involved with future oriented businesses.

Unbending and unyielding on the personal, emotional level, you may find that life at the top is lonely. Though sensitive, you may feel it is weak to let it show and thus others can find you cold and unfeeling, concerned only with achievement and organization, which is where you really shine. This is particularly likely when your Sun occupies the first decanate. The Moon in an earth or water sign shows a softer side which may lead you into service fields like the pioneering nurse, Clara Barton. The Sun in the Virgo decanate can also symbolize an orientation toward service.

Saturn is your Sun sign ruler and its placement in the chart assumes great importance. If it is in an earth or fire sign, you may be quite materially oriented and totally concerned with success. If it is placed in a water sign, you seem much softer in personality, but this may be the reflection of the iron hand in the velvet glove. No one should underestimate your need to succeed. When Saturn is in an air sign, you have the ability to communicate in concise and direct ways and find it easy to get your point across to others.

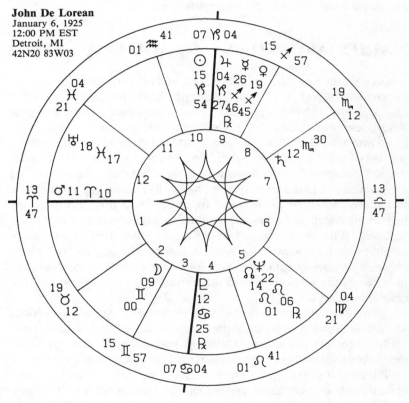

John De Lorean
January 6, 1925
12:00 PM EST
Detroit, MI
42N20 83W03

Source: Gauquelin (A)

With a 9th house Sun, law, finance and big business are good areas for you, as are science and research and any field that involves you in some sort of travel. The Sun in the Taurus decanate also repeats the theme of a financial field or material focus. The Sun in the 10th house corresponds to the ambitious, often merciless business tycoon or politician who stops at nothing to reach his goals but sometimes finds he has won a hollow victory. Organization is your keynote and you energetically fight your way to the top where you function best in the role of capable leadership.

You are blending self will (Aries) with the rules of the game (Capricorn) and what is possible in society. Negative blends are uncomfortable for you (ill, frustrated, feeling blocked) and/or for other people (whom you might step on in your move up in the world). Positive blends mean that you do all you can do, within the realistic limits of our physical world and societal regulations.

ARIES ASCENDANT — AQUARIUS SUN

If you were born between January 21st and February 20th between approximately 9 AM and 11 AM, you may have this combination.

Mentally and physically adventurous, you dare anything — new fields, new people, new challenges. Detached, cool and philosophical (even more so than other Aquarians), you are inclined to hold yourself somewhat aloof from those whom you consider the common people. A good example of this is General Douglas MacArthur. Respected and a great achiever in the military field, he hardly engendered warmth and friendliness in either his personal or professional life. Saturn is just behind his Ascendant and further indicates his potential austerity and coldness. With the arrogant Leo decanate rising, there is even more emphasis on the Aquarian Sun and it is in its own house, the 11th, which suggests even more detachment. With Uranus, the ruler of Aquarius in Virgo in the service-oriented 6th house, you can see how well the chart fits the man.

You know your weaknesses and in typically Aquarian fashion, work to improve them by education, question asking and reading, especially if Mercury (the planet that shows your reasoning capacity) is in either Aquarius or Capricorn. If Mercury is in Pisces, you seem to pick up information through a process of osmosis. You set great store by mental qualities, philosophy and learning and do not relate well to those who do not. Therefore you make every effort to communicate your philosophical ideas to others, as does evangelist, Oral Roberts who has this combination. You have very definite ideas whatever your field and you do not respond well when these ideas are challenged. If the Sagittarius decanate is on the Ascendant, you may even be considered dogmatic and unapproachable by those who don't know you well. Whatever your field, it embraces large groups of people and you pioneer new methods and ideas, especially when the Aries decanate rises.

The Sun in the 11th house or in the third (Libra) decanate may correspond to government service in some capacity, from serving in the armed forces to working for the post office. The Sun in the 10th house suggests a career in politics, social service or charitable work of some kind. Socially secure, you maintain your own standards which are quite unique and you may at times, seem austere and unapproachable. In fact with the Sun in the 11th house, you are often the loner who enjoys going your own way in the face of society's expectations.

Douglas MacArthur
January 26, 1880
10:13 AM LMT
Little Rock, AR
34N45 92W16

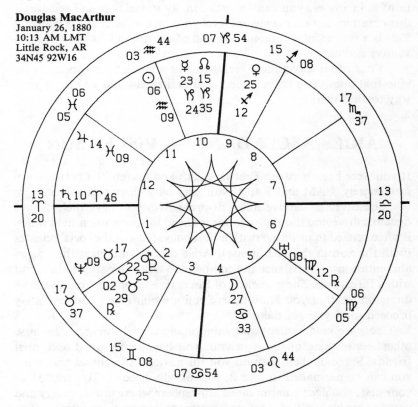

Source: Church of Light "rectified by Williams" (DD)

The Sun in the first decanate (Aquarius) denotes a great capacity to skim the surface, picking up bits of vital information from here and there. The Sun in the third decanate (Libra) usually corresponds with a bit more personal warmth and concern for the relationships with other people. But it can also be highly competitive.

The planet Uranus, your Sun ruler, is a key here and the house and the sign it is in may indicate a field of interest. If it is in an air or fire sign or house, it seems to emphasize your independent nature and desire for variety. If Uranus is in earth or water by sign or house, material goods are more important to you and you know how to focus your energies into a societally approved outlet.

Your insatiable curiosity often drives you to unlimited self-education; you have a constant need to learn especially with the Sun in the Gemini decanate. Unless Venus (the planet of love and affection) is in Pisces, you can be emotionally unyielding and seemingly disinterested, but on the mental level you can engender much warmth. This is a very mental combination and often symbolizes literary or inventive genius.

Your life is a continual seeking of new challenges, especially intellectual ones. You crave variety and excitement and go out of your way to find them.

ARIES ASCENDANT — PISCES SUN

If you were born between February 20th and March 21st between approximately 7 AM and 9 AM, you may have this combination.

Sensitive, perceptive and self-protective, you nevertheless have dynamic drive and the ability to forge ahead in your chosen field which is often related to medicine (with a 12th house Sun) or the social sciences (with the Sun in the 11th house). Aries rising symbolizes the energy and enthusiasm to balance the compassion and sympathy so inherent with a Pisces Sun. The gentleness of Pisces benefits much from the Aries direction, so that you know where you are going and you resolutely proceed until you get there.

You are kind, ardent and emotionally straightforward. Because others sense these qualities in you, you have many good and loyal friends. Some of them lean on you for advice and counsel and when you can be persuaded to give it, it is usually heeded. To function at your best, you need a harmonious atmosphere where music, poetry and dancing are highlighted if not as a career, at least as an avocation. You may be subject to emotional mood swings, due to the fiery Aries versus watery Pisces. You may be up with the fire, down with the water side of your nature, until you learn to balance expression and holding back; optimism and pessimism.

This combination often indicates the super athlete, especially when the Sun is in the 11th house or the Aries or Sagittarius decanate is on the Ascendant. This is the one Aries rising where drugs and alcohol can be problem areas. Drugs or alcohol may be used as an escape, to run away from life. Or, when this combination is improperly used, your attitude could surface as, "If I can't do it my way, I won't play." There is the possibility of confinement at sometime in the life with the Sun in the 12th house, if you are not using the energy in a positive way. However, this placement of the Sun usually shows great inner strength which can be called on when the need arises.

Jim Backus
February 25, 1913
7:30 AM CST
Cleveland, OH
41N29 81W42

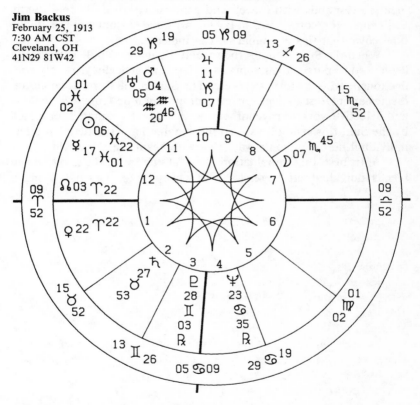

Source: *Contemporary Sidereal Horoscopes* (A)

Neptune is very important in the assessment of this combination because it rules the Sun sign. With Neptune in Gemini or Libra, there is a tendency to let tomorrow take care of itself. The creative imagination is usually strong, with the potential of a good blend of the rational and idealistic. Excessive romanticism in personal relationships is a danger to be resisted with Neptune in Libra. When Neptune is in Cancer or Scorpio, your intuition and perception are often strong and you may surprise yourself with your accurate hunches. If Neptune is in Leo or Sagittarius, it suggests some dramatic ability which can be used to act, sell or teach. Neptune in Virgo and Capricorn symbolize feet on the ground which can stabilize the Aries drive and Pisces imagination and provide some direction.

With the Sun in the 12th house, or the Leo decanate rising, there is often an interest in the performing arts and many times this placement corresponds with a deep and compelling voice. Singer Johnny Cash and actor/comedian Jim Backus are good examples of the unique type voice that this combination can indicate.

When the Sun occupies the second decanate, people often feel a deep need to pursue their roots — in terms of genealogy, family connections, saving historic sites, etc. The Sun in the third decanate indicates an interest in depth investigation: anything from archaeology and detective work to psychotherapy. If the first decanate is occupied by the Sun, this symbolizes even more potential aesthetic talent. The individual needs, in some way, to create beauty in the world.

At its best, this combination feels "at one" with the universe and blends individual self-expression with sensitivity for the whole cosmos.

CHAPTER TWO

TAURUS ASCENDANT

Pleasant, easygoing, accepting, and likable, people find it easy to be with you because you can be so relaxed and undemanding. Known for your stability and dependability, others are assured that when you say you will do something, you will — no matter what. Fond of material pleasures, you are often eager to share indulgences with others.

People may see you as somewhat slow, if not actually physically slow moving, at least deliberate in your thinking. You may appear phlegmatic, stolid and firm and are often known as the "strong, silent" type. But you are, in reality, acutely sensitive with deep, strong feelings that you protect with a deep reserve or occasional belligerence.

Of all the Ascendants in the zodiac, you respond most to gentleness and affection. You prefer life to be comfortable and harmonious. You may ignore potential trouble and hope it goes away. Your emotions are powerful and you have a profound need for security, both emotional and physical. You tend to throw yourself emotionally into your work, which is often creative or financial.

You are persistently loyal in your devotion, once given, whether to a person or an idea, deserving or not. If hurt, you tend to simply ignore who or whatever has caused the problem and rather than hate, you become somewhat unforgiving and resentful. You may deliberately avoid personal commitments at times, perhaps after early hurts. Dependable, responsible, hardworking, wholeheartedly responsive, you are often bullheaded and do not enjoy opposition.

Taurus is persevering, creative, artistic, domestic and usually musical. Pleasure-loving, even self-indulgent, you are nonetheless, practical; you plan ahead carefully and once your ideas are formulated, you are not easily swayed. You seldom go where you don't want to go or do what you don't want to do. When urged or cajoled, you can just fold your arms, dig in your heels and stay put.

You prefer to learn at your own pace. When pushed, you can become nervous and irritable and at times, physically ill. For you, the best bet is a steady, regular schedule. Once you grasp a concept and thoroughly understand it, it is yours forever and you can enlarge upon it and share it with others. If your Sun sign ruler or Venus are poorly placed (showing the potential of low self-esteem), you can be the most negative and pessimistic of all the signs, looking at the dark side of things and operating as if a little black cloud is following you around. You must remember to enjoy life and appreciate yourself even when not totally comfortable. When accepting of yourself, you can be most tractable and willingly responsive. You seldom worry, fret or chew your nails and are not generally the nervous, twitchy type unless your Sun sign suggests some irritability. You take things pretty well in stride and are rarely moved to sudden action.

Taurus rising women can be the most talkative of all the signs, seeking a sense of security through charming others, while the men can be just the opposite. They may need to be conversationally prodded since they tend to equate security with strength and silence in traditional male roles. Taurus is one of the square signs in appearance having a broad physical structure. It is the sign of great beauty, being ruled by Venus. You are usually short and often stocky, unless Venus is in a tall sign such as Gemini or Sagittarius. Your chin is often round; you may have dimples and almost always have regular, symmetrical features with prominent, round eyes, luxurious hair and small ears. You tend to have a short neck and powerful shoulders, frequently giving you the appearance of a bull. You may have a separation between your two front teeth and your teeth are usually small, white and even. You generally take great care of and pride in your appearance, trying always to dress in the latest style.

Usually healthy with a strong constitution, it takes a lot to get you down, but once down, you may not recuperate too rapidly. Often this is due to your stubborn refusal to do what the doctor says. Your cold can turn into a sore throat, laryngitis or tonsillitis. The throat is your most vulnerable area. Throat problems are a clue that you may be overdoing or under satisfying your need for pleasure. You love to eat and must take care not to overdo on rich foods or you may have to deal with gout, lethargy and/or obesity. You might play the role of the hypochondriac, being very concerned with your health and worrying about it a good deal.

Practical, stable and resolute you may like to garden and are often attracted to the earth sciences, since you relate so strongly to the earth element. It has been said of Taurus rising that they are very down-to-earth. The trick is not to become so bogged down in material needs and attitudes that you fail to enjoy the more ethereal things that life has to offer.

Kind, gentle and easygoing, you are the salt of the earth and can be depended upon to exert a calming effect in all your dealings with other people.

TAURUS ASCENDANT — ARIES SUN

If you were born between March 21st and April 20th between approximately 7 AM and 9 AM, you may have this combination.

Masterful is the word for you. This is a very powerful combination and you may project a pronounced self-oriented attitude. Generally frank and outspoken in your views, you are often daring and persistent with a surprisingly self-confident willfulness. You are rarely satisfied with anything less than influencing everyone in your sphere, although you would be astonished and nonbelieving if this were pointed out to you. Capable, driving, determined, you rarely miss your goals.

With the Sun in the 11th house or the Taurus decanate rising, management is where you shine . . . in art, business, science, publicity or the creative fields. You are alert, responsive, ambitious and can override anyone or anything that gets in your way, especially if the Sun is in the assertive Aries decanate or if the driving Capricorn decanate rises. If the third decanate is rising and the Sun is in the 12th house, you may be interested in the entertainment field and you have the drive and tenacity to make it to the top doing your own thing, like actor Lon Chaney and singer-entertainer Pearl Bailey.

Temperamentally you can ignore what you don't like, so people who do not agree with you do not usually hang around for long. You can be the head person surrounded by "gofers" and "yes men," or else a very lonely person unless you learn the lesson of tolerance. Your opinion of yourself is usually good; you may need to develop an appreciation of others.

Jealousy and possessiveness are traits that may be overemphasized to your detriment. There is a tendency toward bossiness, particularly if the Sun occupies the Leo decanate, indicating a desire for center stage. You have the ability to do everything well and always be right . . .

which is difficult for others to handle. Your strength **and** weakness is that you can make everyone believe you're right so you **must** be and this is sometimes a troublesome row to hoe.

With a 12th house Sun, if you use your executive and concentrative ability, you can be a behind-the-scenes power to be reckoned with, though sometimes you may feel thwarted and restrained, believing that opportunity is passing you by. This feeling seems to be more prevalent when the Sun is in the Sagittarian decanate which often indicates unreasonable expectations or when the self-critical Virgo decanate is on the Ascendant.

Pearl Bailey
March 29, 1918
7:00 AM EST
Newport News, VA
36N59 76W26

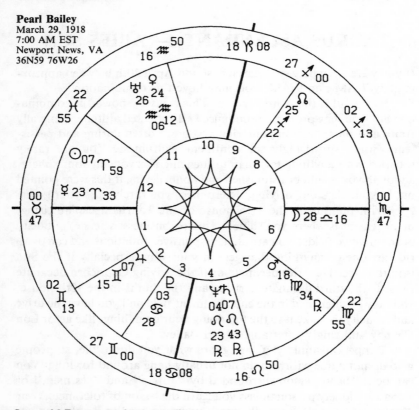

Source: McEvers quotes her personally (A)

Your Taurus indefatigability and Aries initiative indicate a lot of push and you usually get where you're going by the shortest route possible.

TAURUS ASCENDANT — TAURUS SUN

If you were born between April 20th and May 20th between approximately 5 AM and 7 AM, you may have this combination.

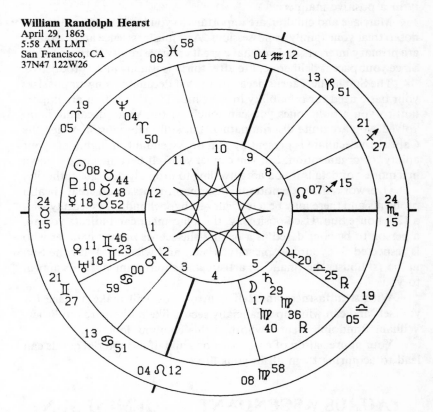

William Randolph Hearst
April 29, 1863
5:58 AM LMT
San Francisco, CA
37N47 122W26

Source: *Sabian Symbols* #444 (C)

Responsibility is the keyword here. If you aren't careful, you take on too much of it, biting off more than you can chew, but sincerely wanting to be helpful, preferably on your own terms. One key to how you handle this combination is Venus, the ruler of both your Sun and Ascendant. If it is in Aries or Gemini, there is some flexibility available to you and a bit of restlessness. If Venus is in Taurus, your appetites and emotions are strong and need proper outlets if you are to avoid the pitfalls of self-indulgence and simple stubbornness. Money and material assets are very important as you tend to rely upon them for your fundamental feeling of security. Creating beauty is another potential forum for expressing Venusian themes. If you have satisfying outlets for feeling a sense of pleasure, beauty, and ease, you are less likely to fall into Taurean lethargy. Express your desire for comfort and security in a positive manner.

Marriage and children are important to you but you must take care not to treat your family as possessions. Art, music, science and literature are primary interests and you have great creative ability in these fields. Since your pace is deliberate, life after thirty is usually more productive.

The Sun in the Taurus decanate or that decanate rising emphasizes your basic need for tangibility in your life. The things that are important to you are the ones you can touch. If the Virgo decanate is involved, you are quite discriminating, but still materialistic. When the Capricorn decanate is present by Sun or Ascendant, it highlights your ability for organization. But you can let yourself become bogged down in a morass of details if you are unwilling to properly delegate authority.

Overwork and/or emotional disappointments could create health problems and there may be a tendency to hypochondria, especially with a 12th house Sun. Used positively, this placement can indicate you are a person to be considered as a behind-the-scenes money handler who is respected for your perspicacity, vision and wisdom. With the Sun in the 1st house, the financial, artistic and entertainment fields appeal to you.

With steadfastness and self control, you will make a place for yourself and can wind up financially secure like millionaire publisher, William Randolph Hearst who had this combination.

Your appreciation of ease, harmony and life's material goods can lead to acquiring them all in your life.

TAURUS ASCENDANT — GEMINI SUN

If you were born between May 20th and June 21st between approximately 3 AM and 5 AM, you may have this combination.

Conversation, sociability and wit epitomize the Gemini Sun and Taurus Ascendant combination. You live to talk, often speak out of turn and can be sarcastic, but with such wit and humor that all is forgiven. F. Lee Bailey, the famous trial lawyer is a good example of this pairing. You can enhance your innate Gemini cleverness by cultivating your Taurus persistence. Though you are not usually particularly ambitious (unless the Capricorn decanate is rising) once your interest is aroused, you can forge to the head of the class. You put up a good front and seem to be a very solid citizen, but you have an underlying need to explore all avenues of opportunity.

F. Lee Bailey
June 10, 1933
2:00 AM EDT
Waltham, MA
42N23 71W14

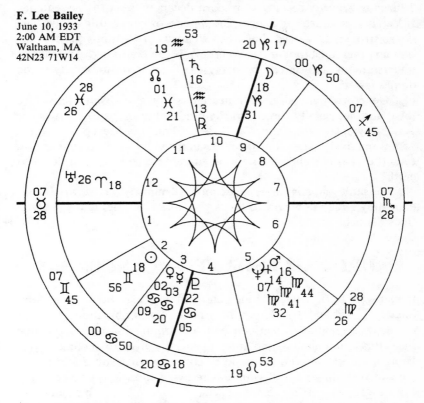

Source: Ruth Hale Oliver, from his mother who specifically said standard time, although daylight time was in effect (C)

    With the Sun in the 3rd house, mental occupations are good: any field that demands ease and facility of expression... writing, proofreading, teaching, lecturing. With your interest in bits and pieces of information and the changing scene, you make a good salesperson. This is emphasized with the Sun in the amiable Libra decanate. With Gemini curiosity and dexterity and Taurus patience and eye for detail, scientific fields may hold a challenge for you, especially when the Sun is in the intellectual Aquarian decanate. This is a good combination for mental achievement and you work best among people rather than off by yourself somewhere, especially if the Sun is in the articulate Gemini decanate or the Virgo decanate is rising.

A 2nd house Sun suggests that you are a good financial advisor or business manager and this is doubly emphasized if either the stable Taurus or security seeking Capricorn decanate is on the Ascendant. If Venus is in Taurus or Cancer, the chances of your settling down early are strongly increased, but when Venus is in Gemini you may feel that any relationship that ties you down is too confining. An older or understanding spouse can be a big asset until you are ready to be domesticated.

Generous, impulsive, warmhearted, social and hospitable, you're loyal and not readily fooled, as the practicality of Taurus settles the variability of Gemini. Once you've decided on your life's path, success comes relatively early, but like all Geminis you thrive on change and even the Taurus stability cannot be guaranteed to bring you down to earth.

Versatile and adaptable as are most Geminis, your Taurus Ascendant shows you know how to focus your many abilities into a productive channel.

TAURUS ASCENDANT — CANCER SUN

If you were born between June 22nd and July 23rd between approximately 1 AM and 3 AM, you may have this combination.

Friendly and unpretentious, with a charming disposition, you like the status to remain quo and are not generally given to making waves. Diplomatic and tactful, you tend to cover up what you don't like to see and you will go out of your way to avoid showdowns and coming face-to-face with issues. It isn't a lack of realism as much as an inner compulsion to avoid confrontation. This is reaffirmed when the Sun is in the self-protective Cancer or sensitive Pisces decanate.

Basically you're a realist (especially with the Taurus decanate rising) and if forced to, you can fight for what you want. To you, the best offense is a good defense and you keep your defenses up especially with the cautious Capricorn decanate on the Ascendant or the Sun in the controlling Scorpio decanate. You may appear to be somewhat self-centered and overly possessive, but it is only because you are seeking to ensure a sense of security.

Domestic, sociable, a good cook, fond of entertaining particularly when the first decanate rises; home and family are important to you and you rarely stray far from the family pattern. Background, heredity and antecedents all figure into your scheme of life and your home is your castle. Sensitive, affectionate and somewhat clinging, you are more sentimental than ardent and this is strongly evident if the practical Virgo decanate is rising. Though you may appear unoriginal, you are really not lacking in imagination but are in full realization of your talents and your limitations. Ex-president Gerald Ford embodies many of the characteristics of this combination.

Gerald Ford
July 14, 1913
00:43 AM CST
Omaha, NE
41N57 95W57

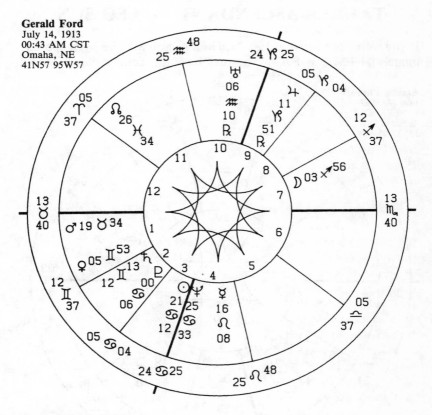

Source: Baby Book (C)

With the Sun in the 2nd house, you may be in civil service work, handling finances in some way or in banking. The Sun in the 3rd house can be a mail deliverer, furniture or home appliance sales person or repairman. If the Virgo decanate is on the Ascendant and the Sun is in the Scorpio decanate, you are often the meticulous, orderly housewife who is well organized and a valuable, stable and worthwhile community member. Regardless of the house placement, fine paintings and great music move you deeply and you may have a beautiful singing voice.

Home-loving, often patriotic and with a true sense of beauty, you are endearing to those around you because you are so good at smoothing ruffled feathers, soothing hurt feelings and creating an aura of calm.

TAURUS ASCENDANT — LEO SUN

If you were born between July 23rd and August 23rd between approximately 11 PM and 1 AM, you may have this combination.

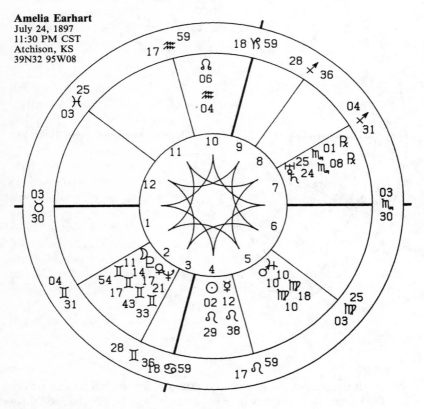

Amelia Earhart
July 24, 1897
11:30 PM CST
Atchison, KS
39N32 95W08

Source: *American Astrology* Magazine June 1960 (C)

You want the finer things in life, but also the thrill of living life on the edge. You seek security, but also pursue the "high" of an adrenalin rush. Taurus adds a note of financial caution to Leo's inherent extravagance and sometimes you are at odds with these two factors of your personality. The Taurus decanate on the Ascendant tips the balance in favor of caution, but if the Sun is in the second decanate, the grandiose side of your nature usually wins out. With the Sun in the 4th house or the Capricorn decanate on the Ascendant, your sense of responsibility is overworked. You may be the star of your circle, but you won't shine for long if you carry the weight of family, friends, relatives and the community on your shoulders. The Virgo decanate rising mirrors your compulsory sense of duty and if you do not learn to pace yourself, your health could suffer.

Pride can be your pitfall. Good looks and noble bearing make you seem quite majestic and somewhat aloof, although when people know you better they see your warm, fun-loving nature. You are very positive, rather set in your ways and have a high sense of integrity. Emotions, intuition and creative power are strong and whatever you do is a product of your own free will especially with the Sun in the Aries decanate. Once committed you are almost always faithful. Capable, generous and indefatigable, you are the person who can manage two or three crises at once without ever coming unglued. Aviatrix Amelia Earhart certainly showed this combination at its best, blending Leo's strength with the Taurus determination to achieve her goals.

The Sun in the 5th house or in the first decanate is highly creative; this is its natural home and it symbolizes great potential here. Acting, costume or dress design, jewelry making, writing plays or children's literature, music, puppetry; all these fields are open to you. You are able to give a singularly personal touch to any creative endeavor especially if Venus is also in Leo. With Venus in Virgo or Cancer, you are particularly good at any profession demanding both flair and painstaking attention to detail. Sometimes you venture where others would never dare and get involved in hazardous or risk taking occupations that require speed, dexterity and quick reflexes.

With your strong forceful personality, you shine socially, at home, at work and with your friends. You are dependable and others know they can count on you when the chips are down.

TAURUS ASCENDANT — VIRGO SUN

If you were born between August 23rd and September 23rd between approximately 9 PM and 11 PM, you may have this combination.

You present a solid front to the world and are the most practical of people. Your modesty and conventional outlook can give you an acceptance of life on all levels. Always willing to put yourself out, you have shrewd common sense and can be depended on to see a job through thoroughly. Actually you're not usually ambitious unless both the Sun and Ascendant are in the Capricorn decanate. The harmony between the Sun and Ascendant generally indicates success without too much of a struggle. Your Taurus rising sign shows that you are more dependent upon affection than most Virgos. Usually you prefer a slow, steady pace with a pleasant job and pleasing companionship. You'll leave the fireworks to others. Your greatest enemy is one that all Taureans have to cope with... inertia.

Taylor Caldwell
September 7, 1900
8:30 PM GMT
Manchester,
England
53N29 2W15

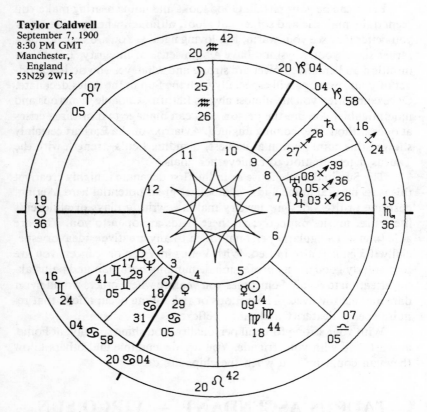

Source: Joylyn Hill in *Mercury Hour*, rectified (DD)

With the Sun in the 5th house, you are often an inspired writer (William Saroyan, Taylor Caldwell) particularly if the Sun or the Ascendant are in the Virgo decanate. If Venus, the ruler of your

Ascendant is also in the 5th house, regardless of the work you do, the combination of your will (Sun) and personality (Ascendant) in the 5th house indicates a creative attitude toward your work. If the Taurus decanate rises, or the Sun is there, you may find a career in the field of music. Whether you are a nurse, writer, musician, teacher or social worker, you get real emotional satisfaction from your job and are probably greatly admired by your co-workers.

With the Sun in the 6th house, you do the same work but with a different attitude; it may be more routine or demand more of your personal attention. This is a good placement for a nurse, doctor, veterinarian, labor union or employment agency worker. You're a dependable detail person, especially when the Virgo decanate is on the Ascendant giving the effect of a double Virgo. You are not usually aggressive or executive, so you may be overlooked when promotions are handed out. Learn to speak up and make yourself heard instead of retiring into the woodwork.

Dedicated, dependable and a loyal friend, spouse or co-worker, others seek you out because you are staunch and solid like the rock of Gibralter. You accept the responsibility of your actions and people sense your trustworthiness.

TAURUS ASCENDANT — LIBRA SUN

If you were born between September 23rd and October 24th between approximately 7 PM and 9 PM, you may have this combination.

With the double Venus emphasis, charm and a love of beauty are often notable with this combination. The ability to please, tact, diplomacy and usually a pleasing appearance all combine to make you the born romantic with a sure public touch. But you can waste your emotional resources in a series of love affairs all with idealistic yearnings that leave you high and dry when they don't work out. With at least a partial emotional outlet in creative work such as the arts or music, you'll have better perspective in your love life.

Your emotional relationships are highly important unless the Aquarian (with the Sun) or the Virgo (with the Ascendant) decanates are involved; then you can be a bit more detached. You never get tired of seeking your ideal time after time. You really **believe** in romance with a capital R. The Taurus Ascendant indicates sensuality and with the Libra Sun you are amorous; the trick is in learning to balance this. Your Libran affability gains a steadfast Taurean quality and this does much to counterbalance the frivolous side of your Libra attitudes. At the same time, it forms a protective overlay for your overly sympathetic nature. If either the Taurus or Virgo decanate is rising, you show more practicality and stability, but you are still an incurable romantic.

With the Ascendant in the Capricorn decanate and the Sun in the 6th house, the military looms as a potential career area, since you are practical in spite of your romantic nature and have executive and business flair. This also indicates the ability to run your own business. With the Sun in the Gemini or Libra decanate or in the 5th house, you're genuinely creative in the decorative arts or music, painting or science. TV personality Suzanne Somers shows the charm and ability to please common with this combination.

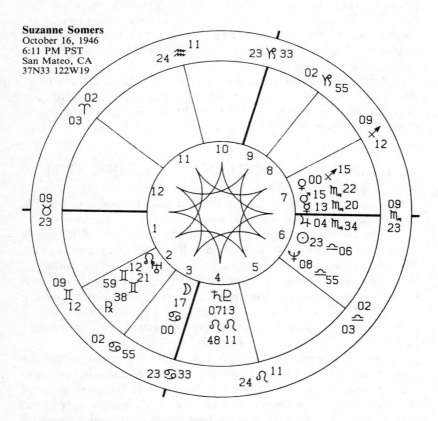

Suzanne Somers
October 16, 1946
6:11 PM PST
San Mateo, CA
37N33 122W19

Source: Moore in *Mercury Hour* cites Birth Certificate (A)

Charm is your keyword and with your easygoing affability, you are usually on friendly terms with everyone in your world.

TAURUS ASCENDANT — SCORPIO SUN

If you were born between October 24th and November 23rd between approximately 5 PM and 7 PM, you may have this combination.

A good fighter; subtle, persistent and acute, you're the right person to get any job done. You are able to bore your way in where a direct attack would fail, especially with the Sun in the Scorpio decanate. You make a good mining engineer, union boss or organizer, or on another level... surgeon, doctor, veterinarian, nurse or occult healer.

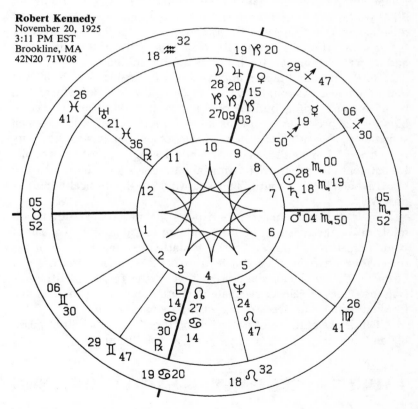

Robert Kennedy
November 20, 1925
3:11 PM EST
Brookline, MA
42N20 71W08

Source: *Horoscope Magazine* 9/70 (C)

You can be somewhat manipulative and fixed in your ways, particularly with the Taurus decanate on the Ascendant. You generally have solid convictions and a great deal of analytical power especially with the Virgo decanate rising. Your motives are not always readily apparent but once you make your move, it results in success. You are learning to balance self-indulgence with self-control, and sex and money are often issues for you. If you do not learn to give, receive and share comfortably with other people, you may end up in struggles for control in your close personal relationships. If the energy symbolized by this powerful combination is not used in a positive way, it can be a most undermining force... as witness Charles Manson, the infamous mass murderer and cult leader.

With the Sun in the 7th house, you can be a dominating, forceful person and a terrifically hard worker. You'll die with your boots on. Since you're an uncompromising driver and usually expect as much of others as you give of yourself, you are often a hard person to work for or with. Attorney General Robert Kennedy had this combination and he was well-known for his drive and perspicacity.

Restlessness and false humility can create problems with the Sun in the 6th house. At your best, you are extremely loyal, but you should broaden your spiritual outlook or your health could suffer. This combination is prone to problems in the regenerative area: women sometimes being subject to irregular menses and possibly the necessity for a hysterectomy and men occasionally developing prostate trouble. Resentment and anger often contribute to illness and you must learn to cultivate a forgiving attitude if you would deal with health matters positively.

With the Capricorn decanate rising, you may have exceptional administrative and executive abilities and you're usually a step ahead of your competition. You can get things started in a big way, but it has to be **your** way; thus you can be a difficult partner in marriage or business. You're the **boss** and no one had better forget it. If the Sun is in the Pisces or Cancer decanate, you are usually more indirect and less blatant in your need to demonstrate your control.

This is one of the most powerful and forceful combinations possible and you are capable of prodigious accomplishment.

TAURUS ASCENDANT — SAGITTARIUS SUN

If you were born between November 23rd and December 22nd between approximately 3 PM and 5 PM, you may have this combination.

A born traveler, writer, lecturer and commentator, you are instinctively drawn to the creative arts, both mental and manual. This is often a very lucky combination and the person who has it seems to lead a charmed life. If you are unable to complete your formal education, study on your own... it comes easily for you. You combine the steadfastness of Taurus with the high-flown Sagittarian philosophy and somehow make it acceptable to your whole circle.

Routine work bores you unless the thorough Virgo decanate is rising. You may quickly lose interest and have the tendency to drift optimistically, waiting for a better day or time to get started on your hopes, dreams and wishes. This is especially evident when the Sun is in the idealistic Sagittarian decanate. There is potential laziness here and the sooner you make the choice between necessity and desire, the more successful you will be. With the Sun in the energetic Aries decanate, you are probably more active and forceful.

Ludwig von Beethoven
December 16, 1770
1:29 PM LMT
Bonn, Germany
50N44 7E05

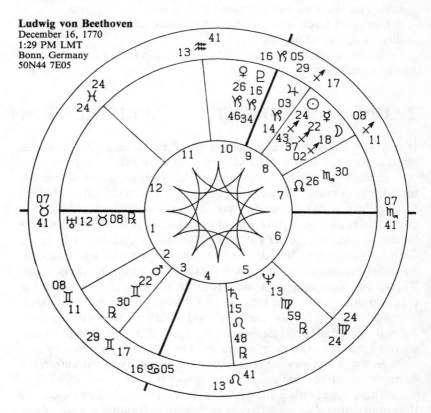

Source: Howard Hammit, Jr., Seattle AFA Convention (DD)

For you to be practical is often the hardest thing in the world, but at times you have moments of method and orderly behavior even though you are bored by trivialities. Generally, though you may chart out a practical course, sticking to it is something else again, unless the Taurus or Capricorn decanates are on the Ascendant. With the Sun in the 9th house, you use the practicality of the Taurus Ascendant to keep from wandering theoretically all over the map. Aspiring and inspirational, you make a good teacher of philosophy, religion, history or any abstract subject if someone else will organize your notes for you.

The Sun in the 8th house suggests practicality may be a little easier to come by. You might gain financially and spiritually through others because of your warm, winning and generous personality. With the Sun in the Leo decanate you are very ardent, warmhearted and companionable and the joys and pleasures of life seem to seek you out.

Composer Ludwig von Beethoven is a good example of the creative ability of this combination.

You are a practical dreamer whose castles in the air have firm and steady foundations.

TAURUS ASCENDANT — CAPRICORN SUN

If you were born between December 22nd and January 21st between approximately 1 PM and 3 PM, you may have this combination.

Though you're no penny pincher, you sure know how to get the most for your money. You can squeeze a nickel until the buffalo hollers "uncle." Your love of comfort and luxury is well supported by your conservative nature. You're willing to work and push your way up the ladder of success especially if either the Sun or Ascendant is in the Capricorn decanate. Recognition and prestige are more important than financial remuneration, but security is the most important thing of all. Taurus and his money are seldom parted. When you finally get to the top, you don't push your luck, so you remain — securely successful.

You're a careful planner with good visualization. Pleasing, tactful and diplomatic, you never tip your hand and rarely make waves, so you tend to startle people who are unaware of your tenacity and your need to be quietly in the center of the picture. When uninterested in any subject, you are indifferent but polite.

With a 10th house Sun, you're often the top of the line executive, the astute manager — objective, practical, administrative — particularly if the Virgo decanate is involved with either the Sun or Ascendant. Martin Luther King, Jr., the advocate of nonviolence and interracial brotherhood, is a fine example of a Taurus Ascendant and a Capricorn Sun.

A 10th house Sun placement indicates you can take good advantage of your opportunities while the Sun in the 9th house, with less apparent drive, shows you can be a wonderful teacher and can influence the minds

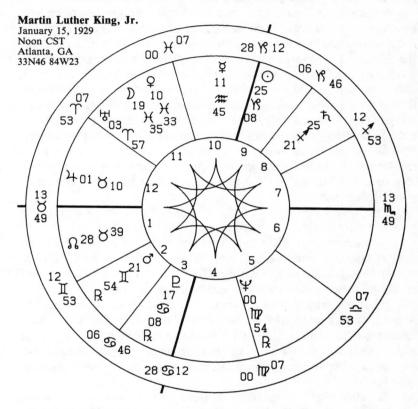

Martin Luther King, Jr.
January 15, 1929
Noon CST
Atlanta, GA
33N46 84W23

Source: Ruth Dewey quotes his mother, "high noon" (DD)

of others. You may seek security in government work. Either placement could be lured into the political field. Laziness may be an issue particularly if both the Sun and Ascendant are in the Taurus decanate. Do not allow your love of comfort to seduce you into taking life too easily; you are capable of the steady drive and endurance necessary for success.

The harmony between the earth Sun and Ascendant suggest a placid demeanor, but no one should underestimate your trenchant capability to get the job done.

TAURUS ASCENDANT — AQUARIUS SUN

If you were born between January 21st and February 20th between approximately 11 AM and 1 PM, you may have this combination.

Extremely philanthropic, you speak like the humanitarian you usually are, in the broad impersonal sense. You have a good mind and are ardent, romantic and loyal. This is one of the Taurus Ascendants that is markedly generous and caring of others. You enjoy people, but do not want to give up any of your personal freedom. So, it is often easier for you to relate to people at large than those you are closest to. You are courteous, generous and hospitable to people in general, but you can be exceedingly high-handed and very dominating in an intimate situation (which is not readily apparent at first acquaintance). You are warmhearted most of the time, but you can be coldheartedly indifferent if you feel someone is trying to tie you down or limit you in some way. You strive for a modicum of security while keeping all your options open.

You have a very high opinion of yourself and others tend to accept you at your own evaluation because most of the time you are correct. Though you don't like to quarrel and can be upset by arguments, your outspoken opinions may embroil you in controversy. Political agitator, Angela Davis and actress Mia Farrow are good examples of strong-minded women with this combination.

When challenged, you are sometimes at a loss which you may try to cover up with a high-flown philosophy. This is especially likely when the Sun is in the Aquarius decanate. It may be difficult for you to accept any opinion except your own. Yet your originality is quite marked and you are capable of bursts of inspiration you then ground with thorough efforts.

The dual fixity of the Taurus Ascendant and the Aquarius Sun indicates that you can be pretty well set in your ways and if you're ambitious for a career, you'll have one, come "hell or high water" particularly with the Taurus decanate rising. Like most Aquarians you are more worldly ambitious than you appear, especially when the Sun is in the 10th house or the Capricorn decanate is on the Ascendant. You're best suited to the professions and the arts, especially music. If the Virgo decanate rises, you also do well in the business field and are an exceptionally good entrepreneur.

With the Sun in the 11th house, you excel in large scale organizational work such as a talent agency or public relations. This is also true if the Sun is in the versatile Gemini or sociable Libra decanate. You feel an overwhelming need to be liked or, at least, noticed. In spite of the conventionality of your Taurus Ascendant, you can be quite outspoken or capable of acting in an outrageous manner if it will afford you the recognition you seek especially if Venus, your Ascendant ruler, is in Aquarius. If Venus is in Capricorn, you are generally much more conservative and when it is in Pisces, you can be a pushover for a sob story, often going out of your way to lend a helping hand.

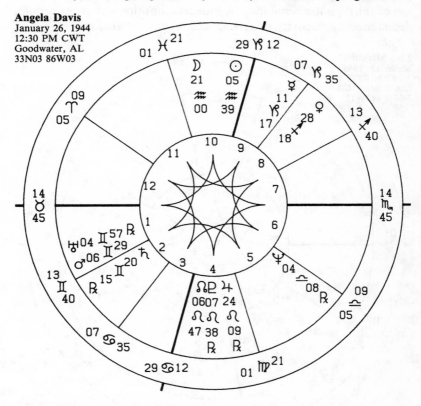

Angela Davis
January 26, 1944
12:30 PM CWT
Goodwater, AL
33N03 86W03

Source: Dana Holliday from Birth Certificate (A)

It is only when people know you well that they can see beyond your kooky exterior to the business oriented, kind person who is really in tune with what is going on in the world.

TAURUS ASCENDANT — PISCES SUN

If you were born between February 20th and March 21st between approximately 9 AM and 11 AM, you may have this combination.

    Emotional is the word for you and you're more dependent than most people on a strong reciprocal affection. You're contented as a clam when you are receiving your share of affection but you tend to depression and an "all is lost" attitude when you feel romantically neglected. The hardest thing for you to cultivate, especially before the age of thirty, is discrimination in your relationships with other people, detachment, objectivity of feeling and a sense of realism.

Liza Minelli
March 12, 1946
7:58 AM PST
Los Angeles, CA
34N03 118W15

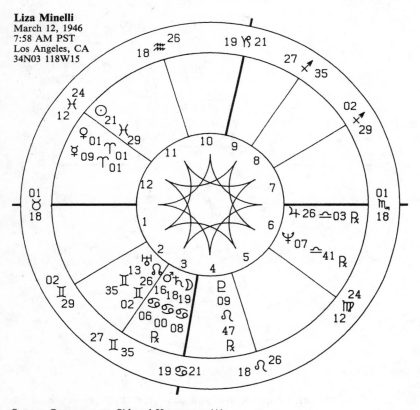

Source: *Contemporary Sidereal Horoscopes* (A)

    Brooding and self-pity can be your downfall and giving in to emotionalism can have a negative effect on your health. This is most noticeable when the Sun is in the Pisces or Cancer decanate. Your self-protective attitude might breed a high degree of self-righteousness which others can find hard to cope with. You may close your mind in rigid stubbornness, and with the Taurus or Capricorn decanate rising, deny what you don't want to understand and be hard and unyielding. If you blend the common sense of Taurus with the romantic idealism of Pisces, you can make a winning combination.

With an 11th house Sun, you are extremely compassionate and the recipient of everyone's troubles and woes. Overprotective of those you love, you do attract some rather queer ducks. You are often found conducting a refuge for wayward pets and underdogs. Your intuition and sensitivity may draw you to the occult and metaphysical and many good astrologers have this combination. This is especially true when the Sun is in the delving Scorpio decanate or the dedicated Virgo decanate is on the Ascendant.

With the Sun in the 12th house, music usually plays a strong role in your life. If you're not musically creative, you are musically expressive or, at least, you enjoy listening. Music, a garden or work that takes you out of yourself is a necessity. Though you need time alone, like all Pisces, to dream and rummage about, when you feel down, don't feel sorry for yourself. Do something for someone else, get busy, talk it out. Do not sit alone and brood. Be positive.

Actress-singer Liza Minelli has this combination.

Soft, gentle and compassionate in a practical way, your friends feel that they have benefitted from having known you.

CHAPTER THREE

GEMINI ASCENDANT

Mentally and physically active, you are interested in everything and everyone and are happiest when you have a finger in every pie and a phone in each hand. With endless curiosity, your favorite words are "who, what, when, where and why." You can be an interfering busybody, but most of the time your sincere friendliness shines forth and others welcome and even approve of your seeming meddling. You can do two things at once with less effort than it takes most of us to do one. All intellectual pursuits — science, invention, teaching, lecturing, literature — are your forte. Anything that requires mental agility, manual dexterity and physical coordination is your bag. You're a great storyteller and a fascinating conversationalist.

Achieving real success depends on directing your many diverse abilities into constructive channels and not scattering your forces to the wind. Your innate restlessness can make you shallow, glib, changeable and unreliable. This is an area that needs careful and constant handling. Naturally, an earth sign Sun (Taurus, Virgo, Capricorn) is going to modify this tendency a bit, but if the Sun is in either a fire or air sign, one of the traits you will have to work on is tenacity. But whatever your Sun sign, your clever and agile Ascendant symbolizes quickness, alertness and flexibility. Any kind of routine is a drag for you and your restless nature demands constant change and excitement.

You are usually tall, slender and lanky with long arms and legs. Your hands, as well as the rest of you, are always in motion and you have been known to wave them around in conversation to get your point across. You rarely put on weight (unless your Sun sign contradicts this), are somewhat narrow in build, but like all the mutable signs you may tend to be a bit wide in the hips. You have a pointed chin, a ski nose (Bob Hope is a Gemini) and wide-set, alert eyes. Many Gemini Ascendants have pronounced knobs on the temples of the forehead and you probably refer to them as your "intelligence bumps."

You need a lot of sleep but don't always get it, as many times you suffer from insomnia . . . your mind never stops even when your body does. Nervous exhaustion is a potential threat and plenty of fresh air and sunshine is really important. You are susceptible to accidents involving hands, shoulders, arms or fingers, especially when moving too fast or trying to do too much at once. Your lungs and intestines can also be vulnerable areas. You really should **not** smoke. Your mental outlook has much to do with your physical health and you prefer overactivity to inactivity.

GEMINI ASCENDANT — ARIES SUN

If you were born between March 21st and April 20th between approximately 9 AM and 11 AM, you may have this combination.

Quick scene changes and constant activity are what you seek. You're the original "get up and go" personality. In a state of constant motion, you may even find it difficult to sit still through a whole meal; you are always leaping up for some forgotten item. You know everyone's first name and don't hesitate to use it.

You are often aware of the intimate details that make everyone your immediate friend and confidante, until you move on to the next group of acquaintances. Your friendly, outgoing personality makes you an excellent salesperson as you have the easygoing approach that covers your shrewdness and you can get the best of the bargain without offending anyone. Your worst fault is your lack of deliberateness — the piles of unfinished business you leave behind, as you flit from one thing to the next. If Mercury, your Ascendant ruler, is in Taurus you are likely to have more fixity of purpose. If Mercury is in Aries, or the Sun is in the Aries decanate or you have the Gemini decanate rising, you are likely to be extremely restless.

Your greatest asset is your ability to do prodigious amounts of work without apparent effort and you find it easy to stimulate others to do the same, especially if the Ascendant is in the Libra decanate. A 10th house Sun shows that you are a natural for politics and public life. With the Sun in the 11th house, you can often be the head of a large corporation or a social director. The ideal position if the free-spirited Aquarius decanate rises, or if the Sun is in the friendly Sagittarius or fun-loving Leo decanate, is cruise director on a luxury liner as this allows you to be mobile and gregarious at the same time.

Actor Gregory Peck has the deep, resonant voice and the ability to project it well, that this pairing often indicates.

Gregory Peck
April 5, 1916
8 AM PST
La Jolla, CA
32N50 117W12

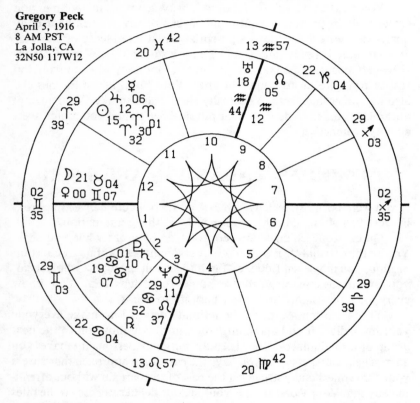

Source: AFA quotes Birth Certificate (C)

Articulate, energetic and seemingly inexhaustible, you have enough mental and physical energy for ten people and are often able to accomplish accordingly.

GEMINI ASCENDANT — TAURUS SUN

If you were born between April 20th and May 20th between approximately 7 AM and 9 AM, you may have this combination.

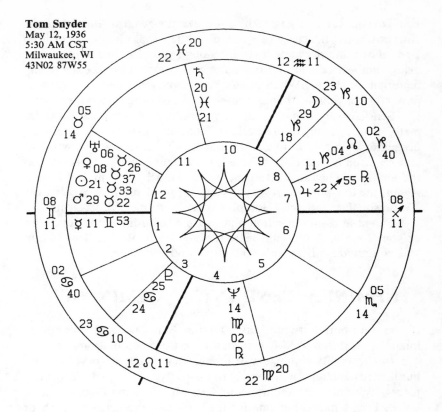

Tom Snyder
May 12, 1936
5:30 AM CST
Milwaukee, WI
43N02 87W55

Source: Robert Jansky (C)

Lighthearted, casual and loving, you seek pleasure from people and from ideas and conversation. Pleasant, friendly and nonaggressive you're a little slow at making the first move but you are usually remarked as a "nice" person which pleases you. You need to go your own way at your own pace, which is not as fast as the usual Gemini Ascendant. Your Taurus Sun slows down your Gemini mobility.

With the Sun in the 11th house, you make and keep many friends as you are an interesting conversationalist, yet rarely a gossip or talebearer. Humble in your evaluation of yourself, recognition usually comes without being sought, especially when the Sun is in the hardworking Virgo decanate. The Aquarius decanate on the Ascendant shows great versatility. However, this decanate combined with a first decanate Sun can take a while to establish itself in a field and is often noted as a "late bloomer." This (11th) house placement often finds you working for a large organization like the government, a big aircraft company, the space program or in the social services. When the Gemini or Libra decanate is rising, though you give the impression of being lighthearted and carefree, under your flippant surface is a strong materialistic streak. When others know you well they can see your powerful convictions that are based on a need for material security.

Sensible, sane and discriminating, you're a loyal and dutiful child, mate, friend and employee especially if the Sun is in the stable Capricorn decanate. With a 12th house Sun, the creative fields suit you well and you are usually musically oriented, the Gemini agility affording you the ability to play an instrument without much thought and effort. Again, the low-pitched, resonant voice is prevalent. Tom Snyder, the TV personality and actor Joseph Cotton both have this pairing.

Fluent in communication and capable in business, the versatility of your Gemini Ascendant belies the steadiness of your Taurus Sun and you amaze others with your drive and persistence.

GEMINI ASCENDANT — GEMINI SUN

If you were born between May 20th and June 21st between approximately 5 AM and 7 AM, you may have this combination.

Intellectuality is the keyword here. Mental activity is your forte, but it needs guidance and control to protect you from scattering your forces, especially if Mercury should also be in Gemini, suggesting a quick, bright mind, but one inclined to skim the surface. With or without a formal education, you usually develop a high degree of manual skill and mental dexterity. Your fondness for people makes you friendly, approachable and sympathetic. When either the Ascendant or Sun is in the Libra decanate, your sociability is often outstanding, but like quicksilver you are volatile and somewhat hard to pin down. Agile, restless and nervously excitable, you are intelligent, rarely dull and often given to inspirational flashes. Quick-wittedness is noticeable when the Gemini decanate is rising or the Sun occupies it. If you can chart your course and stay on it you could easily become a genius in your field, once you decide what it is.

With a 1st house Sun, you like to work with others and your willing ear hears all sides of any story, while your diplomacy gives you a tactful tongue. While you do love to talk, if Mercury is in Taurus or Cancer, you don't indulge much in gossip and people tend to trust and confide in you. With the Sun in the 12th house, science, politics (Henry Kissinger, Hubert Humphrey), acting (Laurence Olivier) and writing (Arthur Conan Doyle) are all possible fields for you. Anything that requires technical precision, whether manual or mental suits you. This is highlighted when the Aquarian decanate is involved.

Henry Kissinger
May 27, 1923
5:30 AM CET
Fuerth, Bayern
 Germany
49N28 11E00

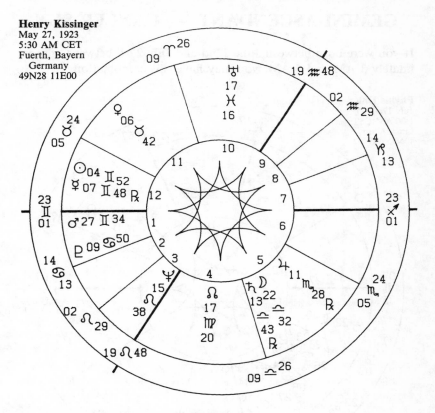

Source: Astrological Association — London (C)

The duality of the Gemini Sun and Ascendant may lead to two careers or vocations at once, or two marriages or even twin children. Too many people and too much activity tend to frazzle your nerves and you need some quiet time each day to yourself, especially with a 12th house Sun. If you use the energy symbolized by this combination in a negative way, you can be devious and manipulative, depending on your charm to extricate you from any difficult situations you may talk your way into. But used positively, this pairing shows charm and the ability to communicate your feelings and ideas to others in a way that they find acceptable and illuminating.

Bright, versatile, multi-talented, you can learn to do almost anything.

GEMINI ASCENDANT — CANCER SUN

If you were born between June 22nd and July 23rd between approximately 3 AM and 5 AM, you may have this combination.

Phyllis Diller
July 17, 1917
1:00 AM CST
Lima, Ohio
40N45 84W07

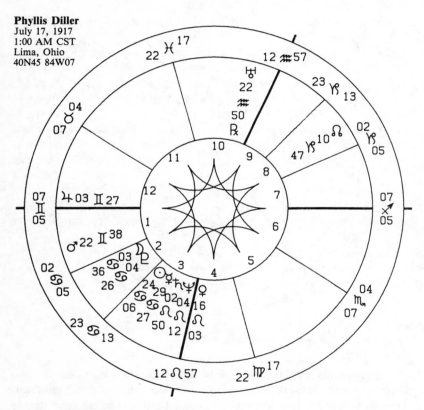

Source: Lockhart quotes her secretary (C)

Emotionally sensitive and responsive, you like people and are well liked in return. Your Gemini eye for detail and coordination plus the Cancer ability to see things whole and in their ultimate value, work well in this combination. You are often exceptionally well attuned to children; your Gemini Ascendant symbolizes a childlike quality in your personality while your Cancer Sun shows a need to provide mothering to someone. You are easily taken in by anyone who has a problem and your heart goes out to the underdog. If the humanitarian Aquarian decanate rises, this is even more pronounced.

Responsibility often comes early in your life and with it a deep need for security, especially with a 2nd house Sun. You are most likely a good money manager and you can stretch a little into a lot with a bit of financial manipulation, particularly when the the Sun is in the Scorpio decanate. With the Sun in the 3rd house, or the Gemini decanate rising, civil service, clerical or postal work may appeal to you. You can be quite dramatic, and often have good eye-mind-hand coordination. This can lead to a career on the stage, in mimicry, pantomime or puppetry. Witty and chatty, you may seem to be somewhat superficial, but you often use this as a facade to cover up your deep Cancer feelings, particularly with the Sun in the sensitive Pisces or emotional Cancer decanate.

Your detached way of offering advice and criticism is seldom held against you because with either the Gemini or Libra decanate rising you are tactful and considerate. If the Sun is in the Scorpio decanate you may have to guard against being too caustic at times. You exhibit the usual Cancer self-protectiveness and an uncanny ability for sidestepping embarrassing situations, usually by turning them into a joke on yourself, like comedienne Phyllis Diller who turned this knack into a lucrative career.

Your friends and acquaintances think of you as comfortable and fun to be around and your genuine caring and concern for others marks you as thoughtful and considerate.

GEMINI ASCENDANT — LEO SUN

If you were born between July 23rd and August 23rd between approximately 1 AM and 3 AM, you may have this combination.

Your Sun really shines as you are warm, friendly and popular. You earn your well deserved popularity because of your true concern for others. You want the best in life, not just for yourself, but for all those close to you. With the skill of Gemini and the determination of Leo, you can get what you want. You are usually the most important person in your circle and justifiably so, as you actively strive for harmony among friends and neighbors. It would take extremely negative behavior for your warmth and outgoingness to be diminished.

With the Libra decanate rising, you rely strongly on the love of

your family for inner support. You are willing to work hard for them
with all the Leo drive, but you must take care that your Gemini nerves
don't wear you out. If the Gemini or Aquarius decanate is on the
Ascendant, the force of your personality carries you far and you have
unlimited creative ability especially in any field where dexterity, a unique
approach and dramatic ability come into play.

With the Sun in the 4th house, your roots go deep and your existence is based on stability and personal love. You are much more
domestic than you seem at first meeting and you have a strong interest
in affairs of the home. Julia Child has this placement. Not only is she

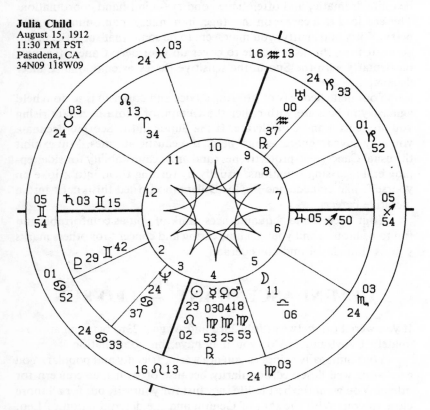

Julia Child
August 15, 1912
11:30 PM PST
Pasadena, CA
34N09 118W09

Source: *Contemporary Sidereal Horoscopes* (A)

a superb cook (4th house Sun) but she is able to write and talk about
it (Gemini). Her Aries decanate Sun suggests entrepreneurship.

With a 3rd house Sun, you are the traveler supreme (Neil

Armstrong, the first man to walk on the Moon), the communicator, the actor, the writer and any or all of these abilities are demonstrated with great flair and panache. Sales ability and advertising or promotional skills are common particularly with the Sun in the Sagittarius decanate. If your Sun is in the Leo decanate you appear as an extroverted, theatrical individual who holds the world in the palm of your hand.

Witty, extroverted and entertaining, you are often the life of the party. Friends love your ability to laugh.

GEMINI ASCENDANT — VIRGO SUN

If you were born between August 23rd and September 23rd between approximately 11 PM and 1 AM, you may have this combination.

This is the classic combination of service rendered: in the clerical, technical, stenographic and secretarial fields. Or for that matter, in any job that while requiring skill, adaptability and dexterity, also involves a lot of routine. Though restless, like all Geminis, you usually channel your boundless energy into many occupational or domestic changes. Once you get by your chronic initial dissatisfaction and really concentrate, you'll progress rapidly because you are quick, agile and a great detail worker.

With the proper education, you would make an excellent executive secretary, an inspiring teacher or an acute and penetrating critic. This is emphasized with the Sun in the painstaking Virgo or careful Capricorn decanate or with the bright Gemini decanate on the Ascendant. With the Sun in the 5th house, writing is often a good field — of the critical, reportorial or factual kind, rather than creative. So is music; the Sun in the Taurus decanate usually indicates that you have a well developed sense of rhythm and an excellent voice. A 4th house Sun suggests that you are somewhat a creature of habit: neat, capable and efficient with a strong sense of duty toward those you love.

Mercury in Leo or Libra indicates added warmth and dramatic force with your otherwise rather cool detached attitude; so does the Libra decanate rising. You are genuinely interested in and like people, yet your critical and analytical faculties may keep others from warming up to you, especially if Mercury happens to be in Virgo. You'll find that if you analyze people less, they'll like you better. This combination is talkative, has a need to communicate and is often good at handicrafts, especially with the Aquarian decanate rising.

Cass Elliott is a good example of the beautiful voice that this pairing can indicate.

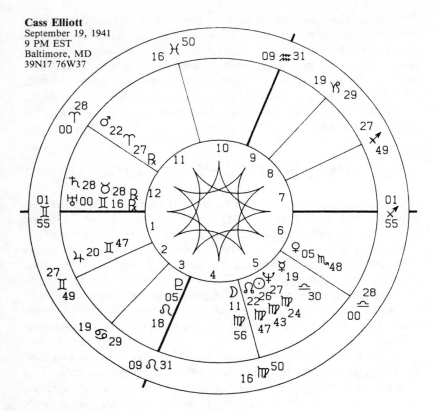

Cass Elliott
September 19, 1941
9 PM EST
Baltimore, MD
39N17 76W37

Source: Steinbrecher quotes Birth Certificate (A)

Capable and hardworking, other people look to you for answers and because you are usually well informed, you seldom disappoint them.

GEMINI ASCENDANT — LIBRA SUN

If you were born between September 23rd and October 24th between approximately 9 PM and 11 PM, you may have this combination.

Naturally gregarious, articulate and intellectually skilled, you can excel in a number of mental pursuits. Literary and artistic creativity added to a charming personality make you very idealistic, versatile and humane, but possibly inclined to lay back and take it easy. The harmony between the Sun and Ascendant may support the willingness to let others do for you — a preference for verbal or mental gymnastics over any actual labor. The drive to achieve can be suggested by Venus or Mercury, your rulers, being in Scorpio. You are a pleasant person to have around and you get places on sheer charm and good luck, so you feel you don't have to exert yourself too much. Romantic, ardent, tactful and persuasive, you have the ability to say the right words at the right time and this talent makes you seem wiser than you are.

With the Sun in the 4th house, in the companionate Libran decanate or with this decanate rising, your social aptitude is your greatest asset. Music and the arts are excellent fields for you. As examples we have novelist Fannie Hurst and opera composer Guiseppe Verdi.

Guiseppe Verdi
October 10, 1813
8 PM LMT
Roncole, Italy
45N01 10E04

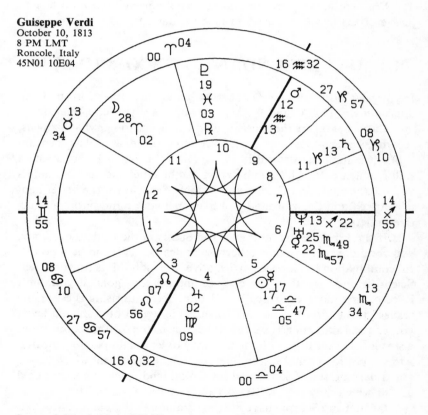

Source: *Sabian Symbols* #285 (C)

With a 5th house Sun teaching, composing, commercial and costume design and dramatic arts all have appeal for you. This is even more likely when either the Sun or Ascendant is in the versatile Gemini decanate. Your inherent weakness is a lack of drive and depth; you have a tendency to skim the surface instead of delving deeply into life. If Saturn is well placed in your chart, it indicates the ability to still be charming, but also more business oriented, willing to work and not quite so content to rely on your charm and wits to get ahead.

When either the Sun or Ascendant is in the Aquarius decanate, you may use your ability to communicate through large organizations or in the political arena. Whatever you do, you are a joy to have around and can be an entertaining host or hostess or the guest who livens up any party.

Your social skills are considerable and your ability to soothe and please others can be an asset in many situations.

GEMINI ASCENDANT — SCORPIO SUN

If you were born between October 24th and November 23rd between approximately 7 PM and 9 PM, you may have this combination.

Curious, you are the experimenter who wants to see what happens, regardless of the consequences. Clever and capable, as well as deep and subtle it is important to fulfill your youthful promise by following a well planned path. This combination can be cruel and ruthless unless you use the analytical Gemini and probing Scorpio for the betterment of yourself and those around you. Channel your mind into constructive outlets.

If the Libra decanate rises or the Sun is in the Cancer decanate, you are more social than is otherwise indicated. This can be a powerful combination but it needs affirmative direction if it is to work well. Scientific and inventive, you can accomplish your goals if you don't lose yourself along the way. The Gemini decanate rising is especially restless and curious. If not sufficiently stimulated on a mental level, you can fall into superficialities. The Sun in the 5th house indicates a strong, creative urge with the tendency to let sex dominate your life. Ardent, passionate and susceptible, you can be inconstant which makes you a hard person to know and love. You tend to blow hot and cold at will which may turn others off to your romantic overtures.

Gemini and Scorpio have little in common so this combination has to work to get it together. Your experimental energy turned to the scientific fields would enable you to use creatively your capacity for detail, follow through and subtlety. General George Patton was a good example of the way this works. His Scorpio energy and drive were diversified through his Gemini Ascendant. Besides going up rapidly through the ranks in the Army, he designed a tank that revolutionized the tank corps at that time. The Aquarian decanate rising emphasized his inventive ability and the Sun in the Pisces decanate showed his psychic perception.

George Patton
November 11, 1885
6:38 PM PST
San Marino, CA
34N07 118W06

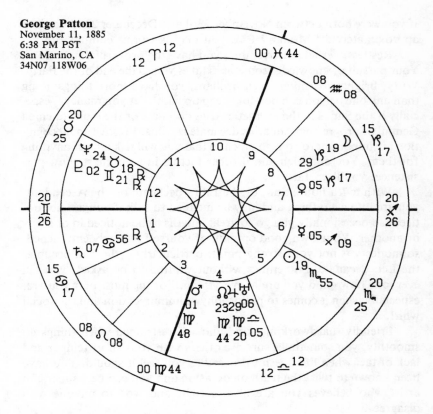

Source: *Patton* by Ladislas Farago (B)

With the Sun in the Scorpio decanate or the 6th house, you may have mental, physical and occult healing power and you can be the top doctor, surgeon, nurse or psychiatrist, providing you don't become too personally involved with your patients. Heart surgeon Christiaan Barnard epitomizes this position with the cool, detached, yet incisive approach to his profession that allowed him to pioneer a field that had challenged medicine for years.

Your Gemini need to communicate combined with Scorpio's drive and discernment indicate that once you set your course, you can convince others of your dedication and forge ahead to great achievement.

GEMINI ASCENDANT — SAGITTARIUS SUN

If you were born between November 23rd and December 22nd between approximately 5 PM and 7 PM, you may have this combination.

Restless, verbal, entertaining, you have the proverbial itchy foot. Your pursuit of knowledge sometimes takes you to the end of the Earth. Witty, bright, charming, even brilliant, you have more things going than any one person can possibly keep up with. Yet you manage, especially if the Sun is in the energetic Aries decanate or the multi-talented Gemini or progressive Aquarius decanate is rising. Prestige and recognition are important to you; so much so that you will risk almost anything for them. You aim high and if other factors in your chart show persistence, you'll go far.

With a 7th house Sun, or the Libra decanate on the Ascendant, you are into everything and may be inclined to sulk if you are not noticed, so occasionally you go to great lengths to be noticed in one way or another. Your own good opinion of yourself is firmly entrenched, so modesty is not your strong point, particularly if the Sun occupies the Leo decanate. Sometimes without waiting to be asked, you tell everyone how good you are at everything. For the most part you are, especially when it comes to philosophy, communication and the social whirl.

Friendly, hardworking, kind and self-restrained when things go smoothly, you sometimes surprise others with your short temper and lack of tact when life doesn't proceed as you feel it should. You have been known to twist the truth on occasion and you can be a super con artist who believes you are always right and woe to anyone who disagrees.

Innately you are the intellectual, inspirational type who often opens the way for others to broaden their own views. The Sun in the Sagittarius decanate almost guarantees this. With the Sun in the 6th house, you are a good idea person, experimenter, pioneer, planner (with someone else to work out the details) always seeking with enthusiasm the new, different and far reaching. Many good sales people combine the mental agility of Gemini with the eagerness of Sagittarius and make it to the top of their field. Aviator Jimmy Doolittle, commentator William F. Buckley and composer Hector Berlioz are three diverse individuals who share this combination.

James Doolittle
December 14, 1896
4:25 PM PST
Alameda, CA
37N46 122W15

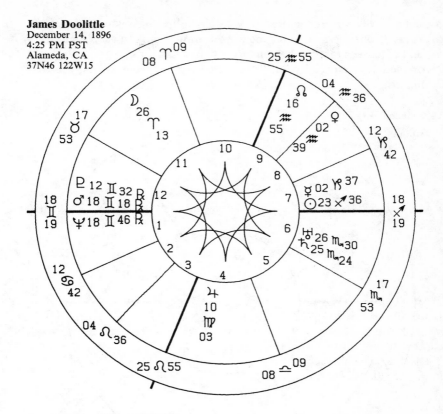

Source: *Sabian Symbols* #285 (C)

Insatiably curious, you are the perpetual student — always seeking, constantly learning and always willing to share your knowledge with others.

GEMINI ASCENDANT — CAPRICORN SUN

If you were born between December 22nd and January 21st between approximately 3 PM and 5 PM, you may have this combination.

Shrewd and matter-of-fact, with a clear, logical mind, you're pleasant, modest and hard working. While you don't seek the limelight, you usually rise to a position of importance within your own circle especially if the Sun is in the ambitious Capricorn decanate. Gemini and Capricorn seem to work well together in spite of the fact that these signs have little in common. Mentally objective, you fool neither yourself or others. You do speak your mind but with such diplomacy that offense is rarely taken and thus you would make a good diplomat or tactician, especially if Mercury and Saturn, your rulers, are well placed.

Johannes Kepler
December 27, 1571
2:30 PM LMT
Weil, Germany
47N36 7E39

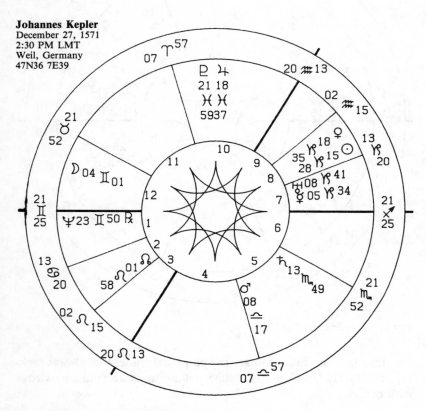

Source: Lockhart quotes *Kepler* by Caspar (B)

The Sun in the 7th house or the Libra decanate rising indicates an unusual amount of charm (which is not generally a Capricorn characteristic) that you are able to use in a very businesslike way. The combination of Mercury and Saturn symbolizes a ready and wicked wit beneath a rather austere and forbidding exterior. The blend of earth and air seems to channel the diversity and changeableness of Gemini into the Capricorn direction and capability, to provide a sensible and commanding personality and a person who is comfortable in any area needing grace, tact and dependability.

Persistent and subtle, your approach is oblique rather than direct and you always seem to accomplish your goals without tipping your hand. Dependable, humane, fair-minded and honorable, with an 8th house Sun or in the money-minded Taurus decanate or the Aquarius decanate rising, the business, financial or scientific field are naturals for you. The latter is even more likely if the Sun is in the thorough Virgo decanate. A 9th house Sun or the articulate Gemini decanate on the Ascendant suggests the law and teaching in an advisory capacity. Since you are surprisingly creative, you may do well as a writer or composer. Johannes Kepler, the astronomer and mathematician, is a good example of the dedication and diversity that this combination symbolizes.

Serious, but with a gift of gab, you can be an entertaining after dinner speaker and function well in any situation that demands a sense of responsibility and mental acuity.

GEMINI ASCENDANT — AQUARIUS SUN

If you were born between January 21st and February 20th between approximately 1 PM and 3 PM, you may have this combination.

Democratic and humanitarian, you have an air of distinction and breeding that seems to place you above your background, even if it was menial or insignificant. Tremendously charming, interested in everyone and everything that is going on, you are clever, altruistic, romantic, and artistic.

With the Sun in the 10th house, this combination indicates a leaning toward literature, music or the arts, as well as advertising, science, mechanics and teaching. If in business, you generally have an artistic hobby for a release from daily tension especially with the restless Gemini decanate involved with either the Sun or Ascendant. Personable and modest, you generally achieve your goal without too much conscious effort. The trine between the Sun and Ascendant indicates much ease and flow, especially where people and ideas are concerned.

Since both your rulers, Mercury and Uranus are such mental and highly changeable planets, you need to develop singleness of purpose to focus your many talents and abilities, otherwise you can fritter your life away in a series of meaningless affairs and menial jobs. A good example of the trifling away of talent and ability native to this combination is John Barrymore, the "Sweet Prince" of American drama who had both the Sun and Ascendant in the Libran (relationship oriented) decanate.

John Barrymore
February 15, 1882
12:33 PM EST
Philadelphia, PA
39N57 75W11

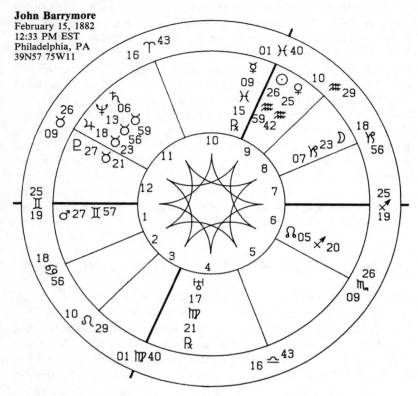

Source: Dana Holliday (DD)

With the Sun or Ascendant in the Aquarian decanate, you enjoy doing for others and thus you are often imposed upon, but your truly deep feeling for human frailty makes you tolerant... up to a point. No one had better push you. When others expect your indulgence and take you for granted, you back off and the Aquarian detachment sets in. Basically, you are easygoing, generous to a fault and always willing to do a friend a favor.

Bright, sharp and a good communicator, your mental alertness can bring rewards to you and your many associates.

GEMINI ASCENDANT — PISCES SUN

If you were born between February 20th and March 21st between approximately 11 AM and 1 PM, you may have this combination.

You appear self-reliant and assured because you have natural digni-ty and are responsive, expressive and can bend flexibly to any situation — too flexibly at times. However, you may quake and trem-ble inwardly because self-confidence is not usually your strong point, no matter how others see you. Even with Mercury and Neptune, your rulers, well placed, this lack of self-confidence often seems inherent perhaps because your ego is not very well developed. Developing more self-esteem is something you may have to work on.

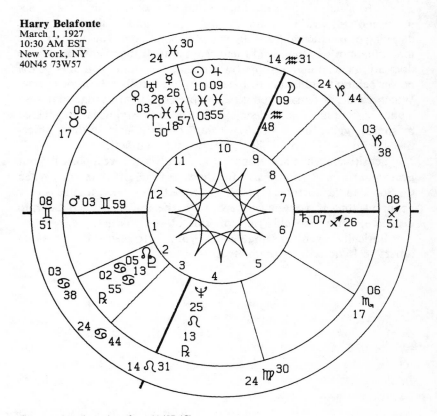

Harry Belafonte
March 1, 1927
10:30 AM EST
New York, NY
40N45 73W57

Source: *American Astrology* 11/57 (C)

Often a born reformer, you protect the weak and defy the strong — a veritable Robin Hood. With an 11th house Sun, you frequently seek a career in institutional or philanthropic work, professionally or through fraternal groups. This is especially noticeable with the Aquarian decanate rising or if Mercury is in Aquarius. Emotional and intuitive, you are often gifted in music, literature, poetry, the mystic and occult. The latter is particularly likely with the Sun in the Pisces or Scorpio decanates. If the Gemini decanate is on the Ascendant, you may be quite adept with your hands and play an instrument well. The Libra decanate on the Ascendant often shows an ability for the art field in some capacity.

Two very well known performers have this pairing — Dinah Shore and Harry Belafonte.

A 10th house Sun can indicate that you work behind the scenes in the movies, writing (John Steinbeck), designing (Gilbert Adrian), directing or producing. Basically you are not a leader; you would rather manipulate others than lead them. If you are a married woman who does not have an arena of her own in which to shine, you may be the power behind a politically or business minded husband, or vice versa. Whether male or female, you generally prefer an indirect road to power. Your biggest fault is a tendency to chatter endlessly, usually triggered by some nagging fear or doubt within. You must learn to think objectively, know when to be silent, decide and then act.

Sensitive, feeling and empathetic, you always have a place in your heart and room at your hearth for those less well off than you. When the Sun is in the nurturing Cancer or gentle Pisces decanate this is very apparent, but if you have the Sun in the self-controlled Scorpio decanate, you try to hide this soft side of your nature.

Basically a gentle caring person, your forte seems to be making others feel good about themselves.

CHAPTER FOUR

CANCER ASCENDANT

Whatever sign your Sun is in, a Cancer Ascendant shows sensitivity, caution and a desire for security. You need to work from a safe and known base. You love the water and unless there are other factors in your chart denying this you will choose to live near it. Domestic and maternal even if you are a male, family loyalty is instinctive in your makeup and though you're rarely in it, your home is your haven. You move indirectly, always circling, rather than in a straight line. This tendency to overcaution may inhibit you in realizing your life's dream unless your Sun is in a strong, aggressive sign like Aries, Leo or Capricorn.

You are essentially realistic and tenacious in pursuing and grasping what you believe to be rightly yours. You don't yearn for the spotlight like the fire signs do, but you have an uncanny sense of publicity and it pleases you to be noticed especially if it will help you to get ahead.

Your self-protectiveness manifests as caution, canniness and an ability to manipulate people and affairs with acute astuteness. Your memory is formidable; you never forget a slight, so once others know you well they tread lightly where your feelings are concerned. You are the most environmental of people, responding strongly to peaceful and harmonious conditions and reacting emotionally to anything upsetting. You reflect feelings like a mirror but will rarely turn loose of tangibles. What is yours belongs to you and the older it is, the more value it has for you.

You need to exercise care in your associations and mode of living.

Sentimental, imaginative and sympathetic, change is your keyword and you have the ability to adapt to your environment. Much, of course, depends on the placement of the Moon, your ruling planet. If it is in a fixed sign, your moodiness is held somewhat in check. If it is in a cardinal sign, you are the doer *par excellence*; in a mutable sign, you may be quite indecisive and be too easily distracted by your multitude of interests.

Cancer in appearance, is one of the short signs, all other factors considered, and like all the water signs, you are round rather than angular. Often you are barrel chested or full bosomed with a slender undercarriage, so that you look a bit top heavy. You generally have a full, round face and beautiful, full-lidded eyes which on occasion are green. Many Cancers are distinguished by a short turned up nose and small hands and feet. As you get older, you may have to watch your weight, especially around the middle. Since Cancer has some rulership of the stomach, some Cancers have a tendency to hold one hand pressed to the stomach. Many tend to walk in a sidewise manner like their namesake, the Crab.

Your emotions are often stronger than your physical body. Worry makes you ill and your vulnerable areas are your stomach and digestive system as well as the breast, chest and skin. Many Cancers develop skin problems when exposed to the Sun. You practically invented ulcers. Emotional support is important for your health. Closeness, caring and being cared for by others will help you maintain good health. Though you may enjoy poor health, as a sign you cling tenaciously to life and are usually very long lived.

Sensitive, emotional and very caring and feeling for others, you have a knack for knowing what the public needs and wants, so are often successful in any field where you can deal with people.

CANCER ASCENDANT — ARIES SUN

If you were born between March 21st and April 20th between approximately 11 AM and 1 PM, you may have this combination.

Aries vigor and enthusiasm usually override your Cancer conservatism and conventionality, propelling you to a position of prestige which really makes you happy. Often this involves changing the established order of things. The Aries need for pioneering something new seems to win out over Cancer old-fashionedness. Of course, much depends on the placement of your rulers, Mars and the Moon. Aries administration and Cancer carefulness make you both a planner and a doer, but your methods of getting ahead (Aries) are indirect (Cancer) and sometimes surprising. What seems simple to you because you push aside obstacles, doesn't appear simple to others, who are often left reeling at your sheer and overwhelming magnetism.

A born promoter, especially when the Sun is in the Aries or Leo decanate, you do well in service fields. With either a 9th or 10th house Sun, you are creative in music and art as were pianist William Backhaus and composer Johann Sebastian Bach.

William Backhaus
March 26, 1884
10:30 AM LMT
Leipzig, Germany
51N20 12E20

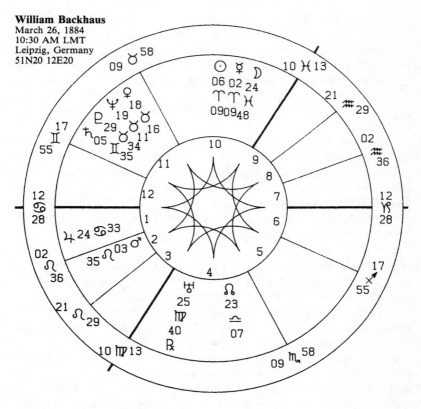

Source: Lockhart quotes him (A)

With the Sun in the 10th house, your best professions are those where you have the freedom to develop new concepts for old methods. You may assume early responsibilities. If you do, you stick with them, especially with the Ascendant in the Cancer decanate. You may have a double code of honor, one for home and another for the public, particularly if the Sun is in the Sagittarian decanate or the Ascendant is in the Pisces or Scorpio decanate. You are often drawn to the political field and you shine when in the limelight.

Sensitive, though bold, your drive and dynamism are cloaked in gentleness and discretion.

CANCER ASCENDANT — TAURUS SUN

If you were born between April 20th and May 20th between approximately 9 AM and 11 AM, you may have this combination.

Pleasant and friendly, your charm and affectionate manner hide a deep self-determination and ambition. Because you are somewhat non-committal and tend to preserve the niceties, you seem meek and variable, but your purpose is firm. There is no mistaking that. Without displaying a great deal of push, you nevertheless achieve your aims with a minimum of fuss.

Domestically oriented, you usually have strong maternal ties. Home and family are vital to you. Thus you rarely remain unmarried, but you do want your own home, married or not. And this home is tastefully decorated where you often display your green thumb with many beautiful plants and a garden that defies description. Artistic, musical, often manually skillful, teaching in any field is a natural for you. You, more than any other Taurus, need emotional and social security, someone to cling to and do for, especially if the nurturing Cancer decanate is on the Ascendant or the Sun is in the helpful Virgo decanate. If the strong-willed Scorpio decanate is rising, you are more independent but you still equate happiness with home and family.

Your home is the base of your life and with the Sun in the 10th house, if you can somehow connect home and career, you are quite content. The real estate field, dressmaking, tailoring, caring for other people's children; anything that enables you to stay home and work is suitable. The Sun in the 11th house indicates much sociability. An aptitude in the financial field is noticeable if the Sun is in either the Taurus or Capricorn decanate. You are a good money manager and invariably have a nest egg tucked away for a rainy day. Both Taurus and Cancer are very financially oriented. In fact, even people who know you well are surprised by your uncanny ability for economics. If your Ascendant is in the Pisces decanate, your biggest problem may be a tendency to hypochondria, but you have a marvelous creative imagination and a strong feeling for beauty.

Composer Peter Tschaikovsky, entertainer Cher, artist Salvador

Dali and inventor Guglielmo Marconi are some of the various personalities who share this persistent combination.

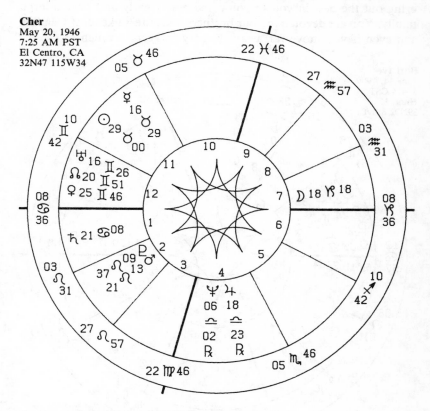

Cher
May 20, 1946
7:25 AM PST
El Centro, CA
32N47 115W34

Source: From her to Quinn, 2/77 Birth Certificate (A)

Warm, comforting and steady, others find in you a firm, guiding influence and you can always be depended upon for help, encouragement and a bowl of chicken soup when necessary.

CANCER ASCENDANT — GEMINI SUN

If you were born between May 20th and June 21st between approximately 7 AM and 9 AM, you may have this combination.

Mental and emotional, this combination shows insatiable curiosity along with deep feelings. Your independence and itchy foot take you away from home early and you may spend the rest of your life trying to establish a home base. You need responsibilities and obligations to bring out the best in you so you often marry early and have a large family. You are devoted to your brothers and sisters like most Geminis and even if you move far away, you try to keep in touch.

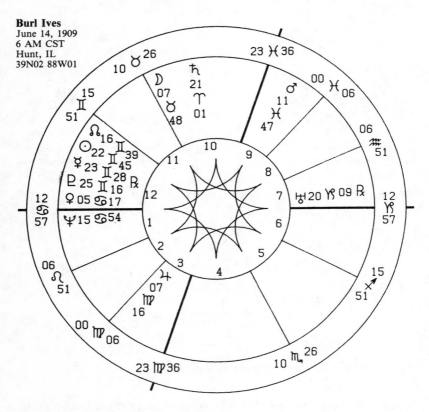

Burl Ives
June 14, 1909
6 AM CST
Hunt, IL
39N02 88W01

Source: Autobiography — *Wayfaring Stranger* (B)

At your best, you are expressive, responsive, flexible and sympathetic, quick and hardworking. This combination sometimes indicates a delicate nervous system. If your equilibrium is upset, your health may suffer, leading to problems with ulcers, skin rashes and stomach disorders. This is most often true when the Sun is in the Libra decanate or the Pisces decanate rises. Either combination mirrors the potential of excessive self-sacrifice, trying to please and appease others. Handling your need for others positively with commitments which support you emotionally, but leave you free to explore the world will help maintain good health.

You have endless capabilities but are often so modest and even uncertain, that you may flounder around seeking your rightful place particularly when the Sun is in the Gemini decanate, reiterating the theme of restlessness and the tendency to be interested in everything and anything. The need for security of the Cancer Ascendant is somewhat at odds with the devil-may-care attitude of your Gemini Sun.

With a 12th house Sun you have fine resources, a deep feeling for the underdog and the ability to work well in social and institutional fields. This is enhanced when the Sun is in the humanitarian Aquarian decanate or the probing Scorpio or supportive Cancer decanate rises. You are never happier than when working with animals, large or small. Thus you would be a good pet groomer, dog show judge or veterinarian. You are gifted with manual skills as well as a flair for words. Misused, this placement may indicate deep-seated psychological problems leading to hospitalization or confinement of some kind. You may wind up on the psychiatrist's couch trying to understand yourself and your motivation.

With the Sun in the 11th house, the professions and arts are your best bet and you may have an aptitude for reportorial writing. An early start in the right direction is imperative or you muddle about trying first this and then that and never getting truly directed. Folk singer Burl Ives is a good example of the informal communicating ability of this versatile combination.

Your need for social activity motivates you and you are at your best entertaining your many friends and acquaintances in your home.

CANCER ASCENDANT — CANCER SUN

If you were born between June 22nd and July 23rd between approximately 5 AM and 7 AM, you may have this combination.

Warm, friendly but a bit shy as a young person, as you mature you may become very involved with public affairs, particularly on the community level. Affectionate, kind and sympathetic, yet often you won't go out of your way for others unless you see some benefit for yourself in the outcome. Your life revolves around your family and if you're not careful you can limit and confine yourself too narrowly. Your children are lovingly spoiled, (the original Jewish mother probably had this combination) and nothing that you can provide is too good for them, especially with the Sun or Ascendant in the Cancer decanate. Giving others constant care and attention makes you happy as a clam — oops, Crab.

Tenacious and clinging, you are enchanted with old things like antiques, history and ancient artifacts. You are very acquisitive and possessive, and try to make sure that you get your share, one way or the other, especially if the Scorpio decanate is involved with the Sun or Ascendant.

Extreme sensitivity is often apparent with this placement, particularly if the Pisces decanate is rising or if the Sun is there, although a strong Mars indicates you know how to hold back the ever-ready tears.

Henry Cabot Lodge
July 5, 1902
4:20 AM EST
Nagant, MA
42N25 70W55

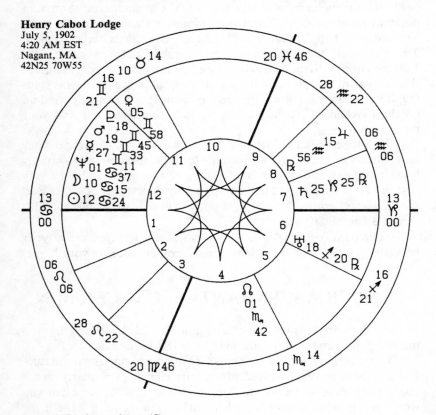

Source: AFA data exchange (C)

Self-pity and loneliness are negative traits which should be overcome so that you can achieve your dreams which are either ideal or practical, depending on the sign the Moon is in. You probably outgrew the early introversion that is often present when the Sun or Ascendant is in the Pisces decanate.

With the Sun in the 1st house, you are more personally oriented and have a great need to be noticed. The placement of the Moon is particularly important with this combination because it rules both the Sun and the Ascendant. If the Moon is in a fire or air sign, you will not be less sentimental and sensitive, only better able to express it. The Moon in water or earth signs seems to be quite emotional and inward. Wherever the Moon is, you are deeply intuitive and perceptive.

Usually a shrewd and capable businessperson, your vocational choices have a wide range — the professions, arts and commerce. This often is a very musical combination. Tact and diplomacy are second nature to you and you may do well in the diplomatic field like Henry Cabot Lodge who was US ambassador to both South Vietnam and West Germany.

You come across to others as caring, considerate and thoughtful, one who can pour oil on troubled waters, so often you act as a coordinator or peacemaker.

CANCER ASCENDANT — LEO SUN

If you were born between July 23rd and August 23rd between approximately 3 AM and 5 AM, you may have this combination.

This is a warm and romantic combination; you are able to dramatize yourself due to impressionable Cancer and creative Leo and are almost always colorful and theatrical in all you do, especially if the Sun is in the Leo or Aries decanate. Dynamic actress Lucille Ball has this pairing and she certainly knows how to put herself across well to the public with the attention-getting ability of Leo and the canny public awareness of Cancer.

Often poetic and always heartfelt in speech, with the Sun in the 3rd house, you have a certain unself-conscious sincerity that allows you to be sentimental but not maudlin. Though deeply and affectionately tied to your family, you are very self-sufficient with enough warmth for everyone around you. A good cook, whether male or female, you can be a gourmet chef, vocationally or avocationally. This is especially noticeable when the Cancer decanate rises. If the Sun is in the Sagittarian decanate, you are more than willing to try unusual recipes from foreign cultures. As well as liking to cook, you like to eat and when you eat out, you prefer to frequent only the best restaurants. You also love to entertain and do so royally.

Lucille Ball
August 6, 1911
4 AM EST
Jamestown, NY
42N06 79W14

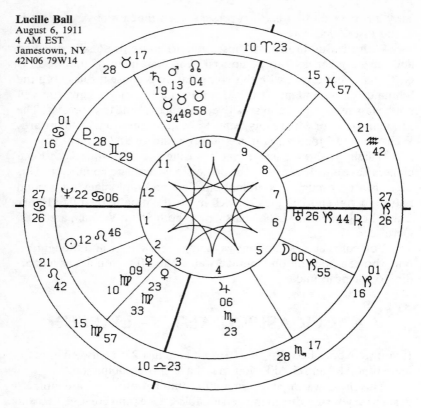

Source: Church of Light quotes Drew (C)

A 2nd house Sun indicates high aims and ideals and you often have a very good opinion of yourself which others readily accept due to your integrity and faithfulness. You are frequently attracted to metaphysical beliefs which you don't hesitate to put into practice, especially with the Ascendant in either the Scorpio or Pisces decanate. You are a firm believer in positive thinking but if you are using the energy negatively, you can be the gloomiest of negative thinkers. You have common sense as well as artistic ability, especially if the Sun is in the 1st house, and a keen eye and ear for politics. Women with this combination may prefer homemaking to the limelight, but can be very successful in a career if that is their choice.

Home-loving, yet outgoing and dramatic, you may be the epitome of graciousness, cordiality and courtesy. You are welcome at all gatherings because of your warmth and friendliness.

CANCER ASCENDANT — VIRGO SUN

If you were born between August 23rd and September 23rd between approximately 1 AM and 3 AM, you may have this combination.

Lily Tomlin
September 1, 1939
1:45 AM EST
Detroit, MI
42N20 83W03

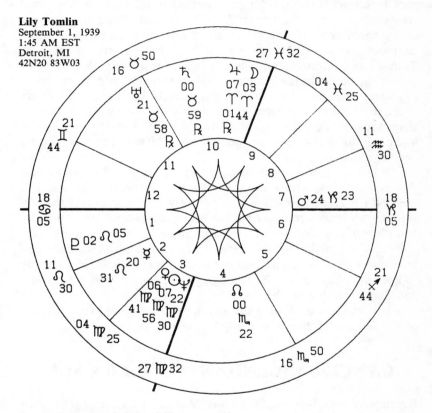

Source: *Contemporary Sidereal Horoscopes* (A)

You're mentally bright, adaptable, alert and quick and like to be involved in everything that's going on around you. Ever willing to help others, you are at your best when a friend is in need. The combination of water (Cancer) and earth (Virgo) indicates a need to nurture, a Mother Earth quality, that comes across as genuine concern. Physically you may not be too robust and you should avoid strain, both physical and mental. You can be moody, volatile and touchy and tend to take yourself far too seriously, particularly with the Sun in the Capricorn decanate or with the Scorpio decanate rising. You function best when you learn to pace yourself and not take everything on your own shoulders.

You often have a green thumb and farming, gardening and all related areas usually appeal to you. With the Sun in the 3rd house, you may be attracted to cashiering or clerking in the food or restaurant trades. Here we also find writers (Leo Tolstoi) and columnists who write about food, cooking and diet. Supply and maintenance workers in hospitals and institutions as well as band leaders, comedians (Lily Tomlin) and entertainers frequently have this combination.

If the Sun is in the Taurus or Virgo decanate, you are far more organized than most Cancer Ascendants. If the Cancer or Pisces decanate is rising, you come across with more feeling and sensitivity than is usually noted for Virgo. Versatility seems to be your keynote and naturally the positions of the Moon and Mercury, your rulers, are very significant.

When antagonized, you can be stubborn and will seldom admit that you could be wrong and though you are generally likeable, you are best left alone when you're in one of your "moods." If the Sun is in the 4th house, you may do well in the real estate field or with investments of any kind in land. You are known for your perceptive mentality and your ability to view things with detachment yet warmth. You have a wry sense of humor and can poke fun at yourself in company to keep up a good front. But though you're laughing on the outside, you may be crying on the inside.

Steady, sincere, capable and warm, others respond to you because of the feelings of caring and helpfulness you exude.

CANCER ASCENDANT — LIBRA SUN

If you were born between September 23rd and October 24th between approximately 11 PM and 1 AM, you may have this combination.

Sociability is your keyword. Cancer rules the home and Libra rules the public and you do like to bring others into your home, which is well appointed and usually well maintained. In your personal relations, while your social sweep is large, you like to dig out fundamentals and you have a need to please others. You are a good listener and others know they can trust you with their secrets so they seek you out to confide in you and get your advice. When you can be persuaded to give it, your counsel is fair, balanced and keyed to the emotions.

If the Sun is in the sociable Libra decanate or the homey Cancer decanate rises, when you entertain, you do it in style. If your Sun is in the fluent Gemini decanate or the imaginative Pisces decanate is on the Ascendant, you may be more talkative and less inclined to listen. Usually easygoing and tactful, you accept surface values as long as the surface is smooth and you put yourself out to be charming and keep things calm and peaceable. Author, bon vivant Truman Capote is a good example of Libra's charm combined with lunar intensity.

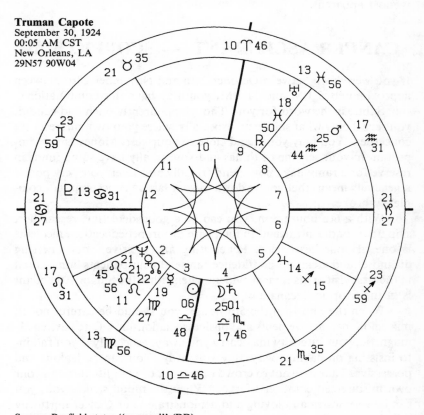

Truman Capote
September 30, 1924
00:05 AM CST
New Orleans, LA
29N57 90W04

Source: Penfield states "personal" (DD)

With a 5th house Sun, you're usually very romantic and between Cancer impressionability and Libra adaptability, you can let your emotions run away with you. Learning deliberate discrimination may be necessary, lest you be easily led down the garden path. With the Sun in the 4th house, you make a good historian, anthropologist or museum curator; all studies that go back and search out the beginnings of humankind intrigue you. Other fields which may prove rewarding are social director, decorating and the military. If the Sun is in the Aquarian decanate or the Scorpio decanate is rising, there can be a marked stubbornness to your otherwise tractable personality. Those placements indicate tremendous strength of will.

Sensitive, witty and entertaining, you are a gracious host or hostess and an always welcome guest since your ability to charm and entertain is most apparent.

CANCER ASCENDANT — SCORPIO SUN

If you were born between October 24th and November 23rd between approximately 9 PM and 11 PM, you may have this combination.

Subtle is the word for you. Though apparently open and candid, you reveal only what suits you, especially where your own interests are concerned. You play your hand close to your vest. Money is very important in your scheme of things and you usually have some funds in reserve for a rainy day. You spend frugally and when you "cry poor" it generally means that you're down to your last bank account, not completely broke.

With a 6th house Sun, you can be a good detective, researcher, skip tracer or diagnostician. In fact, with the proper education, medicine is one of your best fields. Penetrating and incisive, your unerring diagnoses and great self-confidence can send your patients home cured in the first visit. This is most evident when either the Sun or Ascendant is in the Scorpio decanate.

When the Sun is in the 5th house, you should be careful not to mix emotional involvements and business relationships. Often extremely magnetic, your intensity may carry you away, especially if you fall into insisting on having everything your way. You can be jealous and possessive. Take care not to crowd others out of your life through your own misdirected emotional fervor. When the mood strikes you, you can be very warm and loving and demonstrate your Cancer nurturing urge toward all those you are close to.

Though very self-protective if either the Sun or Ascendant is in the Pisces decanate, you are highly impressionable and not always discriminating. This can leave you open for criticism. And the criticism may be hard for you to handle; you tend to be better at dishing it out than taking it. With the Cancer decanate involved with either the Ascendant or Sun, you are perceptive and intuitive, like most Cancers and Scorpios and may experience clairvoyant episodes. Depending upon the placement and aspects to your ruling planets, there can be a tendency for you to have to deal with the law, either as an officer like former police chief Ed Davis of Los Angeles, or as a criminal like the Chicago child murderer, William Heirens.

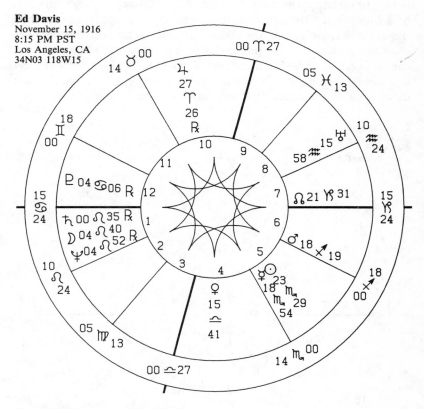

Ed Davis
November 15, 1916
8:15 PM PST
Los Angeles, CA
34N03 118W15

Source: Holliday quotes his mother (C)

Of all the Cancer Ascendants, you are the most trenchant and foresighted. You find it easy to appear calm and collected in the face of daily upheaval.

CANCER ASCENDANT — SAGITTARIUS SUN

If you were born between November 23rd and December 22nd between approximately 7 PM and 9 PM, you may have this combination.

Warm yet restless, you seek close sharing with others but enough freedom to pursue your quest for the meaning of life. Many times this combination indicates beauty of the classic kind: the soulful, liquid eyes, the Mona Lisa type smile and a straight, short nose. Though seemingly shy, timid and withdrawn (Cancer), you have surprisingly high goals of achievement (Sagittarius). More outgoing and approachable than the average Cancer, you are casually friendly with everyone, but are close to only a select few, preferably those at the top. When you want something, you shrewdly and tenaciously hang in there until you get it, especially when the Sun is in the Aries decanate or the Scorpio decanate is on the Ascendant. You think big, have your own code, do

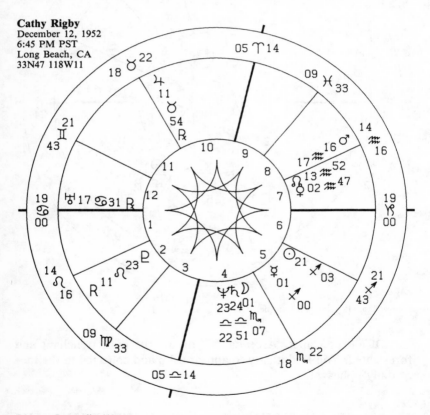

Cathy Rigby
December 12, 1952
6:45 PM PST
Long Beach, CA
33N47 118W11

Source: Gauquelin (A)

pretty much as you please and will go to great lengths to reach your ideals.

If the Ascendant is in the Pisces or Cancer decanate, your seemingly easygoing, placid and calm exterior can hide a lot of drive and ambition which astonishes others when they become aware of it. A 5th house Sun can indicate the inveterate gambler, the lucky speculator or the truly gifted musician, athlete, artist or writer. With the Sun in the 6th house, you have a flair for long range planning, organization and business. You think on a grandiose scale and usually have an ace or two in the hole, especially with the Sun in the Sagittarius decanate. Money is very important to you as it is to most Cancers. But to really get a lot out of life, you need to develop a more genuine interest in people than things or you may wind up lonely and unhappy in spite of your financial success.

Often this combination indicates an interest in what makes people tick and where they originate, so you may become involved in the study of astrology or genealogy. You are curious, intrepid and not afraid to try anything once. Gymnast Cathy Rigby has this combination with her Sun in the showy Leo decanate, so gymnastics was a perfect vehicle for her to show off her athletic skills and fearlessness.

Emotional, sensitive and perceptive like all Cancers, your Sagittarian Sun symbolizes prophetic vision and a broad philosophic and ideological outlook.

CANCER ASCENDANT — CAPRICORN SUN

If you were born between December 22nd and January 21st between approximately 5 PM and 7 PM, you may have this combination.

Stability is the keynote of this combination. Natural business and executive flair indicate that you have the ability to handle people well, socially as well as in the corporate world. You work hard, not just for the money and prestige, but for the satisfaction of a job well done. This is especially apparent when the Sun is in the dedicated Virgo or pragmatic Capricorn decanate or the persevering Scorpio decanate rises.

You understand and relate well to other individuals and thus would do well in sales, law and counseling, especially when the Sun is in the 7th house, which suggests a Libran overlay to your individuality. Tact, diplomacy and genuine warmth are your best attributes, but you can have a cutting tongue and the biting sarcasm of theater critic Alexander Woollcott.

With a 6th house Sun you can be more subtle and indirect but you are rarely accused of manipulation or double dealing unless your Ascendant is in the Pisces decanate and you are not handling the issues symbolized by Neptune very well. Be clear about your ideals and do

Alexander Woollcott
January 19, 1887
3:30 PM EST
Phalanx, NJ
40N22 74W32

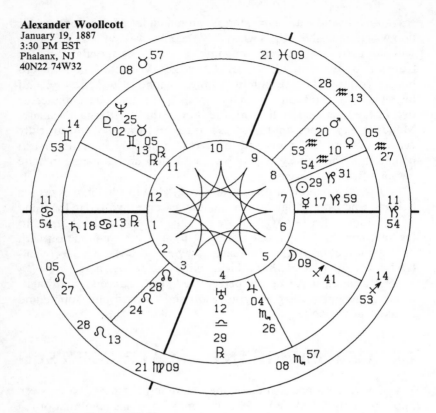

Source: *Constellations* 1977 (C)

not cloud the issue with evasions or half-truths.

The tendency with this combination is to marry late, but a solid early marriage is a good sound base for you to build on especially with a 7th house Sun. If the Cancer decanate is rising or the Sun is in the Taurus decanate, you seem to need to establish your nest early.

You function capably in all fields relating to the public: selling, acting and teaching, as you are well able to present yourself in an acceptable way. You may feel torn between playing the role of the stern, realistic father versus the gentle, forgiving mother. Avoid either extreme. Take care not to be too caustic in your approach to others, so they are not put off by your brusqueness. Also avoid being overly sweet. Balancing your need for achievement in the outer world with your need for emotional sharing and a home is vital.

Your businesslike attitude provides a good balance for your Cancer tenderness and thus you are able to function well as a caring and concerned but no-nonsense person.

CANCER ASCENDANT — AQUARIUS SUN

If you were born between January 21st and February 20th between approximately 3 PM and 5 PM, you may have this combination.

Bishop James Pike
February 14, 1913
3:30 PM CST
Oklahoma City, OK
35N28 97W31

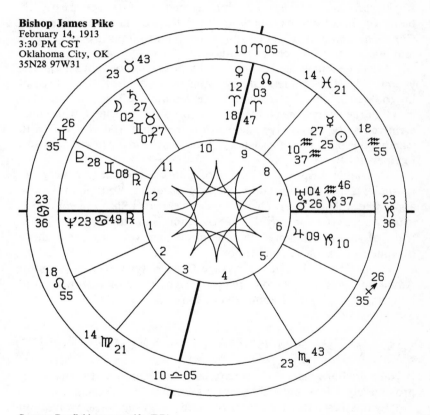

Source: Penfield quotes wife (DD)

You sometimes appear dreamy and idealistic, but beneath your tolerant, philosophic facade, you are determined, practical and you know well how to maneuver for position. William Tecumseh Sherman, the Union General illustrates this well. He was an exceptional military strategist. You are always seeking the deeper meaning of life, through the religious and sometimes the mystic and occult like Bishop James Pike, who after his son's death, used many occult methods to try to establish communication with him. Bishop Pike's Sun in the 8th house and the Pisces decanate rising further indicated his obsessive interest in life after death.

You are more interested in people as a group than as individuals especially if the Sun is in the Aquarian decanate, but your warmth and insight attract friends to you, even though you don't go out of your way to seek them. Since you don't like to get too close, you are usually better off in impersonal relationships unless you happen to have the Cancer decanate rising. Then your need to nurture takes over and you may have many very close friends.

With the Sun in the 7th house or in the Gemini or Libra decanate, you are a kind and understanding counselor or advisor, rarely becoming too personally involved with those you advise. The Sun in the 8th house or the Scorpio decanate rising seems to be associated with much creative ability, especially in acting or composing. And as always with Cancer, this placement spotlights your ability to handle money and deal in financial fields.

Romantic, inspirational, fond of comfort and not too energetic, it usually takes a bit of prodding to get you started. Your philosophical approach, when properly channeled can help you to achieve your great expectations. If Uranus (ruler of your Sun) is angular and the Moon (ruler of your Ascendant) is in a fire or air sign, you may be far ahead of your time in those expectations.

More detached than the average Cancer, yet warmer than most Aquarians, you are able to develop the right blend of nurturance and impartiality in most of your relationships.

CANCER ASCENDANT — PISCES SUN

If you were born between February 20th and March 21st between approximately 1 PM and 3 PM, you may have this combination.

Sympathetic, domestic, sensitive and somewhat conservative, you like to follow family tradition and are usually proud of your heritage. If it's not a heritage you can be proud of, you sometimes invent one that is. Roots are particularly important when the Cancer decanate is rising. Ever the romantic, you are in love with love and enjoy being patted, fondled and touched unless the Moon (your Ascendant ruler) is in Gemini or Aquarius which show that you can be somewhat detached and standoffish.

If either the Sun or Ascendant is in the gentle Pisces decanate, shyness sometimes keeps you from expressing your needs and desires but you function well in a partnership relationship and generally marry young. You must learn to tell your partner what is troubling you and what you are thinking, if you want to solve problems and avoid long silences and moodiness.

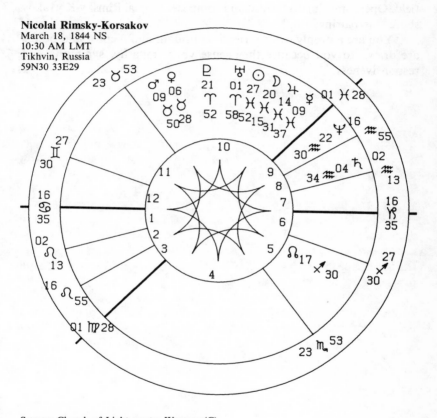

Nicolai Rimsky-Korsakov
March 18, 1844 NS
10:30 AM LMT
Tikhvin, Russia
59N30 33E29

Source: Church of Light quotes Wemyss (C)

Tactful and diplomatic, you seem pliable and somewhat detached from everyday affairs. You have a neat way of avoiding unpleasant issues as you say what is expected of you rather than voice your own opinions unless the trenchant Scorpio decanate is involved with either your Sun or Ascendant. With the Sun in the 8th house or in the Cancer decanate, you're very intuitive, sometimes psychic, clairvoyant or clairaudient (able to hear a voice that is not present but which has objective reality).

You are especially perceptive when it comes to money and investments and you should learn to follow your hunches in these areas. With a 9th house Sun, you can be a good lawyer, teacher or actor; the Sun in the 10th promises success in some field, as this is a competent and capable combination. It often indicates a special talent in the music field. Opera star Enrico Caruso and composer Nicolai Rimsky-Korsakov share this pairing.

You are a deeply caring friend, confidant and mentor and others are drawn to you because they sense your empathy, sympathy and responsiveness.

CHAPTER FIVE

LEO ASCENDANT

Generous, kind and friendly with a genial disposition, you like to make magnanimous gestures that often seem larger than life. A natural leader, you prefer to be in command, and if you do not feel that you are the center of attention, you can quickly lose interest in what is going on. However, because of your striking personality, it rarely happens that others are not tuned in to you. Generally, your sunny, smiling presence is welcome at any gathering.

A super organizer and a wise distributor of duties, you know well the value of delegating work to capable assistants to whom you express your approval generously. Leos are often very childlike in their approach to life and the best way to get around these lions is to flatter them. Humor Leos and they will eat out of your hand. Just like the bull, you are stubborn and cannot be pushed. You are very proud and if someone makes the mistake of belittling you, you may forgive, but you'll never forget. You are convivial and romantic and there are very few Leo spinsters or bachelors. You are almost constantly in the throes of amour.

You must take care not to become arrogant and domineering in your dealings with others, as you have a tendency to say, "We'll do it my way or not at all." Since Leo is a fixed sign, you are determined, persistent and firm in your beliefs and quite unswerving in your views. Wherever Leo is in any chart, there is a need to project the individuality in a very personal way. This can lead to great achievement but also to extreme egotism when Leo colors the Ascendant. You are an outgoing extrovert; it is said there are no introverted Leos, only Leos who pretend to be introverted.

In appearance you have a large, square body and a large head, but you can be the shortest sign, unless your Sun sign or hereditary background suggests height. Your body is muscular, especially with the Aries decanate and people are in some way aware of Leo's hair which you often toss around like a mane. Occasionally the reason others notice your hair is because you are totally bald. Or it may be an unusual color — like Lucille Ball's or Mae West's. You have wide shoulders and narrow hips, a loud, cheerful voice like a lion's roar and lively sparkling eyes which are sometimes green like a cat's. Leo men develop very high foreheads when they start to bald.

Like Aries, Leo is prone to high fevers, accidents and sudden violent illnesses (especially when not channeling your anger and aggression outward in a constructive release) but rarely to long, chronic illnesses. You might have either a very strong heart or a weak one that might be subject to rheumatic fever, etc. Keeping challenging but reachable goals in your career and love life will help keep a healthy heart. . . along with proper diet and exercise. Your back is a vulnerable area and you may suffer from disc or spasm problems, especially if Saturn is in the 1st or 6th houses. This shows the potential of "carrying the world on your back" and the psychological sense of pressure and excess responsibility can contribute to your back problems. You recuperate well and probably wouldn't get sick in the first place if you'd quit fooling around and take better care of your health.

Whatever your Sun sign, it will express very strongly through the first house of personality and also bring the characteristics of the house in which it is placed into prominence.

LEO ASCENDANT — ARIES SUN

If you were born between March 21st and April 20th between approximately 1 PM and 3 PM, you may have this combination.

You have the ability to project your personality almost to the point of overwhelming others. That's a lot of fire you have going for you and the only thing that would dampen it a bit would be if Mars, your Sun sign ruler, was placed in a water sign. There is a romantic quality to your nature and sometimes a daydreaminess that needs and usually finds an avenue of expression either in gambling, speculation or the arts. This is most prevalent if the Sun or Ascendant is in the Leo decanate. Warm, pioneering and dramatic, you can explore new fields of endeavor in any direction, particularly if both the Sun and Ascendant are in the Aries decanate.

With an 8th house Sun you are often the dedicated doctor, law enforcer or financier. With the Sun in the 9th house, travel, law and sports fields attract you. An example is sports announcer Howard Cosell. Many times, with either house placement, this is an actor's or politician's chart such as Charlie Chaplin and singer-evangelist, Anita Bryant.

Anita Bryant
March 25, 1940
3:10 PM CST
Barnsdall, OK
36N34 96W09

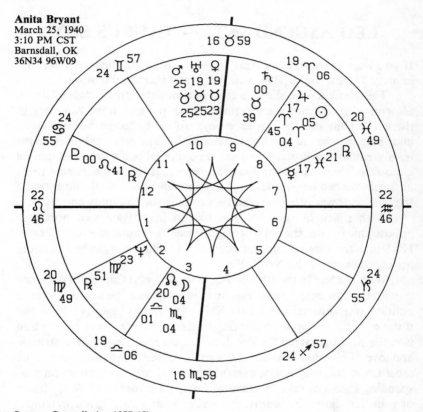

Source: *Constellation* 1977 (C)

A good education is important with this combination but there is a tendency to laziness and self-centeredness. Often you are not willing to work hard enough or wait long enough to obtain the necessary schooling to enable you to succeed in your career field. You prefer to get by upon your warmth and charm and usually you do. Pleasant is one of your keywords, but you must take care not to laze through life as the perennial house guest or tennis bum. Especially with the Sun or Ascendant in the Sagittarius decanate, the good life may appeal, but don't expect others to do everything for you. You have the drive and initiative to achieve if you choose to apply it.

Determined, fiery and always ready to take a chance, others are drawn to you because you are an exciting person to be around, with such good ideas for ways to have fun.

LEO ASCENDANT — TAURUS SUN

If you were born between April 20th and May 20th between approximately 11 AM and 1 PM, you may have this combination.

This combination shows a great deal of determined, dogged drive. Slow-moving and not always quick to grasp a situation, you hang in there and your sheer persistence pays off in the long run. Materially and socially oriented you like the best in life and will work hard to get it. A great host or hostess, you are at your regal best when entertaining a crowd of your friends and acquaintances. If the Leo decanate rises, at times you can be overbearing, haughty and egotistical, but most of the time your warmth and steadiness endear you to family and friends.

With a 9th house Sun, you like to investigate vast horizons: philosophical, educational or geographical like explorer Robert Peary. His Sun in the Virgo decanate indicated his ability to organize and equip his expeditions to the North Pole.

With the Sun in the 10th house, in the forceful Capricorn decanate or with the dynamic Aries decanate rising, you may be a leader: social, political or industrial like Henry Kaiser. Self-indulgence is a potential if the sometimes opportunistic Sagittarian decanate rises or if the Sun is in the comfort loving Taurus decanate. But your good-time attitude and love of pleasure can also make you a valued guest and friend. Like most Leos, you may not be careful with your cash and can go on wild spending sprees or take spectacular financial gambles. If Venus (ruler of your Sun sign) is in Taurus, the desire for stability might help temper your extravagance. But there may be a certain blind side to your nature; a difficulty in seeing another's viewpoint which can, at times, make you seem unkind and unfeeling. Your orientation tends to be towards ease, comfort and stability but you need to realize not everyone enjoys the kind of comfort and ease that you do. If Venus is in Aries or Gemini, you are probably more relaxed and quite a bit more flexible. However, the potential of overdoing your risk-taking activities is greater with these placements. Keep a balance between your need for the good things in life and your gambling instincts which can overreach.

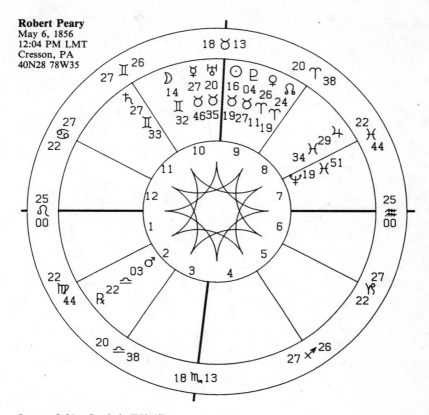

Robert Peary
May 6, 1856
12:04 PM LMT
Cresson, PA
40N28 78W35

Source: *Sabian Symbols* #759 (C)

You operate in a courteous, sociable and mannerly way which can endear you to everyone you come into contact with.

LEO ASCENDANT — GEMINI SUN

If you were born between May 21st and June 21st between approximately 9 AM and 11 AM, you may have this combination.

Gracious, friendly and talkative, popularity is your keynote and you are a welcome addition to any social gathering. Many entertainers, actors, singers and performers have this combination including Guy Lombardo, Rise Stevens, Senator Henry Jackson and the incomparable Marilyn Monroe.

Urbane, witty and a whiz at keeping the conversation going, the

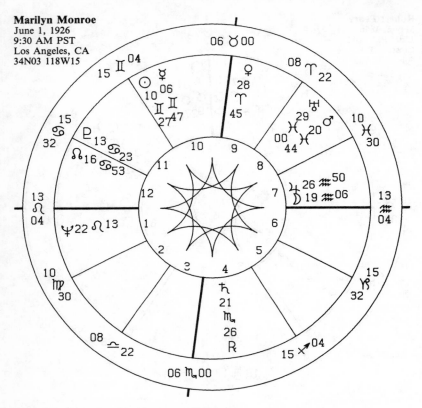

Marilyn Monroe
June 1, 1926
9:30 AM PST
Los Angeles, CA
34N03 118W15

Source: Photo of Birth Certificate in biography (A)

trick for you is in knowing when to keep quiet. You are capable of much tact and diplomacy, writing and speaking ability and are well able to handle most social situations.

With a 10th house Sun, educational, literary and sales fields may attract you. If your Sun is in the 11th house or in the Aquarian decanate, you might consider the diplomatic corps, government service or politics. Whatever you choose, you will make good use of the Gemini Sun charm and versatility and the Leo Ascendant warmth and persistence. Like all Leos, you have a love of teaching, of showing others how to do things. This is especially noticeable if the Sagittarius decanate is rising or the Sun is in the Gemini decanate. With the proper education, you could end up as a counselor or psychiatrist as you have an ability to smooth things out for others. This is most likely if the Sun is in the Libra decanate.

Women with this combination are charming hostesses whose guests always feel welcome. Shallowness and a tendency to exaggerate are your pitfalls and you should try, in telling your stories, not to dramatize them out of proportion. Like most Geminis, you are active and on the go, rarely wanting to stay in one place too long. If the Leo or Aries decanate is on the Ascendant, you may show an interest in the sports field as your Gemini Sun suggests dexterity along with your Leo need to show off.

You have the ability to get your point across in a most acceptable way and others seem to gravitate to you and are willing to listen to your sparkling, informed communication.

LEO ASCENDANT — CANCER SUN

If you were born between June 22nd and July 23rd between approximately 7 AM and 9 AM, you may have this combination.

Your home is important to you and if you can afford it (and you generally can) it is large and lavishly furnished. You love to entertain and nothing pleases you more than when your friends feel free to drop in at any time of the day or night. The only thing is, they should also feel free to help themselves, as in true Leo fashion, you will not necessarily wait on them.

This is a very domestic and maternal combination. Both Leo and Cancer are known for their attachment to children and you must take care not to smother your offspring with love. Surprisingly, sometimes this combination chooses not to have children, feeling that they will not be responsible and secure enough to raise a family successfully. Home-loving, patriotic and astonishingly materialistic, you are a good money earner and handler and usually quite intuitive about investments especially if the Moon is in Taurus, Cancer or Capricorn, or the Sun is in the Cancer decanate.

With the Aries or Sagittarius decanate rising, you can be quite liberal in outlook which is not necessarily a Cancer trait. You are more inclined to engage in activities which support your feelings of independence and freedom. The Leo decanate, by contrast, highlights dramatic ability, but indicates that loving and being loved are of paramount importance.

With an 11th house Sun, you may be active in community affairs, politics or government work. If the Sun is in the 12th house or the Pisces decanate, you are capable of a great deal of manipulation and behind-the-scenes preparation and so you would do well in movie or TV production and direction or financial planning. Since Leo and Cancer are both monetary signs, any field where you could handle money would offer great opportunity. Although you operate with typical Leo extravagance, your Cancer Sun indicates that you are a shrewd and capable manager of other people's assets, especially when the Sun occupies the Scorpio decanate. Though sensitive, you have the Leo aptitude for drama, so this is a good combination for acting as in the case of Olivia de Havilland.

Olivia de Havilland
July 1, 1916
8:40 AM JST
Tokyo, Japan
35N40 139E45

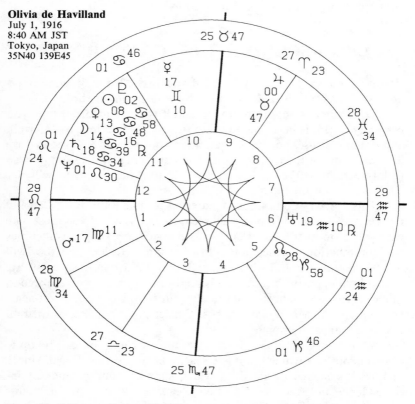

Source: Penfield states "personal" (DD)

Dramatic and perceptive, you often astonish friends and acquaintances with your keen grasp of the political and financial arenas.

LEO ASCENDANT — LEO SUN

If you were born between July 23rd and August 23rd between approximately 5 AM and 7 AM, you may have this combination.

Alex Haley
August 11, 1921
4:55 AM EDT
Ithaca, NY
42N27 76W30

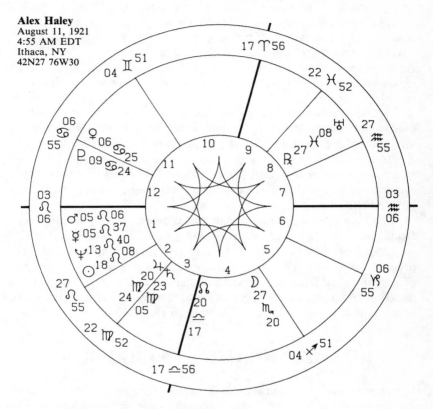

Source: Kaye in *Horoscope Magazine* quotes Birth Certificate (A)

Dramatic, you give the effect of being on stage at all times and you have a flair for showing your best side. Seemingly always in command, especially with a 1st house Sun, you attract others to you by your sheer magnetism and authoritative presence. Affable, outgoing and generous, you have many friends and they are important to you, but things must be run on your terms or you lose interest quickly and turn to some new fields to conquer. Your staying power is highlighted when both the Sun and Ascendant are in the Leo decanate.

Your biggest fault is pride and it can lead you to a fall if you are unaware of other's wishes and feelings. Naturally, the aspects to the Sun are of great importance because with this combination, you have all your eggs in one basket, so to speak. Instead of blending two signs, we are dealing only with Leo and so you act very much as a pure typical Leo — arrogant, generous, extroverted, proud and playful.

With the Sagittarian decanate on either the Sun or Ascendant, you may be quite visionary and philosophical, but in a typical Leo way, you have developed your outlook from your own experiences. If the Aries decanate is prominent, you are quite an entrepreneur and your predilection for anything new and showy may involve you in some far reaching ventures.

If the Sun is in the 1st house, acting (Mae West), writing (Alex Haley) and politics (President Benjamin Harrison) are naturals for you; any field where you can project your vibrant Leo personality. With a 12th house Sun, you are a great social director, restaurant host or hostess, entertainer or dancer (Agnes deMille). The best way for others to persuade you to their line of thinking is through flattery. Vanity is your Achilles heel.

You are open and dramatic and what others see is what they get from you. You can also be very loving; your ego is vulnerable to response from others and you want to feel loved, admired and appreciated in return. You are capable of giving as well as getting lots of psychological strokes. Vibrant and charismatic: you seek love, admiration and attention from others, but are as generous and giving of praise and adulation as you are willing to receive it.

LEO ASCENDANT — VIRGO SUN

If you were born between August 23rd and September 23rd between approximately 3 AM and 5 AM, you may have this combination.

A natural money handler, which Leo is often not, you can earn and invest well and thus seldom have financial worries. Combining your enthusiastic, inspired side (Leo) with your pragmatic and realistic side (Virgo) can result in impressive accomplishments in a number of areas. You radiate caring, generosity and warmth, but are well able to suppress your emotions when it suits you to do so and then you must take care not to appear coldly critical and indifferent.

When the first decanate rises, or the Sun is in the 1st house the dramatic impact of Leo holds full sway and you have a well defined ego, sometimes bordering on the dictatorial and ostentatious. Just think of President Lyndon Johnson and his regal bearing and high-handed ways.

With Mercury, your Sun sign ruler in Virgo or the Sun in the Virgo decanate, you have analytical talent but can go overboard with troublesome details and little odds and ends in typical Virgo fashion, ignoring the large scale problems that need your attention. With Mercury in Leo, you may be more relaxed and a great storyteller, but a trifle pompous. If Mercury is in Libra or the Sun is in the Capricorn decanate, you like to lead a very socially active existence. The 1st house Sun position can also symbolize work with children, entertainment, advertising, investment or any field where you hold power and teach or persuade others.

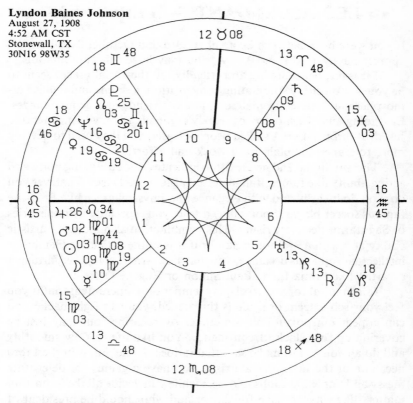

Lyndon Baines Johnson
August 27, 1908
4:52 AM CST
Stonewall, TX
30N16 98W35

Source: Doris Chase Doane (DD)

The Sun in the 2nd house or Taurus decanate often finds you in designing, jewelry or manufacturing fields or in any job in which you can serve the public in some way. There is more Virgo humility apparent in this house position, but Leo charm and affability lend a nice balance to the traditional Virgo diffidence and timidity. The Sagittarian decanate rising may emphasize the urge to roam far and wide, and if the Aries decanate is there, you are more dynamic and forceful than most Virgos. The Leo self-assurance is a good balance for your Virgo often too modest approach to life.

Blending your Leo confidence and need to do more with your Virgo practicality and willingness to work, can result in a highly capable and creative combination.

LEO ASCENDANT — LIBRA SUN

If you were born between September 23rd and October 24th between approximately 1 AM and 3 AM, you may have this combination.

Pleasant, peace-loving and friendly, all the social graces seem to be yours. You enjoy stimulating conversation, a serene and relaxed atmosphere and the congenial company of friends and acquaintances. Easygoing and pleasure-loving, rarely argumentative, you may tend to just drift through life. A skilled people-pleaser, you may need to develop more tolerance for plain hard work and effort.

The Sun in the 2nd house often indicates a good singing voice and acting ability like famed Italian actress, Eleonora Duse. Whatever you do, you do it easily and with elegance and physical grace like Pele, the famous soccer player. Sports may attract you especially with the Aries or Sagittarius decanate rising. This combination also indicates artistic ability and with a 3rd house Sun or if it is in the articulate Gemini or intellectual Aquarius decanate, you may be a writer, composer, arranger or artist like Franz Liszt, Paul Simon or Eugene O'Neill.

It is unusual for you to display temper or temperament, but if you feel your self-esteem or pride is threatened, you can fight back. You can appear outspoken and sometimes overbearing, but may just be covering up for a lack of confidence. You like life to flow smoothly and do all you can to make sure that it does. If the Sun is in the Libra decanate or the Leo decanate rises, you have a genius for delegating messy and unpleasant jobs to others while you decide all the important matters like what to have for dinner and who should be president of the country club.

A partner is necessary for you to feel fulfilled but with the typical Leo desire for power, you prefer the partnership to run on your terms. In spite of your Libra Sun, you seldom lean on others, but instead prefer to be leaned on if the leaner can do it graciously and with appeal.

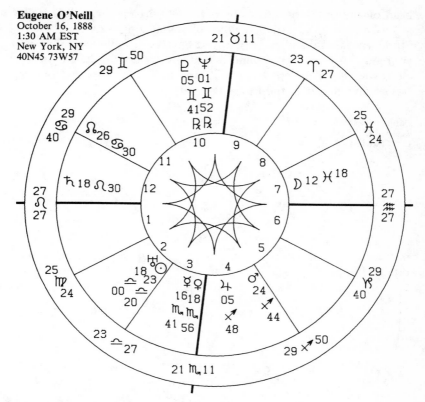

Eugene O'Neill
October 16, 1888
1:30 AM EST
New York, NY
40N45 73W57

Source: Allen in *American Astrology* (C)

Charming, magnetic and intuitively diplomatic, you can be a party favorite: social or political.

LEO ASCENDANT — SCORPIO SUN

If you were born between October 24th and November 23rd between approximately 11 PM and 1 AM, you may have this combination.

This is a very dynamic mixture. Power is your watchword. Your drive needs a constructive channel in the outer world lest you dominate those around you. Hot-tempered, active, compelling and forceful, you see to it that things go your way and you can be extremely dictatorial. You rarely function well in a subordinate position as it is hard for you to take orders and therefore you either act in a starring role or at the head of any endeavor, especially if the Leo decanate is rising. If the game isn't played according to your rules, you don't want to take part. Stubborn, intense and persistent, you have no trouble accomplishing your aims. All that fixity connotes that you are not always easy to get along with as you are not very pliable or acquiescent to another's ideas, unless your Sun is in the Pisces decanate.

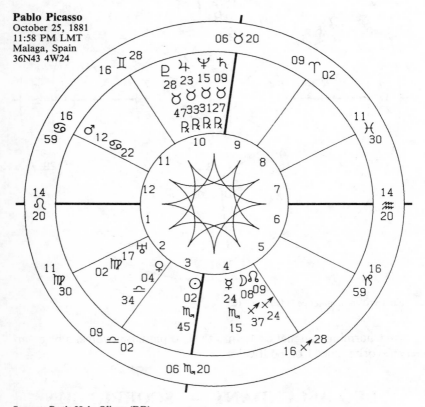

Pablo Picasso
October 25, 1881
11:58 PM LMT
Malaga, Spain
36N43 4W24

Source: Ruth Hale Oliver (DD)

You may appear to put great emphasis on the pursuit of pleasure (particularly with a 5th house Sun) but you are really more concerned with matters of lasting value. This is especially noticeable with the Sun in the penetrating Scorpio decanate or the idealistic Sagittarius decanate rising. You can be very creative; in art (Pablo Picasso), music (Art Garfunkel) or writing, but you are usually a slow starter, going at your own speed and can seldom be hurried by anyone.

With the Sun in the 3rd house, any field where you can communicate your very pronounced and definite ideas is good. A 4th house Sun, or if it is in the Cancer decanate can be quite patriotic and often you will serve your country in some capacity — as a top sergeant in the Army, for instance. Military service is often symbolized by the Aries decanate rising as well. The Sun in the 5th house indicates athletic and management ability and very often we find satirical comedians with this placement. Usually Leo's roar is worse than his bite, but the Scorpio note here makes you a worthy and caustic opponent in any fight.

Some very prominent world leaders have this combination: Hermann Goebbels of Germany, Leo Trotsky of Russia, Indira Gandhi of India, the Shah of Iran and Prince Charles of Great Britain. Whatever your choice of career, you execute it well and rise to the top through sheer diligence and desire. Your dignity is important to you and you make every effort to maintain it.

If someone wants a job well done, you are the person to call upon because you are so dedicated once you are committed to any project. You demonstrate the qualities of dependability and steadfastness better than any other blend of signs.

LEO ASCENDANT — SAGITTARIUS SUN

If you were born between November 23rd and December 22nd between approximately 9 PM and 11 PM, you may have this combination.

This blend is often found in the charts of royalty and it does indicate dignity and noble bearing. Once you decide on your direction and apply yourself you can achieve endlessly. A natural leader and joiner, you may be active in sports as a player, coach or manager especially with a 5th house Sun or if your Sun or Ascendant is in the Leo decanate. Fun-loving, quite philosophical, creative and proud, you would also do well in the educational or political fields. You are very open and kind and you love fun and games; sometimes to the exclusion of productivity. When you work, you work hard but when you play, you play hard and often your problem is that you would rather play than work.

You have a tendency to drift impatiently through life always seeking the pot of gold at the end of the rainbow especially if the Sagittarian decanate is involved with either the Sun or Ascendant. A gambler and risk taker, your motto could well be, "Nothing ventured, nothing gained." With all the fire in your chart your attitude could easily be, "I know what I want and I'm going to get it. Out of my way world!"

With the Sun or Ascendant in the Aries decanate, self-confidence is your strong point; you believe in yourself and your philosophies and don't like to be challenged. With a 4th house Sun, contracting, home decorating, animal husbandry and forestry are all good fields for you. Many people in the jewelry trades have this combination. With such an unrestricted chart (the Sun trine the Ascendant sign) it is easy for you to take the effortless way that may lead to a life of crime, due to your ability to charm your way into and out of situations like convicted rapist-murderer, Theodore Bundy. Jane Fonda has put the energy of this combination to better use.

Jane Fonda
December 21, 1937
7:57 PM EST
New York, NY
40N45 73W57

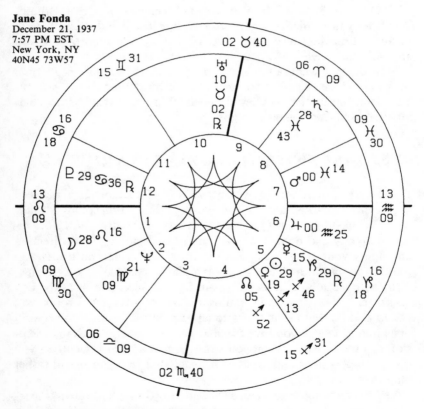

Source: Carol Tebbs quotes a mutual friend (C)

Your positive attitude and well developed ego make it easy for you to accomplish your not inconsiderable goals.

LEO ASCENDANT — CAPRICORN SUN

If you were born between December 22nd and January 21st between approximately 7 PM and 9 PM, you may have this combination.

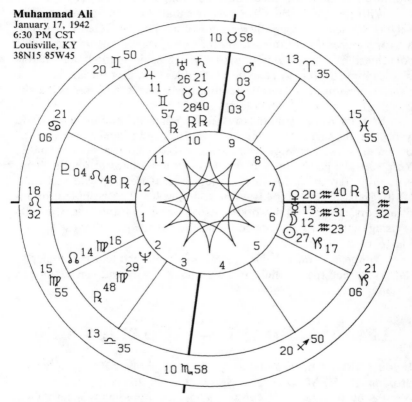

Muhammad Ali
January 17, 1942
6:30 PM CST
Louisville, KY
38N15 85W45

Source: Steinbrecher quotes Birth Certificate in *Mercury Hour* (A)

You display all the qualities of leadership and then you back up your show of authority by your natural enterprise and responsible attitude. Usually gifted with a good sense of humor, you respond well to others. This combination shows a blend of warmth and charm (Leo) with careful efficiency (Capricorn). Strongly individualistic, you go your own way, doing your job thoroughly and competently in your chosen field. With a 5th house Sun or the Leo decanate on the Ascendant, this could be acting, teaching or competing in sports.

The Sun in the 6th house or the Virgo decanate often finds you in editing, publishing or journalism. Not generally very creative, unless it is in music, you do well in a position of management in the business or professional world. Until you arrive at a top level position, it is not easy for you to take orders and this shows a need to learn submissiveness and humility or it will take you much longer to reach the top.

With the Sun in the Capricorn decanate, you can climb to great heights as you are a doggedly determined hard worker (Capricorn) with a strong sense of the dramatic (Leo). One if the best examples of this combination is boxer Muhammad Ali. He projects the image of one who cannot possibly lose, so he rarely does. The Sagittarian decanate rises, indicating he naturally tends to exaggerate and mirroring the potential of his religious interests.

You are not as spontaneous as your Leo Ascendant makes you appear on the surface and are more cautious and prudent than you like others to know. You may even tend to negative attitudes occasionally. You want the good things in life and will work hard to obtain them, especially if your Sun is in the Taurus decanate, and you feel that, "whatever is worth doing is worth doing well." This combination indicates one of the hardest working Leos, especially if the Aries decanate is rising. Much of your Leo roar and flash is tempered by the steadying focus of Capricorn.

Competent and capable, yet with lots of dash and the ability to dare, you seek the spotlight in a businesslike way and can surface as a leader in anything you do.

LEO ASCENDANT — AQUARIUS SUN

If you were born between January 21st and February 20th between approximately 5 PM and 7 PM, you may have this combination.

People oriented, that's you! Friendly and outgoing, you have your helping hand out to others whether or not they want it. You are somewhat contradictory in your attitudes; at one moment you are concerned for appearance and what others think (Leo) and at the next you could care less for propriety and convention (Aquarius). Exuberant and extroverted, you rarely meet a stranger and your warmth comes across in your genuine kindness and concern for another's well-being.

Often a trendsetter in a new field, especially with the Aries decanate rising or the Sun in the Aquarius decanate, you are attracted to large groups working in humanitarian endeavors. A typical example of this combination was Jackie Robinson who pioneered the black man's participation in big league baseball. His Sun in the Gemini decanate indicated the mobility so necessary to an athlete.

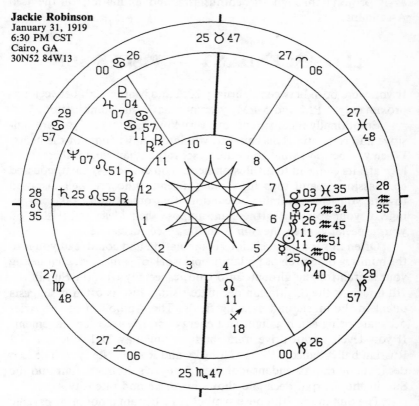

Jackie Robinson
January 31, 1919
6:30 PM CST
Cairo, GA
30N52 84W13

Source: *Wait Til Next Year* by C. Rowan (B)

The Sun in the 7th house or in the Libra decanate symbolizes counseling, psychological and psychiatric, with the proper training and education. With a 6th house Sun, or if the Leo decanate is rising, the entertainment field often attracts you. In any undertaking you choose, you are persistent and often brilliant. Romantically you can get carried away and prudence should be developed in personal relationships. With the Ascendant in the Sagittarian decanate, you are quite sociable and a fun-loving bon vivant. If the potential is mishandled, you can be a revolutionary kook going your own way and doing your own thing with little regard for others' thoughts or feelings. You are capable of pulling the Aquarius affability together with your Leo personality and seeing things in their entirety.

This is one combination where the Aquarius Sun is really gregarious as it projects through the enthusiasm and animation of the Leo Ascendant.

LEO ASCENDANT — PISCES SUN

If you were born between February 20th and March 20th between approximately 3 PM and 5 PM, you may have this combination.

Emotionally inconsistent, but very kind and loving, you are sensitive and romantic. This can lead you into many affairs of the heart. When you perceive what you want to see rather than what is there, your love affairs can lead to disillusionment. You are very sympathetic and compassionate and thus have many friends who are well disposed toward you. But you must be cautious that others don't take advantage of your seeming softness and impose their ideas and wishes on you, especially when the Sun is in the Pisces decanate.

Often this is a very religious combination and could lead you into the ministry or church or philanthropic work of some sort, channeling your search for the ultimate into God, especially with the Sun in the 7th house or the Sagittarian decanate rising. Just as often it suggests talent in the music and dancing fields. The symbolism of the Aries decanate rising can highlight vast energy and the need for movement. If you develop your drive, fame and fortune may find you, as it did Russian ballet dancers Vaslav Nijinsky and Rudolf Nureyev. The Leo decanate on the Ascendant indicates Nureyev's dramatic flair and the Sun in the Scorpio decanate shows his drive and intensity.

The Sun in the 8th house symbolizes a certain amount of psychic and intuitive ability which could be channeled into a positive direction somewhat along the line of seer Edgar Cayce. Sailors, fishermen and maritime workers may also have this placement, especially if the Sun is in the Cancer decanate. With a 7th house Sun, once your partner is chosen, you can become the most faithful of spouses, due to your inherent Pisces need for emotional stability and your Leo fixity and affection. This is a very good pairing for any career in the acting and dramatic professions because of your ability to express the Pisces pliability through the Leo creative energy and you slip so easily into any role and make it your own.

You have a tendency to look for the beautiful dream, ideal love that does not exist. You are the original believer in the fairy tale of "living happily ever after." Your search for infinite beauty can be directed to art. Beauty is more likely to satisfy ecstatic yearnings than

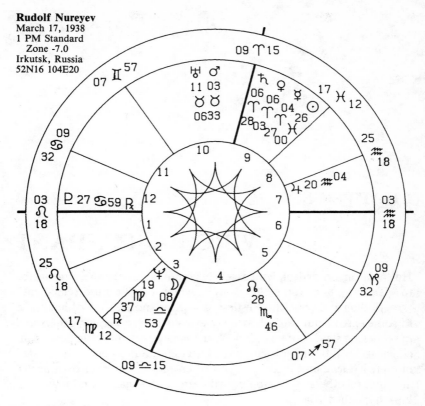

Rudolf Nureyev
March 17, 1938
1 PM Standard
Zone -7.0
Irkutsk, Russia
52N16 104E20

Source: Derek and Julia Parker (C)

hoping for the perfect partner or spouse who does not exist.

This is the most dramatic of all combinations. Leo drama and Pisces magic can cast any illusion.

CHAPTER SIX

VIRGO ASCENDANT

Hardworking, practical, with excellent common sense, you are dedicated to efficiency and doing things well, which can be misdirected into flaw-finding and criticism. Restless, a worrier and creature of habit and to some extent, puritanical, you are at your best in helping others and in rendering service of any kind. You have a strong belief in your principles and will fight for them to the bitter end. Since you are interested in diet, hygiene and medicine, you often talk about your own health and that of others. Occasionally you are quite negative and may even be a hypochondriac.

Usually you are **not** a leader; you follow through on what others start and can be depended upon to see that a good job is done, working long, steady hours and totally dedicated to the job at hand. Basically uncomfortable in crowds, if you are asked to participate in an event that doesn't intrigue you, you can say no and mean it.

Although you are very methodical and exacting, you have excellent perception, intuition and discrimination. Sensitive to your environment and thoughtful of others, you are somewhat quiet, reserved and may be lacking in self-confidence even if the Sun is in a fire sign. But you are occasionally inclined to give unasked for advice and may be hurt if it is not followed or when it is suggested that you mind your own business.

The placement of the planet Mercury is very important because it is your ruler and it can often add dimension and scope to the whole chart if well positioned and/or aspected. Though externally cool and collected, inwardly you can be a mass of anxiety which can lead to ragged nerves. Though you observe a good diet, you tend to stomach upsets and your sign single-handedly keeps the Tums company in business. In spite of your interest in health and hygiene, or maybe because of it, you are surprisingly healthy and most of your illnesses stem from worry, fatigue and mental tension. Often you are a vegetarian and know exactly how food should be cooked for the best nutritional advantage. Staying relaxed and not subjecting yourself to excessive pressure will also help you keep healthy. Virgo symbolizes the need to be efficient. If that need is overdone, illness can be an unconscious way to take a vacation. If the push for effectiveness is underdone, illness allows people to not feel guilty about a lack of accomplishment. A feeling of productivity is important to you, but do not overwork.

Virgo is one of the slender, moderately built signs, but you often have long legs, hands, arms, feet and fingers even if you are not tall. You have the length of limb in common with the other Mercury ruled sign, Gemini. Like all the mutable signs, you tend to have a high forehead and you are often characterized by a weak chin and small bird-like features. Many times the women with this sign rising are rather undeveloped and built like a young boy. The most distinctive thing about Virgo's appearance is the eyes, which are usually hooded and rather small, but clear and sparkling. You generally have fine, plentiful hair, a beautiful complexion and your fine bone structure makes you extremely photogenic.

VIRGO ASCENDANT — ARIES SUN

If you were born between March 21st and April 20th between approximately 3 PM and 5 PM, you may have this combination.

This duo indicates great concentration of energies on the technical level. Your energy and ambition can be channeled into any number of practical pursuits. You are able to make an impact in the real world. Aries dares and Virgo hangs back, but by fits and starts, you generally get where you are going sooner or later with Aries drive and Virgo capability. You are ambitious and a conscientious worker, but you don't always follow through like a typical Virgo unless the Ascendant is in the persevering Taurus decanate, or the Sun is in the fixed Leo decanate. You have the broad scope of active Aries and the Virgo attention to detail, but people sometimes have trouble understanding your ability to detach yourself from a situation where you feel too personally involved. On the rare occasion when you do reach out for their help, you may appear too needy and people tend to shy away.

With the Sun in either the 7th or 8th house, human relationships are important, but do not depend on others for your self-esteem. You may also be a nature lover. Since you are understanding and sympathetic, your friends feel they can open up to you and you give good sound advice and actual service, going out of your way to be helpful and compassionate. This is especially noted when the Sun is in the Aries decanate. Your fault is that you may judge too harshly especially when the Ascendant is in the Capricorn decanate. Channel your fault-finding skills into tasks rather than people. You appear more ardent than you actually are; in fact, you are quite discriminating in your personal attachments which is an unusual trait for Aries.

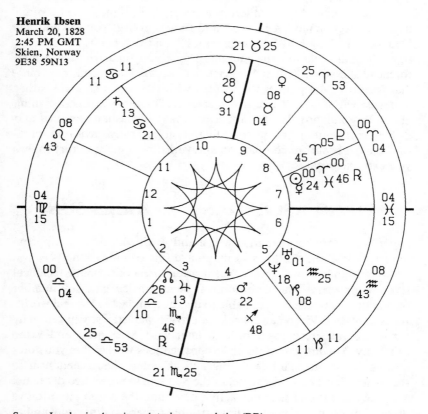

Henrik Ibsen
March 20, 1828
2:45 PM GMT
Skien, Norway
9E38 59N13

Source: Lyndoe in *American Astrology* speculative (DD)

If the Sun is in the idealistic Sagittarian decanate or the hygienic

Virgo decanate is rising, you are often the dedicated doctor or nurse. Many botanists, naturalists and those interested in health and health food are found with this combination. Henrik Ibsen who had this pairing studied medicine and chemistry before he became a poet and dramatist.

Aggressive, yet discriminating, you are quite goal oriented and once on the road to what you want to achieve, you let nothing get in your way until you reach your destination.

VIRGO ASCENDANT — TAURUS SUN

If you were born between April 20th and May 20th between approximately 1 PM and 3 PM, you may have this combination.

Dependable and sincere, practical and conservative, you are not likely to take romantic or professional chances and are certainly not one to throw your money away carelessly. Waste is abhorrent to you and you like to bet only on sure things, if you bet at all. You are the ultimate perfectionist. While method and deliberation motivate you, you have an aptitude for saying the right thing at the right time, especially when both the Sun and Ascendant are in the pragmatic Virgo decanate. When you offer criticism, as all Virgos are prone to do, it is constructive and generally well received. Your orientation is toward the material world. You believe in what you can see, hear, feel and measure. Comfort, security and stability all appeal and you will patiently pursue your planned path to the proper destination. For fullest satisfaction, working with tangible objects is best.

With the Sun in the 9th house, you aspire high, often in the educational or writing fields. The Sun in the 8th house or in the Taurus decanate or that decanate rising frequently shows involvement with the financial or money handling fields such as banking, cashiering or accounting which you take to like a duck takes to water. You, of all people admire achievement in others. The accord between the Sun and Ascendant suggests you are not terribly driven to achieve on your own unless the ambitious Capricorn decanate is involved with either the Sun or Ascendant. What you do, you do well because of your desire for perfection. Novelist Charlotte Bronte and baseball player Warren Spahn are good examples of the dedication to excellence which is so often found in this combination.

Social, literary and often very musical, you are skilled in dealing with physical reality and are a gracious, charming and helpful person.

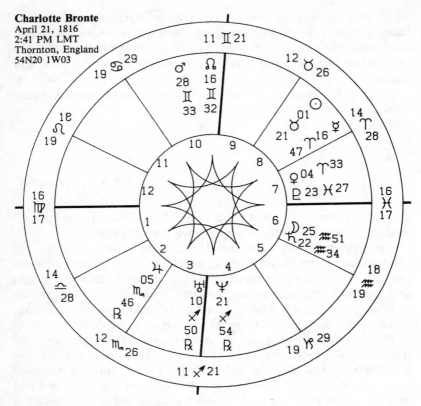

Charlotte Bronte
April 21, 1816
2:41 PM LMT
Thornton, England
54N20 1W03

Source: *Sabian Symbols* #134 (C)

VIRGO ASCENDANT — GEMINI SUN

If you were born between May 20th and June 21st between approximately 11 AM and 1 PM, you may have this combination.

With the double Mercury rulership, all Mercury attributes are emphasized and the aspects to and placement of your ruling planet become all important. Agile, restless, observant, knowledgeable and imaginative, you are never dull and often receive quick flashes of inspiration. You are genial, but warmth is something you need to work to develop. You're talkative, sometimes too much so and you may chatter aimlessly and endlessly about trivial things. You are endowed with a clever wit and you are one of the few Geminis who would never think of being late for a date or appointment.

If your volatile energy is properly channeled, you may be a literary whiz like Nobel prize winner Thomas Mann. His Ascendant in the Capricorn decanate showed his ambition and the Sun in the Libra decanate indicated his interest in and understanding of how people think and feel.

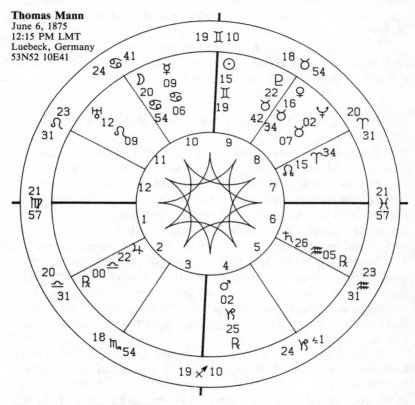

Thomas Mann
June 6, 1875
12:15 PM LMT
Luebeck, Germany
53N52 10E41

Source: *Sabian Symbols* #638 (C)

You have the ability to say the right thing to the right person at the right time, thus helping yourself socially and professionally. The Sun in the 9th house or in the fluent Gemini decanate highlights your literary ability and suggests professions in the editing, publishing, news and secretarial fields. Often this combination indicates a very philosophical approach to life. Rachel Carson with her vital concern for the environment is a good example of this placement.

With a 10th house Sun, you seem destined to make your mark in the world either in business or a profession because you are adaptable, quick and discerning. A romantic butterfly, you may flit from one amour to another and unless Venus is in stable Taurus or the Ascendant is in the Taurus decanate, companionship may be better for you than partnership. If the discriminating Virgo decanate is rising or the Sun is in the Aquarian decanate, your selectivity is even more noticeable and you must take care not to come across to others as cold and snobbish.

You are meticulous, dexterous and quite impartial so you are an asset in your neighborhood, with your friends and especially in your relations with co-workers and bosses.

VIRGO ASCENDANT — CANCER SUN

If you were born between June 22nd and July 23rd between approximately 9 AM and 11 AM, you may have this combination.

Domestic and protective of home and family, you like things to be neat and well ordered. You are discriminating, give careful attention to detail and are anxious to protect those you love and cherish. Once you overcome your Cancer timidity, you are a naturally friendly person and are often drawn into group activities, especially with an 11th house Sun. Many times you are the leader of a group that shares your interests, much as author Ernest Hemingway, whose coterie of friends joined him in his fishing and hunting expeditions. His Sun in the Pisces decanate showed his strong need for approval from others and the Virgo decanate rising suggested his phenomenal recall of facts and happenings.

Somewhat sensitive and vacillating, you nonetheless have a lot of ambition, especially if the Sun is in the Scorpio decanate or the Capricorn decanate rises. With Cancer perception and Virgo discernment, you are able to outguess others without even trying. Thus you are usually able to reach the top in your field whatever it is. Sometimes you even surprise yourself with your success and you may tend to become domineering and overbearing which is not generally either a Cancer or Virgo characteristic. This is particularly noticeable when you feel your security or safety is threatened.

The materialistic Taurus decanate rising or the Sun in the security-oriented Cancer decanate often indicates an interest in economics and you may well seek a career in this or related fields. With the Sun in the 10th house, you are frequently a good salesperson, restauranteur, politician or administrator. Often this combination seems to indicate a photographic memory. Once you achieve an objective outlook and an understanding of your position in the community, no one is kinder or more thoughtful than you.

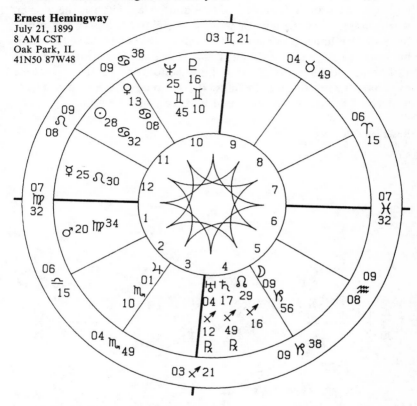

Ernest Hemingway
July 21, 1899
8 AM CST
Oak Park, IL
41N50 87W48

Source: *Ernest Hemingway* by Carlos Baker (B)

Concerned, forgiving and truly helpful, you will go out of your way to see that others are comfortable, comforted and consoled.

VIRGO ASCENDANT — LEO SUN

If you were born between July 23rd and August 23rd between approximately 7 AM and 9 AM, you may have this combination.

Ideally, you need a role where you can give aid to others in a showy and authoritative way. You sometimes have difficulty aligning your Leo individuality to the service oriented Virgo Ascendant. It is not easy for you to fulfill the part of willing helpmeet and often you turn to nursing or counseling as a comfortable way to achieve this, especially when the Virgo decanate rises.

You are usually fond of children and have a gift for the written word; many good teachers or writers of children's books and music have an 11th house Sun placement. Some authors who have this combination are Guy deMaupassant, Edna Ferber and Rupert Brooke. The 12th house position of the Sun requires solitude and some time alone each day to work through feelings. If you do not make sure you have a place of refuge, your emotional balance could be upset.

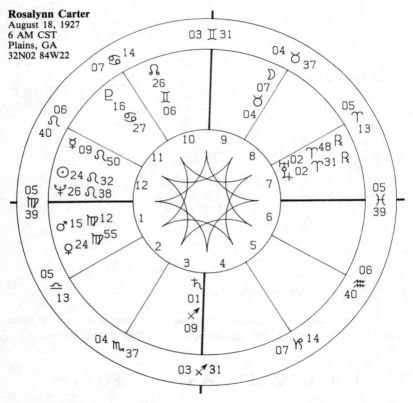

Rosalynn Carter
August 18, 1927
6 AM CST
Plains, GA
32N02 84W22

Source: *Family Circle* magazine (C)

Very creative, especially with the Sun in the Leo decanate, you have strong feelings of right and wrong and you often inspire others to unlimited accomplishment, in the meanwhile letting your Virgo diffidence stifle your Leo confidence. This is not quite so apparent if the Sun is in the Aries decanate (indicating self confidence) or if the Capricorn decanate rises (indicating ambition but possible self-criticism). But it is especially noticeable when the Sun is in the 12th house, suggesting you can fall into wanting things perfect, or not at all. When the Taurus decanate is rising, your creativity may express through handicrafts, especially making objects that are beautiful and add comfort to the home.

Unless Mercury, your Ascendant ruler is also in Leo, or the Sun is in the Sagittarian decanate, you may seem shy and humble, but in reality you usually have a strong ego and are tolerant, hospitable and generous like all Leos. Very often this placement can designate the devoted woman like Rosalynn Carter, wife of the former President, who backs a powerful husband, with wisdom, patience and courage.

Selfless, amiable and supportive, your Leo Sun finds direction through your Virgo Ascendant and you are more extroverted than is expected from most Virgos. Virgo practicality channels Leo creativity for productive results in the world.

VIRGO ASCENDANT — VIRGO SUN

If you were born between August 23rd and September 23rd between approximately 5 AM and 7 AM, you may have this combination.

No other combination in the zodiac gives such attention to detail or has such powers of observation. Your major talent lies in analysis and discrimination. You shine at finding flaws, figuring out what is wrong and how to make things more efficient. But your critical eye can be a problem if directed at people rather than your work. You are extremely self-sufficient, but you must take care not to appear to be too much so, or you can come across as cold and unapproachable, particularly if the Capricorn decanate is involved with your Sun or Ascendant. Schedules, rules and regulations, method and particularity are your gods and you are a marvelous detail worker, but you should watch that all of this does not impair your breadth of scope and your depth of vision. Remember, rules are made to be broken.

You are very sentimental, yet you set intellectual compatibility above the thrill of passion and romantic impulse, especially if your ruler, Mercury is also in aloof Virgo. If Mercury is in companionable Libra, this tendency is modified somewhat, but it is still present and you are a very circumspect and proper person. If Mercury is in fiery Leo, you are more relaxed in your romantic encounters, but still quite discriminating.

You have a strong sense of responsibility so you function well in a position of authority over others as your detachment allows criticism without sting especially if the Sun or Ascendant is in the Virgo decanate. You like to help others adjust to things, so with a 1st house Sun, you work well in a judicial, directorial or advisory capacity. With the Sun in the 12th house, police and detective work may appeal to you as do chemistry, research and computer analysis. This is also a good combination for the competent, efficient office worker. With the Sun or Ascendant in the Taurus decanate, music or finance could be your choice. Whatever field you choose, your employer can expect competent, dedicated service from you.

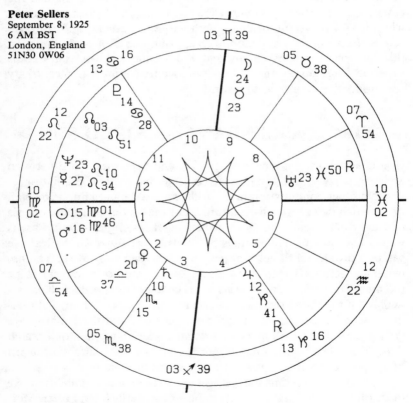

Peter Sellers
September 8, 1925
6 AM BST
London, England
51N30 0W06

Source: Freeman in *American Astrology* 6/71 (C)

Some prominent people with this placement are movie producer Samuel Goldwyn and actors Roddy McDowell and Peter Sellers.

An organizer, neat, serious and systematic, your intellectual outlook is broad and flexible and your life style conservative and traditional.

VIRGO ASCENDANT — LIBRA SUN

If you were born between September 23rd and October 24th between approximately 3 AM and 5 AM, you may have this combination.

Modest, practical and discerning, you know well the value of cooperation. Socially aware, charming and witty, you are very companionable and often a sought after guest. Drawn to the artistic fields, you can excel in interior decoration, fashion design and acting. Your critical capacity is strong and when properly focused, can aid you to a successful career in business, a profession or the arts. However, you should curtail this critical bent in your human relationships where it is not always well received. You would question that others see you as critical, fussy, neat and a worrier, but this is because you may perceive "practicality" or "realism" where others experience criticism. Procrastination can be a danger as Virgo wants it all **right**; Libra wants it fair and even, so you keep gathering more information and put off acting on it. The Libra vacillation seems to be underscored with this combination.

You can be the bubbly extrovert one minute and the coolly detached spectator the next. A tendency to self-pity should be handled or you can cause yourself much unhappiness with a complaining and whining approach to life. Actor Montgomery Clift is a good example of this pairing. He was dissatisfied with himself and the world around him and could find no acceptable way out of his dilemma. The Sun in the restless Gemini decanate suggested the potential of his indecisiveness and inability to settle down.

The Sun in the 1st house or the Libra decanate often does well as a social or cruise director while the 2nd house Sun is creative in almost any field. Either placement is quite expressive and outgoing when the energy is positively used. Companionship is a must for you and you generally marry quite young. But in the contradictory way of Libra, sometimes you choose not to marry at all. The Taurus decanate rising may indicate more stability than is usually present. If the Capricorn decanate rises, the need to achieve status and recognition is more pronounced. If the Sun is in the Aquarian decanate, you are less modest and unassuming, more inclined to go your own unique way. Extreme modesty and self-effacement is symbolized by the Virgo decanate on the Ascendant. You do your work and never dream of blowing your own horn.

Montgomery Clift
October 17, 1920
2:30 AM CST
Omaha, NB
41N15 95W57

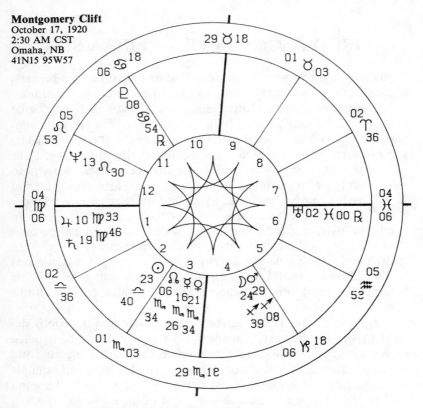

Source: Church of Life from Birth Certificate (A)

The alliance of Virgo propriety and Libran conviviality shows you as a perceptive and quite conventional person whom others respect, admire and look up to.

VIRGO ASCENDANT — SCORPIO SUN

If you were born between October 24th and November 23rd between approximately 1 AM and 3 AM, you may have this combination.

Perseverance is your keynote. You are determined to finish what you start and do it all effectively. Objective, astute and outspoken, you are very competent and capable of great concentration. You should try to direct this concentration into broad humanitarian channels rather than tie yourself to self-serving, trifling areas.

Cool, direct and very self-sufficient, you like the good things in life (like all Scorpios), are ambitious and you can aspire to a position of some importance. Though willing to give service to others, you have an intense and almost neurotic dislike for accepting favors from anyone else. You don't intend to obligate yourself to anyone. This is most likely when the Capricorn decanate rises or when the Sun is in the Scorpio decanate. Both placements symbolize an intense need to control your own life.

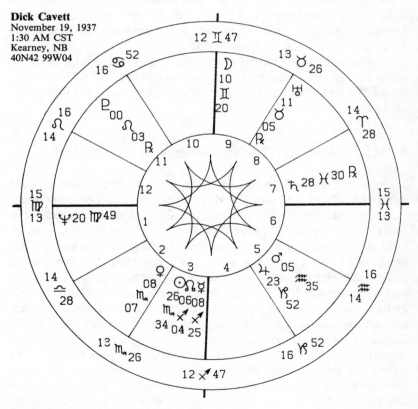

Dick Cavett
November 19, 1937
1:30 AM CST
Kearney, NB
40N42 99W04

Source: Stewart in *American Astrology* (C)

Dependable and reliable, you are aware of your own goals and strive to get ahead on your own, thus you usually go to work when quite young. When the Virgo decanate is on the Ascendant as well, your sense of self is tied to your job and early employment is even more likely. You feel good about yourself when you are being productive and effective. With a 2nd house Sun, or the Taurus decanate on the Ascendant, you usually have an uncanny ability in the financial fields. The Sun in the 3rd house often indicates the executive secretary, electronics engineer or business machine operator. You are quite creative and can turn a hobby into a productive and financially rewarding business. The medical and nursing fields are also a good bet if your Sun is in the Pisces or Cancer decanate.

Emotionally quite well controlled, you can even be cold-blooded if you feel it necessary and so make a detached and objective commentator or TV interviewer like Dick Cavett. By developing warmth and genuine compassion, you will attract more friendliness and sensitivity from those you come in contact with.

Your capable attitude that nothing is impossible for you to accomplish encourages others to rely on you and they are seldom disappointed as they discover your great thoroughness and organizational skills.

VIRGO ASCENDANT — SAGITTARIUS SUN

If you were born between November 23rd and December 22nd between approximately 11 PM and 1 AM, you may have this combination.

Idealistic, clever, often brilliant, you aim high and can achieve your goals with effort and diligence. You have a strong willingness to work hard, an expansive attitude and the ability to express yourself well. Your competence with a 3rd house Sun or the Virgo decanate rising is often expressed as literary or inventive talent, like author Louisa May Alcott and entrepreneur Walt Disney. You are often deeply religious, especially when the Sun occupies the Sagittarius decanate. With your Sun in the 4th house, your roots go deep, but you may suffer from a deeply ingrained inferiority complex which is rarely apparent to others. A perfect example of this was Emily Dickinson, the poet whose works were not published until after her death. Even though her 3rd house Sun was in the (usually confident) Aries decanate, she was a very shy and retiring, but creative person. A domineering father to whom she was devoted, kept her subjugated to his will.

The Sagittarian outlook that feels, "I should be perfect" combined with the Virgo, "Look at all my flaws" attitude can lead to inferiority feelings if you do not make a comfortable blend of ideals and goals

("I'm becoming more perfect") with reality ("These are the necessary, practical steps").

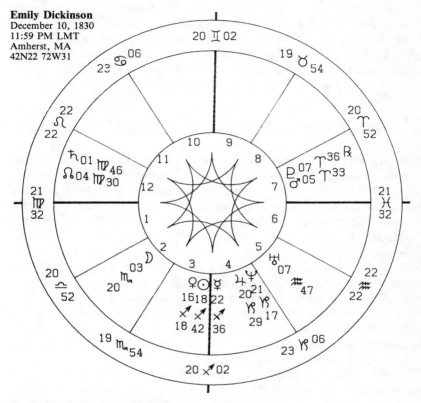

Emily Dickinson
December 10, 1830
11:59 PM LMT
Amherst, MA
42N22 72W31

Source: *Sabian Symbols* #275 (C)

The Capricorn decanate rising seems to emphasize your business ability while the Taurus decanate there indicates musical or artistic talent. You sometimes fail to put yourself across in spite of your broad philosophical reasoning. You must learn to develop your self-confidence and unless the Sun is in the Leo decanate, this may be difficult for you. Allowing yourself to be human helps. Focus on small, reachable steps toward final goals, rather than criticizing yourself for not having it all together. Occasionally this combination signifies a speech problem, stuttering or stammering. Of course, other things in the chart would have to concur.

Romantically dependent, you really shouldn't live alone since personal contacts are vital to you and you sense this and therefore often stay in the bosom of your family much longer than is expected of a Sagittarian. Because of the romantic dependency, you may also, out of misplaced loyalty, stay in a marriage situation you have long since outgrown. Sometimes you are overly talkative and inclined to be critical and tactless, but you are a kind and dedicated friend. You are well suited to the professions — law, teaching, writing, editing and publishing.

Loyal, understanding and duty oriented, you are always willing to reach out and help your fellow human.

VIRGO ASCENDANT — CAPRICORN SUN

If you were born between December 22nd and January 21st between approximately 9 PM and 11 PM, you may have this combination.

Solemn and practical, your life generally runs smoothly and you seem sheltered and protected. The trine between your Sun and Ascendant signs denotes much inner harmony and ease. This doesn't mean that you drift through life aimlessly; on the contrary, you are very hardworking and you take life seriously, sometimes too much so, especially if your Sun or Ascendant is in the Capricorn decanate. Modest, dignified and diplomatic, you conduct yourself in such a way that people know exactly where they stand with you — at least on the surface.

The best example of this combination is Richard Nixon who embodied the "life is serious, life is earnest" philosophy and the belief that he was so upstanding and forthright that no one could ever suspect him of any double dealing.

If either the Sun or Ascendant are in the affectionate Taurus decanate, you are warmer and come across as caring and considerate of others. If the Virgo decanate is prominent with either the Sun or Ascendant, your discriminative qualities may surface as criticism. Romantically somewhat aloof, you must take care not to seem cold and unfeeling. Your dignified bearing can create a barrier between you and those you feel deeply for, unless Venus is in Pisces (where it suggests more softness and romanticism). Learn to relax and unbend so that others may feel your earthy warmth and see your sincere kindliness.

A 4th house Sun often symbolizes an attraction to farming, mining or the real estate business; any field that gives you a feeling of roots and groundedness. If your Sun is in the 5th house, you may have an inclination to teaching, law or politics. Sometimes this is a very musical placement.

You have a businesslike, common sense attitude toward life and can be the most efficient of pragmatists.

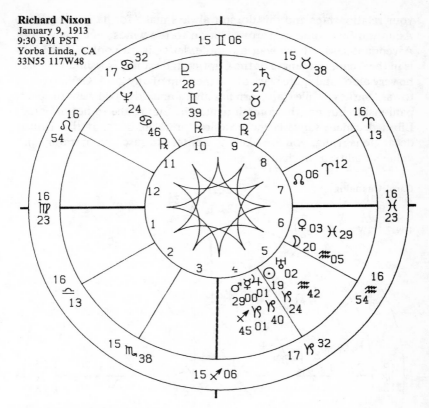

Richard Nixon
January 9, 1913
9:30 PM PST
Yorba Linda, CA
33N55 117W48

Source: Church of Light (C)

VIRGO ASCENDANT — AQUARIUS SUN

If you were born between January 21st and February 20th between approximately 7 PM and 9 PM, you may have this combination.

This is where the Aquarian humanitarianism really shines forth. You have a willingness to do for others, not because of the reward involved but because it seems right and proper for you to do so. This combination seems to correlate with a most striking appearance, not necessarily beauty, but certainly distinction. Friendly, but cool and detached, you appear conventional and restrained (Virgo) but when it is least expected you do or say something incongruous and unpredictable (Aquarius). Your biggest fault is that you can take yourself too seriously and so you must learn to cultivate a sense of humor.

Amicable and genuinely fond of people, you tend to intellectualize your relationships and this doesn't always make for happiness. Your Aquarian Sun wants to throw caution to the winds, but your Virgo Ascendant says, "Now wait a minute, let's play it cool." If the Sun is in the Gemini decanate or the Capricorn decanate is rising, you may be very aloof and quite wary of partnership of any kind. Gemini tends toward variety, while Capricorn has high standards. You want the companionship but not the commitment. The Sun in the (other-oriented) Libra decanate suggests more desire for relatedness. If the Taurus decanate is rising, you are likely to appreciate ease and harmony and value stability over change.

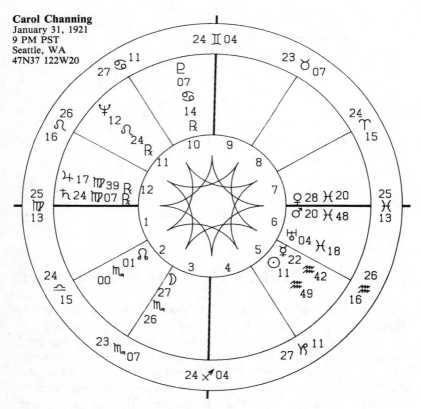

Carol Channing
January 31, 1921
9 PM PST
Seattle, WA
47N37 122W20

Source: *Contemporary Sidereal Horoscopes* (A)

Whether your Sun is in the 5th or 6th house, you can excel in the medical field and social services and also in computer technology. You are often an excellent nurse, therapist or dietician; any line that is

humanely helpful. You may be caught up in the food conveying or catering business as a waitress, waiter, hostess or bartender, especially with
the Sun in the Aquarius decanate or the Virgo decanate rising. Surprisingly, many actors and entertainers have this combination; Tallulah
Bankhead, Ann Sothern, Carol Channing, Zsa Zsa Gabor and Eddie
Cantor, just to mention a few.

Appropriately applied, this blend indicates the realistic revolutionary: someone willing to work to achieve a more open, tolerant world
with equal opportunity for all.

VIRGO ASCENDANT — PISCES SUN

If you were born between February 20th and March 21st between approximately 5 PM and 7 PM, you may have this combination.

You have a very strong, truly compassionate feeling for others,
but you are apt to involve yourself in situations better left alone. You
seek not only to help people, but you literally want to take them under
your wing and look out for them sympathetically and even tenderly.
Thus you can be gullible and easily taken advantage of. You may not
understand why people turn on you and resist your well-meant advice
and concern. Then you feel sorry for yourself and tend to wallow in
self-pity. If you could turn your reforming abilities to practical use in
the social services or counseling fields, they would certainly reward you
in a more positive way. A prime example of the gullibility of this combination is kidnap victim Patty Hearst who was so suggestible to the
demands of her captors.

With a 6th house Sun, if the Sun is in the medical Scorpio or nurturing Cancer decanate or if the hygienic Virgo decanate is rising, you
may choose to be a nurse, doctor, veterinarian or animal groomer. The
Sun in the 7th house often indicates work in the philanthropic or sales
fields. You can be an admirable advice-to-the-lovelorn columnist or
a reforming journalist as you are literate and fluent and usually gifted
with ability for the spoken and written word. This is often quite
noticeable when the Capricorn decanate rises. When the Taurus
decanate is rising, you may be born into the lap of luxury or make it
to that point through your own endeavors.

Occasionally this combination indicates the "unneat" Virgo; your
mind is orderly but your body is untidy and you are careless of your
appearance and surroundings, which is unusual for Virgo. This seems
most prevalent when the Sun is in the Pisces decanate. Romantically
credulous, you often marry someone you can take care of, a weak

Patty Hearst
February 20, 1954
6:01 PM PST
San Francisco, CA
37N45 122W26

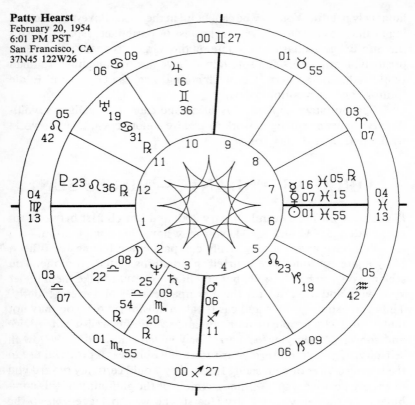

Source: *Contemporary Sidereal Horoscopes* (A)

person who will lean on you. Then, you tend to complain bitterly about being used and taken advantage of. This is most often the case when the Sun is in the 7th house. If you are using the energy positively, you are very idealistic and able to make the best of any partnership. Gentle and good-natured, you are very concerned for others and they sense this and return your sympathy and consideration accordingly.

There is a natural complementary here. Virgo needs Pisces vision to rise above petty details to a sense of higher purpose. Pisces needs Virgo common sense and willingness to work to keep from falling into pure fantasy. Together they suggest the practical idealist.

CHAPTER SEVEN

LIBRA ASCENDANT

Justice and harmony are your keywords and when your sense of propriety and balance is disturbed, you can become vacillating and easily influenced. If you have ever tried to balance an old fashioned two-sided scale (the symbol for this sign), you will understand the precarious position of the Libran personality. The least bit too much on either side creates an imbalance and this is what Libra rising is trying to prevent. You lean over backward to have everything come out even and when it doesn't, you show the other side of your nature — quarrelsome, restless, stubborn and confused. But as long as everything is in balance, Libra is a calm, gracious and good-natured individual whom it is always fun to be around.

You are definitely the white collar or professional type since you don't like to get your hands dirty. There are those rare Librans who are mechanics, oil workers and ditchdiggers, but that's associated with other factors in the chart — not the Libra Ascendant. Generally neat in both appearance and work, you are kind, naive, gullible, generous, idealistic and affectionate. You have a deep-seated need to be appreciated, pampered and admired and there is an inclination to self-indulgence and selfishness. Libra works best in cooperation with another. You always need personal feedback to know when you are performing to the best of your ability and working in harness is the best way for you to achieve this.

Charming, pleasant and naturally refined, you wear clothes well, are usually good-looking and enjoy associating with cheerful, fun-loving friends in lovely and elegant surroundings. You hate to be rude, but you can be if the occasion demands it. You are an exceptionally good listener, even to the point of letting someone bore you rather than hurting their feelings. As good a listener as you are, so are you a good conversationalist — rarely at a loss for words. Often you are aesthetically inclined and the artistic, decorating and musical fields may attract you.

In appearance you are pretty or handsome and even if you cannot claim picture book good looks, you have a very pleasant expression and sweet countenance. Blessed with dimples, either in cheek or chin or at least in the knees; you have a beautiful smile, even teeth and curly hair. Often you have a cleft in your chin. Libra is a tall sign and unless your Sun is in one of the short signs (Cancer, Scorpio or Pisces) or below the horizon, you are generally of at least moderate height, slender but with a tendency to put on weight around the middle as you get older. In the Caucasian race, Libra is one of the blue eyed signs and you have pretty eyes with long lashes. This is the sign of great beauty, but if you allow self-indulgence to run rampant, you can become very obese. Never forget that you are ruled by Venus which also rules sugar, starch and chocolate and you are usually fond of all these good, but fattening things.

You are generally quite healthy, but must watch your diet and be sure that you get enough liquids. Libra has some jurisdiction of the kidneys and you should always be sure to drink plenty of water to keep them functioning properly. When you overindulge, you may be prone to headaches and skin problems. Librans are often known to develop ulcers when their delicate sense of emotional balance is upset. You are healthier than most signs when you behave moderately and don't push yourself too hard or overdo.

LIBRA ASCENDANT — ARIES SUN

If you were born between March 21st and April 20th between approximately 5 PM and 7 PM, you may have this combination.

Dynamic and charming, you are also quite aware of your personal needs. You know how to use other people diplomatically, especially with a 7th house Sun and this talent frequently brings you to the political limelight. Socially oriented and with a strong need for partnership, you should turn your energies outward with charm and reasonableness. This is a combination learning to balance self-direction with a need for other people. Avoid the extreme of accommodating always to what others want (Libra) as well as aggressiveness and vanity (Aries).

With a 6th house Sun, sports, law and commerce are all good fields for you. Occasionally this blend marks outstanding athletes such as Kareem Abdul Jabbar, the prominent basketball center. This is especially true with the Gemini decanate on the Ascendant, indicating dexterity and mobility. His Sun in the Sagittarian decanate shows his attraction to sports and also his interest in religion.

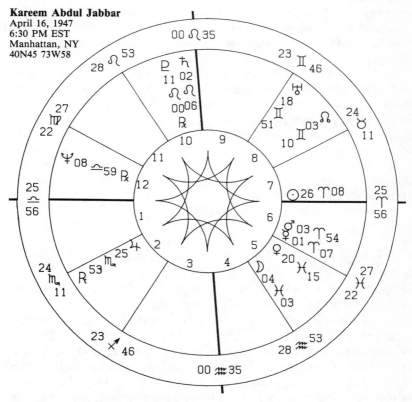

Kareem Abdul Jabbar
April 16, 1947
6:30 PM EST
Manhattan, NY
40N45 73W58

Source: H. Allen in *Horoscope* magazine (C)

Sometimes the internal conflict symbolized by this opposition of signs causes you to feel frustrated and insecure. You can suppress your considerable power to your detriment. You might become picky and faultfinding instead of sociable and friendly. Ardent, passionate and warmly loving, especially if the Sun is in the Aries or Leo decanates, you need a responsive emotional outlet for your physical urges. You may appear unsure and indecisive at times, but with Mars in either an earth or fire sign, indicating practicality and drive, you can certainly make and keep your place on the way up the ladder to success. Mars in an air sign indicates your expression is more in mental or manual pursuits, while Mars in a water sign denotes that you lean towards intense emotional experiences and depth understanding.

Sometimes there is a sense of frustration to be overcome and you must learn to turn your suppressed power in an outward direction and join forces with another person who will help you channel your energies in a positive orientation. This is especially true when the Sun is in the 7th house or the Ascendant is in the Libra decanate showing self-development through relationships. The key is being assertive but not aggressive and willing to compromise without becoming too compliant. When the unconventional Aquarian decanate rises you are less dependent on others and have more definite personal opinions.

Less aggressive and dynamic than the average Aries, this pairing indicates a generally easygoing attitude, but no one should ever mistake your agreeability for weakness.

Direct and expressive as well as charming and diplomatic, you are capable of being exactly who you are while still sharing close relationships with others.

LIBRA ASCENDANT — TAURUS SUN

If you were born between April 20th and May 20th between approximately 3 PM and 5 PM, you may have this combination.

You have a double Venus theme so that even though you appear idealistic, you never stray too far from the practical and essential. You need beauty, comfort and luxury in your surroundings to be truly happy no matter what you may say to the contrary; and Libra can always be depended on to be contrary. You are artistic, social and do best in a pleasant, relaxed atmosphere. Charm is your keyword and when you are so inclined, you can win anyone over to your viewpoint just on your sheer force of personality.

Laziness can be your pitfall. You have a tendency to drift along and enjoy life, especially if the Sun is in the (complacent) Taurus decanate or the (convivial) Gemini or (social) Libra decanate rises. You can rely on others too much to make your decisions for you and may set too much store by material things. Love is very important to you — to give and to receive it, and sometimes this inclination can lead you into a dead-end type relationship.

With the Sun in the 7th house, the law field has appeal to you; making it, breaking it or upholding it. With an 8th house Sun or in the security-seeking Capricorn decanate, you are often attracted to financial fields — management, banking, cashiering. If the Sun is in the productive Virgo decanate or the philanthropic Aquarius decanate is on the Ascendant, willingness to serve in some capacity is inherent. You surprise others with your zest for humanitarian helpfulness.

The double Venus rulership here is very noticeable, so the placement of Venus is very important. If it is in Pisces or Cancer, your sensitivity is highlighted; if it is in Taurus, you may be more materialistic and stable than most Librans; if it is in Aries or Gemini, changeableness is highlighted.

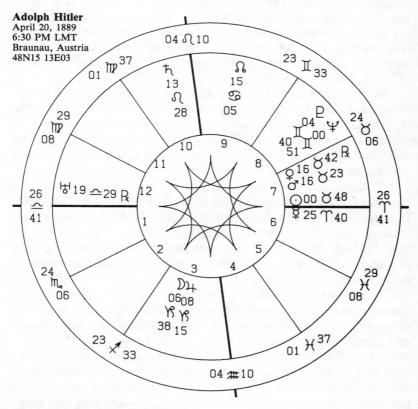

Adolph Hitler
April 20, 1889
6:30 PM LMT
Braunau, Austria
48N15 13E03

Source: *Hitler* by Alan Bullock (B)

Adolph Hitler comes to mind as one who had an insatiable desire for all the negative materialism. He certainly was able to persuade others to see his side of things. He demonstrates the idealism native to this pairing, but his idealism was of the most negative variety.

Whatever you do, you do it with charm, warmth and if you can have your way, with as few upheavals as possible.

LIBRA ASCENDANT — GEMINI SUN

If you were born between May 20th and June 21st between approximately 1 PM and 3 PM, you may have this combination.

Lighthearted, gay and persuasive, you are in love with love and may find it difficult, if not downright impossible, to settle your affections on just one person, especially if your Venus is also in Gemini showing a love of variety. Venus in Taurus suggests more steadiness in love relationships, while a Cancer Venus implies a need to be needed. An Aries Venus often depicts the person who goes from one conquest to the next.

A born socialite and good mixer, you fit well into any group or situation, especially when the third decanate rises or the Sun is in the first decanate (creating a double Gemini note). This blend is noted for verbal ease; being able to chat with anyone about anything. Restless and always changeable, you keep everyone guessing as to what you'll get into next.

With the Sun in the 8th house, or the future-oriented Aquarius decanate involved with either the Ascendant or Sun, you may be drawn to scientific research particularly if it involves field trips, aeronautical research and development or writing about travel. You think fast on your feet and your curiosity provides you with many challenging fields of inquiry and investigation. John F. Kennedy, the versatile, martyred president had this combination.

Gregarious, loquacious and knowledgeable, you are never at a loss for words and thus you make a good writer, lecturer or politician with either an 8th or 9th house Sun. Casual and friendly, you enjoy people and intellectual discussions or trivia quizzes. If the Sun or Ascendant is in the Libran decanate, law or counseling may appeal to you. With your vast people skills, any career in the personnel field could be rewarding. With the Sun in the 9th house, you may be found in the publishing, import-export or advertising fields — anything that keeps you on the move and challenges you mentally.

A good example of the daring and adventurous spirit of this pairing is the undersea explorer, Jacques Cousteau.

Jacques Cousteau
June 11, 1910
1:15 PM Paris time
Ste Andre de Dubzac
France
44N59 0W24

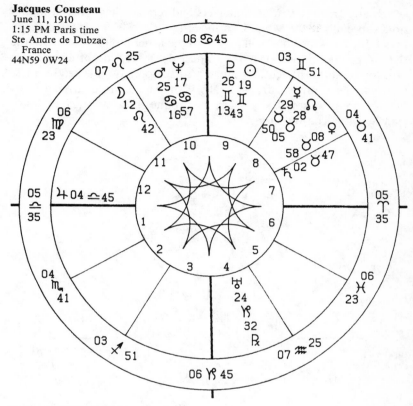

Source: Gauquelin #444 Vol. 3 (A)

Communicative and amiable, you are usually a trendsetter who is noticed and applauded.

LIBRA ASCENDANT — CANCER SUN

If you were born between June 22nd and July 23rd between approximately 11 AM and 1 PM, you may have this combination.

With home and family as a base (Cancer), you reach out through social channels (Libra) and with your warm and winning ways make many friends. You may be interested in music and the arts. You could also be the type who argues for the sake of argument and who is willing to take any side in a discussion just to liven things up.

Many grocers, market managers and retailers have this combination, especially if the Moon is in the 6th house. You have an uncanny knack for knowing what will appeal to the general public and with the Sun in the 10th house, or in the Cancer decanate, you often rise to a position of authority without much effort. You have marked business ability and executive flair, especially if the Sun is in the driving Scorpio decanate. Nelson Rockefeller, the urbane and sophisticated politician had this combination.

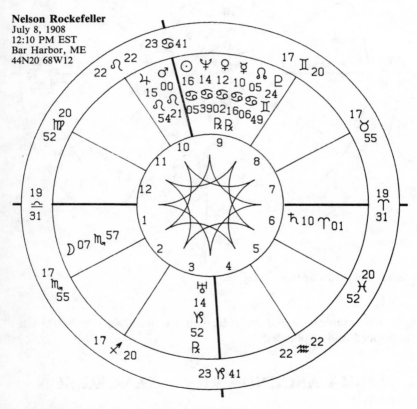

Nelson Rockefeller
July 8, 1908
12:10 PM EST
Bar Harbor, ME
44N20 68W12

Source: *Nelson Rockefeller, A Political Biography* (B)

The Sun in the idealistic Pisces decanate combined with the ambivalent Libra Ascendant symbolizes the indecision and vacillation often present when Libra is strong in the horoscope. With either the carefree Gemini or unique Aquarius decanate rising, you are less conventional than is expected of a Cancer Sun. You are able to innately sense another's abilities or inadequacies and so are a good judge of personnel and this is one of the attributes of the top level executive. Great sociability is most often the case when the relationship-oriented Libra decanate is on the Ascendant.

With a 9th house Sun, you are frequently a world traveler, but you always return to your home base to recharge your batteries. Roald Amundsen, the Norwegian explorer who discovered the South Pole had this placement.

You are a warm and loving person, sympathetic, generous and tactful and these qualities are reciprocated by those you love.

LIBRA ASCENDANT — LEO SUN

If you were born between July 23rd and August 23rd between approximately 9 AM and 11 AM, you may have this combination.

Dramatic, magnetic and completely charming, you have a regal air about you. Maybe it is your height and proud bearing, but even if you are short, you carry yourself with an air of dignity. However, others aren't put off by this, but rather, are drawn to you because of it. Really friendly and outgoing, you are easy to talk to and quite approachable in spite of your considerable self-respect. In fact, dignity is your keyword; think of the very stately and revered actress, Ethel Barrymore who had this duo. The Sun in the Aries decanate and the Aquarius decanate rising symbolized a lady who was pioneering and dedicated in her field.

With the Sun in the Sagittarius decanate, you aim high and take pride in your accomplishments whether on a national, social, domestic or personal level. Ardent, sincere and romantic, you must avoid a dictatorial, benevolent despot role which may come a little too naturally. This is especially likely with a 10th house Sun, if the Sun is in the proud Leo decanate or the Libra decanate rises showing a desire to run your relationships on your terms. You make a good judge, but take care not to sit in judgment of friends and family. Usually though, you are engaging, pleasant and relaxed; at times too much so and that's when your Leo spark can be of benefit.

The Sun in the 10th house suggests your attraction to high places literally as well as figuratively and highlights your Leo pride, but don't forget that pride goes before a fall. When the Gemini decanate rises, you do well in all professions dealing with people. With an 11th house Sun you work especially well with large groups. A 9th house Sun or in the Sagittarius decanate may find you teaching, or working in the travel field. If you don't travel in your work, you will definitely travel as an avocation.

Ethel Barrymore
August 15, 1879
10 AM LMT
Philadelphia, PA
39N57 75W11

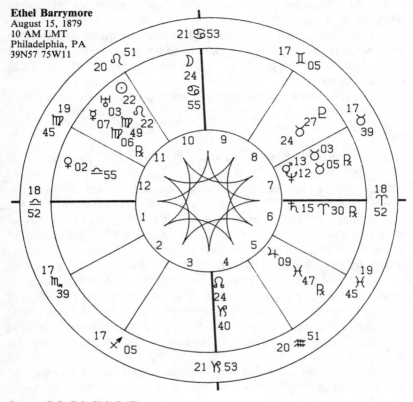

Source: C.C. Zain Vol. 3 (C)

The dramatic ability of Leo and the diplomacy of Libra show that you are a welcome guest wherever you go. You are able to lead with authority, yet still maintain an agreeable and likable demeanor.

LIBRA ASCENDANT — VIRGO SUN

If you were born between August 23rd and September 23rd between approximately 7 AM and 9 AM, you may have this combination.

Your pleasant attitude may hide a rather retiring personality and you are far more critical and discerning than you appear on the surface. Fastidious and painstaking to an almost fanatical degree, you are conventional, prudent and quite often inhibited (Virgo) in spite of your warmth and sensitivity (Libra). You are always striving for affectional acceptance, but you may be hesitant to reach out for love and affection. If Mercury and Venus, your rulers, should both happen to be in Leo, you can be quite extroverted and willing to let your hair down occasionally.

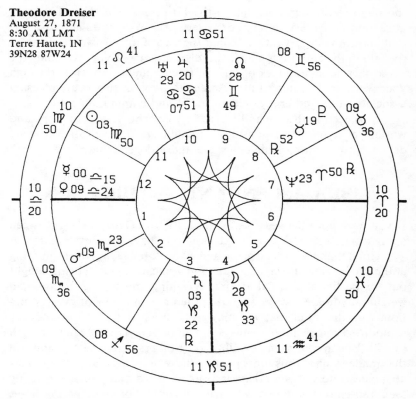

Theodore Dreiser
August 27, 1871
8:30 AM LMT
Terre Haute, IN
39N28 87W24

Source: AFA 3/59 (C)

As with most people having a Libran focus, you are artistically oriented, but your Virgo Sun shows practical application. With the Sun in the 11th house, or the mechanically-skilled Aquarius or dexterous Gemini decanate on the Ascendant, you are often drawn to the graphic arts, hairdressing or decorating. The Sun in the Taurus decanate can also indicate the desire to create something beautiful in the world. Both Virgo and Libra value method, order and neatness and you must take care that this talent doesn't become faultfinding and picky especially with the Sun in the Virgo decanate.

American editor and writer Theodore Dreiser whose works had great impact on the course of modern American literature had this blending.

A 12th house Sun frequently indicates an interest in astrology and related subjects and may also denote that you are an excellent and thorough researcher. The Sun in the 11th house could symbolize an attraction to the service fields or government work as an ambassador, diplomat or civil servant. So could the legal Libra decanate rising or the Sun in the ambitious Capricorn decanate. Once you overcome the Virgo skepticism and lack of self-confidence and can operate through your warm and winning Libra Ascendant, you attract many pleasing associates and find enjoyment in social and community activities.

You need both love and work. The key is loving your work and working at your love relationships (without being too critical). The blend depicts you as an amiable colleague and a dependable spouse.

LIBRA ASCENDANT — LIBRA SUN

If you were born between September 23rd and October 24th between approximately 5 AM and 7 AM, you may have this combination.

Good manners, social grace and a knack for saying the right thing at the proper time distinguish you, and you can count on being sought out for parties and social affairs. Weighing and testing, testing and weighing, you are always analyzing the pros and cons of every situation, with the result that you may seldom take action. This tendency is modified somewhat if Venus is in Leo or Scorpio, showing strength of will. You are more than willing to let others make the decisions on the smaller issues, thus most people find you an agreeable and adaptable companion. Comparison is your keyword and you spend many long and enjoyable hours with friends and cohorts comparing notes on a multitude of interests. All of the above is emphasized even more when the Sun or Ascendant occupies its own Libran decanate.

With the Sun in either the 12th or 1st house, you do well in the acting field as you have a flair for packaging yourself well and putting yourself across to the public. Charlton Heston, Catharine deNeuve and Rita Hayworth are all good examples of this charismatic combination. Your ability to dissemble and pour oil on troubled waters may attract you to the political arena like former president Jimmy Carter. When the Aquarian decanate is involved with either your Sun or Ascendant, you may be drawn to group activities. This can include running for legislative office or simply being very active in clubs or associations.

This double Libran theme is usually musical or artistic and you may be drawn to these fields in some capacity, preferably as a performer. If the Sun or Ascendant is in the Gemini decanate, you may be ambidextrous and capable of doing great things with instruments. John Lennon who was so talented as a composer and performer is another who had this pairing.

John Lennon
October 9, 1940
8:30 AM WDT
Liverpool, England
53N25 2W58

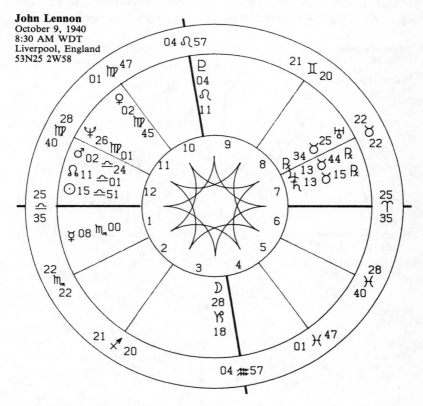

Source: Sybil Leek (DD)

Romantic, cheerful and peace-loving, you respond to an agreeable, loving partner who doesn't make too many demands on you, especially if the Libra decanate is involved with either the Ascendant or the Sun. In fact, you often appreciate it if your partner handles your financial, social and domestic life leaving the "fun" things for you. But to feel fulfilled, you want a partner; someone who can provide the constant feedback that you thrive on.

Balanced and even-handed, your innate sense of justice coupled with a skillful diplomacy and tact are assets in any number of situations.

LIBRA ASCENDANT — SCORPIO SUN

If you were born between October 24th and November 23rd between approximately 3 AM and 5 AM, you may have this combination.

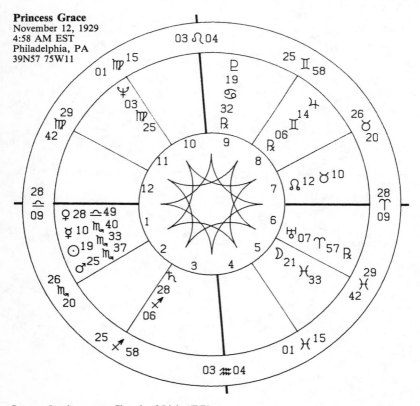

Princess Grace
November 12, 1929
4:58 AM EST
Philadelphia, PA
39N57 75W11

Source: Jansky quotes Church of Light (DD)

Deceptively easygoing and with a good sense of humor and an easy wit (Libra) that belies your penetrating insight into another's intentions (Scorpio), your seemingly easy manner is a cover-up for a shrewd, tenacious drive for success. You know how to make points through both subtlety and apple polishing and your motto could well be, ''It is easier to catch flies with honey than vinegar.''

You do well in any field that requires public relations as you are able to persuade others so as to get the best from them. It helps, of course, if the Sun is in the Scorpio decanate, indicating thoroughness and depth of understanding. With a 1st house Sun, you can succeed in any promotional endeavor especially when the Ascendant is in the fluent Gemini decanate. The Sun in the 2nd house often suggests loan and investment jobs and indicates ability for combining business and social activities to your best advantage. This is even more likely when the Sun is in the Cancer decanate or the Libra decanate rises.

If your Sun is in the gentle Pisces decanate, your reserve is usually more pronounced and you could be drawn to work in the medical or research areas. If the scientific Aquarius decanate rises this interest could be focused in some function dealing with computers or as an x-ray technician. On the personal level you are a little bit hard to know as there is almost always an air of mystery about you. Remember Grace Kelly and her aura of mystical charm. Sometimes this is your way of covering up your Libra indecisiveness. Of all the Libra Ascendants, you are the least indecisive, or at least you do not let it show. A born diplomat, you have a way of utilizing words that takes the sting out of your criticism.

Relationships are important to you, but you generally want them on your terms. Those closest to you are likely to have their deepest motivations probed and desires questioned.

A natural therapist, you instinctively analyze other people and can be a valuable source of understanding and insight into human motivations and behavior.

LIBRA ASCENDANT — SAGITTARIUS SUN

If you were born between November 23rd and December 22nd between approximately 1 AM and 3 AM, you may have this combination.

Mentally oriented, versatile and loquacious, you like to be on the move. You have a highly developed sense of justice; honor, peace and comparison are all important in your scheme of things. You tend to compromise between sentimentality (Libra) and intelligent appraisal (Sagittarius) of a situation, but once you have decided on a certain line of action, you carry through your ideas with clarity and foresight, without a backward glance.

You are very considerate of and amenable to another person's viewpoint and frequently operate as the great compromiser, especially if the Sun is in the friendly Sagittarius decanate or the Ascendant is in the balancing Libra decanate. You can often win friends and influence people with an ease that others envy and can seldom imitate.

Uri Geller
December 20, 1946
2 AM EET
Tel Aviv, Israel
32N04 34E46

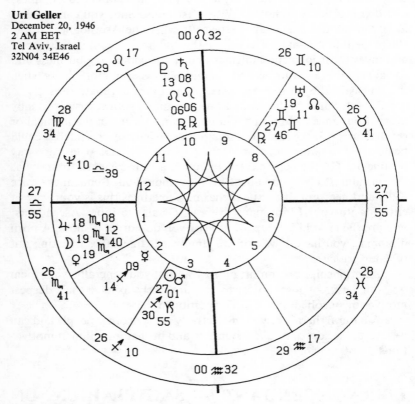

Source: Nolle in *Dell Horoscope* (C)

With a 3rd house Sun, any field where you can communicate — teaching, writing, acting, singing — is a good area for you, especially if your Sun is in the expressive Leo decanate or the articulate Gemini decanate is rising. A 2nd house Sun symbolizes a good sense of material values and often you are interested in economics, art or trade. If the Sun is in the energetic Aries decanate or the freedom-loving Aquarius decanate is on the Ascendant, you can be a real ball of fire, exploring new avenues and ideas and open to unusual pursuits.

Although you are gentle, refined and philosophical, you can be socially indulgent and somewhat lazy. You are outgoing, optimistic, genuinely friendly and well liked and you need people and their approval. If it is withheld you have a way of feeling that it is never your fault.

A couple of very dissimilar people have this combination: telekineticist, Uri Geller and guru, Maharaj Ji.

Both Libra and Sagittarius are people-oriented signs and you are at your best in any social situation that requires you to be congenial and companionable.

LIBRA ASCENDANT — CAPRICORN SUN

If you were born between December 22nd and January 21st between approximately 11 PM and 1 AM, you may have this combination.

Marked business ability characterizes you and you may rise to a position of executive prominence. You are able to combine the ambition and diligence of Capricorn with Libran refinement and social aptitude and make it work well for you in a worldly way. You can be a good administrator and when you are in a position of authority, everyone knows who is boss. The Sun in the forceful Capricorn decanate emphasizes this.

With your warmth and good humor it is easy for you to win both the social and the business esteem to which you feel entitled. You know how to add to your image the necessary qualifications of responsibility, dependability and endurance. Quite conventional, you are nevertheless romantic and warmly sentimental when the occasion arises, especially if the Sun is in the affectionate Taurus decanate or the loving Libra decanate is on the Ascendant.

With a 3rd house Sun, you are an apt politician or actor and publishing and writing could also appeal to you. The potential of your ability with the written word is also indicated by the Sun in the Virgo decanate. Language in general, spoken as well as written, may be a skill when the Gemini decanate is rising.

The Sun in the 4th house frequently finds you in real estate, mining, geology and related fields. This Sun placement symbolizes your devotion to family, tradition and heritage. Some remarkably varied people have this blend: French chemist Louis Pasteur, physician-philosopher Albert Schweitzer, entrepreneur Robert Ripley, politician Barry Goldwater, pop singer David Bowie, and poet Carl Sandberg... all standouts in their respective fields. David Bowie with the Aquarius decanate rising has been recognized in the pop music field for his unique approach as well as his unusual appearance.

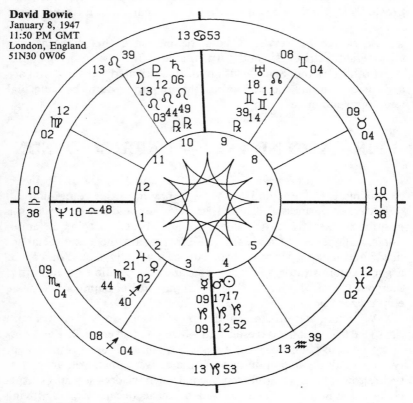

David Bowie
January 8, 1947
11:50 PM GMT
London, England
51N30 0W06

Source: Holliday quotes a bio (B)

The natural square between Libra and Capricorn symbolizes the energy of this combination. You have the drive and confidence shown by the Capricorn Sun plus the *savoir faire* of Libra to make your ambition palatable to others.

LIBRA ASCENDANT — AQUARIUS SUN

If you were born between January 21st and February 20th between approximately 9 PM and 11 PM, you may have this combination.

You are witty, charming and easygoing until someone tries to take advantage of your good nature. Then your spirit of compromise is thrown to the winds and you can become rebellious and challenging. Woe to anyone who gets in your path! A mental combination, your curiosity is often channeled into studying and commenting on other people. Though you are somewhat unpredictable (symbolized by the Aquarian note), you are essentially idealistic and have noble motives, sometimes too noble, bordering on the gullible. You can sometimes be taken advantage of; this is more likely to happen if your Sun or Ascendant is in the (often accommodating) Libran decanate. This combination is great on theory, but not always practical.

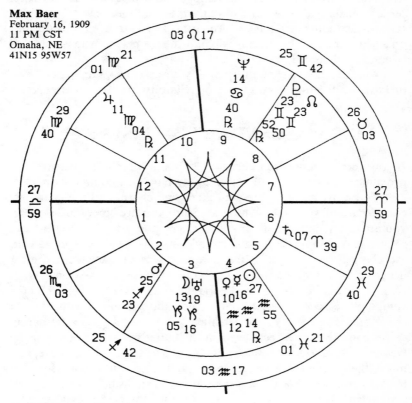

Max Baer
February 16, 1909
11 PM CST
Omaha, NE
41N15 95W57

Source: Church of Light (C)

Generally humane, friendly and creative, if you feel thwarted in your relationships, you can be very jealous and competitive, which surprises anyone who doesn't know you well. Whether the Sun is in the

4th or 5th house, you do well in creative fields: art, acting, music. With a 5th house Sun or if the Gemini decanate is involved, teaching is often your bag and children usually respond well to you because they sense that at heart you are ever young. You may also do well in sports due to your competitive nature. The accord between Sun and Ascendant shows that you may not try hard enough to really star. Max Baer, the famous boxer, is one who did.

You really benefit from a good education and generally continue to study and learn throughout your life. This is especially true if the Aquarius decanate is involved with either the Sun or Ascendant. Warm-hearted and romantic, you idealize love and express it in the broadest sense to encompass everyone you know. Since Libra feels the need for face-to-face confrontation and Aquarius prefers to keep relationships on a broader base, this pairing can indicate the person who is humane-ly concerned for all mankind.

Able to relate to the entire world, your openness, honesty and love of ideas lead you into a number of relationships and experiences.

LIBRA ASCENDANT — PISCES SUN

If you were born between February 20th and March 21st between ap-proximately 7 PM and 9 PM, you may have this combination.

You move through life with grace and charm and are genuinely considerate of your fellow human. Since you are so compassionate, you are easily imposed upon and may give too much for too little in return. A bit too easygoing and easily influenced by those around you, especially if the Sun is in the pliable Pisces or dependent Cancer decanate, so it is most important for you to choose your associates wise-ly. For you, more than most, a good motto is, "We are judged by the company we keep." Select your friends and associates with care.

You are often very fond of animals and make a good veterinarian or pet shop owner, especially when the Sun is in the 6th house or the Gemini or Aquarius decanate rises. With the Sun in the 5th house, act-ing or the art field may appeal to you and since you respond strongly to the symbolism of Venus and Neptune, you are usually quite musical. We often find this combination in the charts of dancers and choreographers.

This pairing seems to promise great beauty as screen sirens Jean Harlow and Elizabeth Taylor share it.

Sentimental, almost to the point of being maudlin, unless the Sun is in the Scorpio decanate, you are "in love with love" and respond

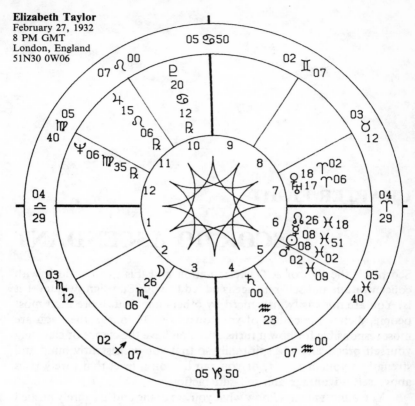

Elizabeth Taylor
February 27, 1932
8 PM GMT
London, England
51N30 0W06

Source: Church of Light (C)

warmly and enthusiastically to romance in all its guises. With the Libra decanate on the Ascendant, you are sociable, agreeable, gentle and kind but you can be inveigled into involvements you never intended. You need to develop good judgment. You rely heavily on friends and companionship and prefer to always have people around you, often as a retinue or entourage.

Gentle, loving and truly sweet, you seek to create and keep an aura of beauty and harmony about you.

CHAPTER EIGHT

SCORPIO ASCENDANT

Scorpio is the sign of self-determination and this quality along with concentration and self-reliance is added to your Sun sign, whatever it is. You are not easily influenced by others and you, more than most people, dictate the course of your own life. Of course, then you are most responsible for how it turns out. You have the choice of elevating yourself practically and spiritually so that you consistently build and strengthen your best self, or you can live on a level that rarely rises above self-advantage and self-satisfaction.

You almost always know what you are doing and are rarely pushed into a line of action due to another's persuasion. You especially do not like to be questioned about your motives. Acute, forceful, subtle, strong, loyal and ardent, you have a tremendous potential for self-help and helping others. However, when your antagonism and latent vengeful nature is stirred, you can be a formidable opponent given to sarcasm, pointed remarks and at times, actual physical violence.

Your self-respect is innate and regardless of what others may think or say, your good opinion of yourself usually remains intact and untarnished. Mostly you take the approval and good will of others for granted. Because of your loyalty, your ability to keep your own counsel and your extreme self-containment, others willingly confide in you and know they can trust your good judgment.

Pluto is the accepted ruler of Scorpio but because this small but mighty planet moves so slowly (it took almost 30 years to transit through the sign Cancer), it is best to use the placement of Mars as well, to judge the Scorpio personality more certainly.

In appearance, Scorpio is another of the square built signs. Like its opposite sign, Taurus, there is often a "no neck" look with heavy shoulders and a short, thick, powerful torso. Of course, if Mars is in one of the tall, lanky signs (Gemini, Libra or Sagittarius) this is greatly modified. Usually average to short in height, you may have a tendency to a weight problem like all the water signs. The water element seeks emotional security. When food becomes a source of safety and reassurance, weight can be a problem. Substituting other sources of support can be helpful.

Your upper eyelids tend to slant at the corner and your eyes have a deep, piercing look that bores intently into others. Your brows may meet above your nose and have a distinct upward point. This is more noticeable in males, as women generally tend to pluck their brows in the current mode. There is great width to your face just beneath the eyes and your nose is often prominent and may have a hump or high, bony bridge. You have a rather square face and frequently there is a sort of bulldog look. Your hair grows low on your forehead and your body may tend to be quite hairy. Your mouth is full, large and sensual.

Normally you are very coolheaded with great composure and a well controlled nature; insults roll off your back and compliments don't move you at all. Though you appear calm, you are extremely emotional inside and you have an "all or nothing" type personality. But one can rarely tell from your expression when you are discomfited, as you seldom give your feelings away by any outward sign such as blushing, fidgeting or grimacing. The great poker face, that's you. Intensely loyal to your friends, you never forget a kindness, but on the other hand you never forget a slight either and seldom rest until it is repaid in kind.

The meaning of Pluto, your ruler, shows up strongly in your health picture. You can harm your health with excesses, a melancholy and defeatist attitude or just plain hard work, but your Plutonian recuperative power is tremendous and you can amaze the doctors with your ability to snap back from serious illness. Your vulnerable areas are the reproductive organs, the nose and throat. Women can have irregular menses, miscarriages and/or hysterectomies, while men are subject to prostate trouble. Scorpio challenges involve being able to give, receive and share where money and sensual pleasures are concerned. Men or women who have not resolved their inner ambivalences about handling the physical sense world and their sexuality may have difficulties with the reproductive area. Learning to give, receive and share resources and pleasures comfortably can help maintain health here.

Varicose veins and nosebleeds are common. Because of the inherent tendency to rush into things which Mars symbolizes, you are often prone to accidents, cuts and bruises. Regular exercise is especially beneficial where Martian themes are involved. It helps express potential aggression positively.

Although your ambition is rarely obvious, you quietly wait for your chance and are ready to seize whatever opportunity comes along to achieve success. When you live up to your potential, which is considerable, you can be an extremely influential person.

SCORPIO ASCENDANT — ARIES SUN

If you were born between March 21st and April 20th between approximately 9 PM and 11 PM, you may have this combination.

This can be one of the most creative combinations in the whole zodiac since Mars, the indicator of initiative, rules both the personality (Ascendant) and the inner self (Sun). You pour yourself out in a myriad of creative endeavors. You might be a businessperson and artist at the same time with a rich and rewarding love life going full steam. You're certainly not a recluse, but live life to the fullest.

Your work is usually worthwhile and since you are surely not a shrinking violet, you don't object to calling attention to yourself. Walter Winchell, the rapid fire reporter and columnist had this combination. With the Sun in the 5th house or in the Leo decanate, you shine in the musical, literary, philosophical and occult fields as well as in science and invention. This placement can distinguish the outstanding surgeon who introduces new techniques or the inventor or perfecter of surgical instruments. This is especially true if the Scorpio decanate rises or the Sun is in the Aries or Sagittarius decanate.

You thrive best as a big fish in a small pond where you can be seen and rise above the crowd. You, especially with the Sun in the 5th house, need to have hobbies like music and sports to insure an avenue of personal expression. If the Sun is in the 4th house, you are very devoted to home and family but want everything on your terms. This can create problems in relating to other family members. You might be a domineering parent or the rebellious child — or both. Teamwork is a skill you need to practice. Doctors, nurses, professional athletes, soldiers, sailors, guards and people who specialize in hazardous work often have the Sun in the 6th house.

Intensely personal in whatever you do, even when engaged in a crusade ala Gloria Steinem, it is important to your ego that you seek personal recognition above all else.

Your emotions are powerful as are your affections and you must

Gloria Steinem
March 25, 1934
10 PM EST
Toledo, OH
41N39 83W33

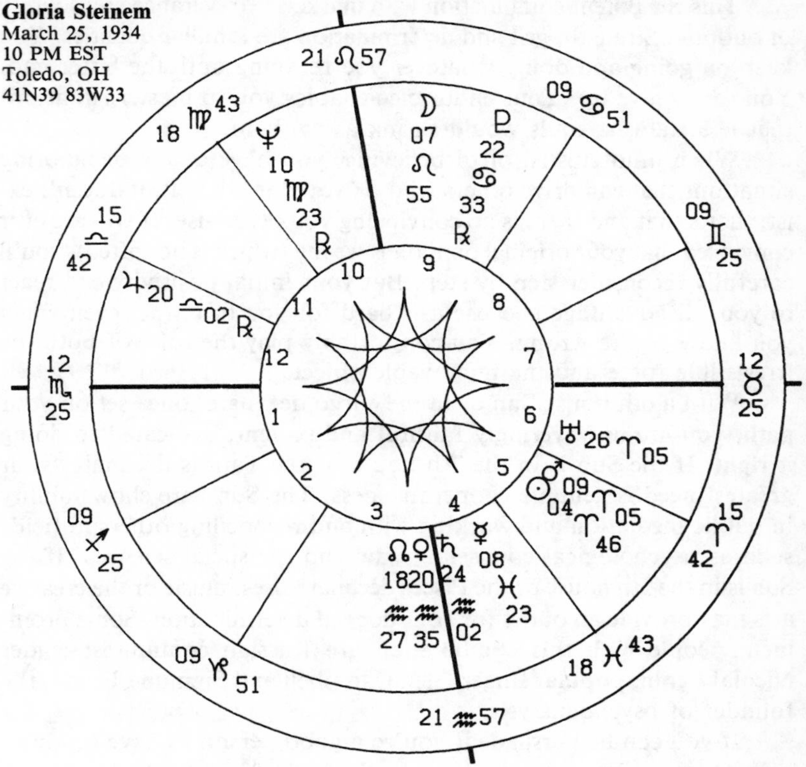

Source: *Contemporary Sidereal Horoscopes* (A)

learn to control this side of your nature and try to depersonalize your reactions. In spite of your warmth and responsiveness, your "me first" attitude may be so strong that you tend to overlook the needs of others and can seldom see your loved ones as separate from yourself. This tendency is modified somewhat if the Ascendant is in the Cancer or Pisces decanate, indicating more sensitivity.

With Aries drive and Scorpio perspicacity, nothing keeps you from reaching a pinnacle of success in your field.

SCORPIO ASCENDANT — TAURUS SUN

If you were born between April 20th and May 20th between approximately 7 PM and 9 PM, you may have this combination.

This is a potent combination with marked perseverance and solidity of outlook. Strength, grit and determination are familiar qualities. You keep on going and doing whatever you're doing until the bitter end. You rarely give up. Your endurance enables you to master situations that less stalwart souls would shrink away from.

When uninterested or disbelieving, you have a way of ignoring situations that can drive others wild. If you don't buy it, it doesn't exist; that's that and there is no convincing you otherwise. If you are ever convinced that your original opinion is wrong (which is not often), you'll carefully reconsider step by step. But your initial positivity can react to your disadvantage because it is hard for you to retract even when you know you're wrong. You comfortably play the roles of both the irresistible force and the immovable object.

With a 6th house Sun or in the Virgo decanate, once set on your path, you are unwaveringly faithful and patient, dedicated to doing it **right**. If the Sun is in the 7th house or the Taurus decanate, your greatest need is genuine cooperativeness. The Sun here shows ability in public mediation and working with and reconciling others in fields such as psychological counseling, law and the social sciences. If the Sun is in the 5th house or the Pisces decanate rises, music or the creative arts may provide an outlet for your dogged determination. Some prominent people with this combination are Russian communist leader Nicolai Lenin, popular singer Glen Campbell and Sigmund Freud, the founder of psychoanalysis.

If you can be persuaded, you're a good person to have on one's side. Once you're committed, particularly in affairs of the heart, you are astonishingly loyal and can cast aside your feelings of independence and your grandiose schemes for yourself with marked abandon. This is especially noticeable when the family-oriented Cancer decanate rises or the Sun is in the faithful Capricorn decanate. In spite of being sensitive yourself, you are not always responsive to the needs or feelings of others. You can at times be petty, jealous and downright mean if you feel others threaten your physical or emotional security. Letting go of resentments may be something you need to do.

"Anything you can do, I can do better" is your motto especially if the Scorpio decanate is on the Ascendant. A competitive outlet of some sort (sports, games, business) would channel your needs for power in a positive direction. You often take the good opinion of others for granted and may be surprised and hurt if they treat you in the cavalier manner you sometimes adopt. You tend to use whatever comes to hand if it serves your purpose and you have been known to regard right and wrong in the same vein. Your persistence helps you overcome the setbacks of what can be a dominating tendency and you mellow with age and experience. You are capable of extraordinary amounts of work and cannot be turned aside from what you see as your duty.

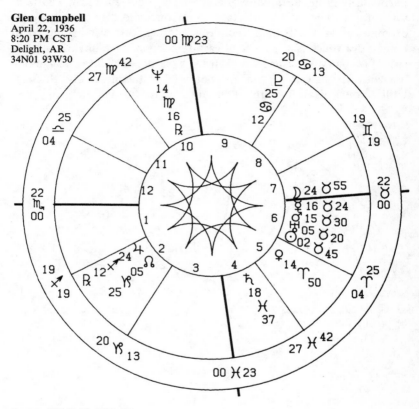

Glen Campbell
April 22, 1936
8:20 PM CST
Delight, AR
34N01 93W30

Source: *TV Guide* 5/70 (C)

Able to concentrate on your own motivation to the exclusion of all else, you are indefatigable in your ability to forge ahead to any goals you set for yourself.

SCORPIO ASCENDANT — GEMINI SUN

If you were born between May 20th and June 21st between approximately 5 PM and 7 PM, you may have this combination.

Your biggest asset is mental keenness and penetration combining the indefatigability and instinctive self-respect of Scorpio with the facility and dexterity of Gemini. This is a mental, creative and scientific pairing and is fairly common with those who deal with the mentally ill, particularly in institutional work. It is also prevalent in the charts of scientific workers and technicians — anyone who digs out, analyzes, examines and presents their findings in another form or meaning. Your biggest drawback is a tendency to scatteredness; too many irons in the fire. If Mercury is in Cancer or Taurus, a bit more stability is suggested, but with Mercury in Gemini the potential restlessness is heightened. Utilize your versatility without succumbing to the dilettante role. You

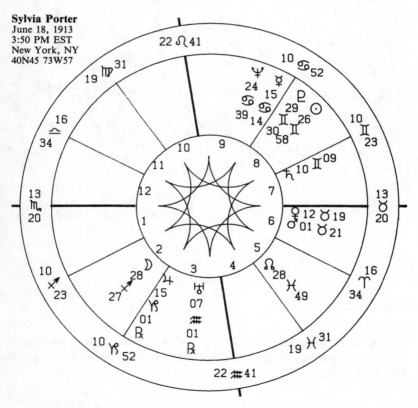

Sylvia Porter
June 18, 1913
3:50 PM EST
New York, NY
40N45 73W57

Source: Jameson in *American Association of Scientific Astrology* (C)

are easygoing and pleasure loving but when you harness your power, you have the magnetism, force and ability to live a constructive as well as an enjoyable life.

This is a double eighth sign combination. Scorpio, the eighth sign is rising and Gemini is the eighth sign from Scorpio. If the Sun is in the 8th house, or the Scorpio decanate rises, there is an even more pronounced Scorpionic emphasis. You are more purposeful, resolute, success oriented and happier if you stick to the analytical, mental and detached side of your Scorpio-Gemini blend rather than becoming involved in its potential for sensationalism. By indulging your 8th house creativity in one sexual affair after another (and you have been known to do this), you create nothing but havoc. Your true creative capacity is strong in writing, particularly the analytical kind (what makes people tick), critical, theatre or even financial like well known monetary analyst, Sylvia Porter.

If the Sun is in the Gemini or Aquarius decanate, you may do well in painstaking lab work that supports and leads to scientific discoveries. With the Sun in the 7th house or the Libra decanate, you have a gift for glib and facile communication and many gifted entertainers (Bob Dylan and Rosalind Russell) have this combination. If the Pisces decanate rises, you may have an interest in medicine or acting; if the Cancer decanate rises, the music field may pique your curiosity.

Anything you do, you do well and your insatiably curious Gemini Sun is grounded by the thoroughness and dedication of your Scorpio Ascendant.

SCORPIO ASCENDANT — CANCER SUN

If you were born between June 22nd and July 23rd between approximately 3 PM and 5 PM, you may have this combination.

Once you're sure of your place in the world, you are generous, helpful and warmhearted. This is a sympathetic and emotional but cagey and self-protective combination with great potential. Your intuition is strong and at your best you are genuinely interested in solving other people's problems with empathy, constructive practicality and good advice based on your strong hunches.

With the Sun in either the 8th or 9th house, you have a powerful mystic streak and a definite interest in mental and spiritual matters, but you may have struggles not only with your own emotions, but also in finding your place in the world. The challenge is acknowledging your strong emotions without repressing them or allowing them to rule your life. Your feelings are powerful, intense, deep and you are proud as well as ambitious.

The subtlety and cunning of the combination of Scorpio and

Cancer can keep you constantly plotting your course no matter how modest and unassuming you may appear on the surface. If either the Ascendant or the Sun is in the Cancer decanate, you can be extremely intuitive and perceptive even bordering on the psychic.

If the Sun is in the 9th house, you may be an inspired philosopher like Henry David Thoreau. With an 8th house Sun or the Scorpio decanate involved with either the Sun or Ascendant, you tend to apply your philosophies in more practical terms like playwright Clifford Odets or Helen Keller, who with Scorpio perseverance overcame her severe handicaps to become a renowned author and lecturer.

Clifford Odets
July 18, 1906
1 PM EST
Philadelphia, PA
39N57 75W11

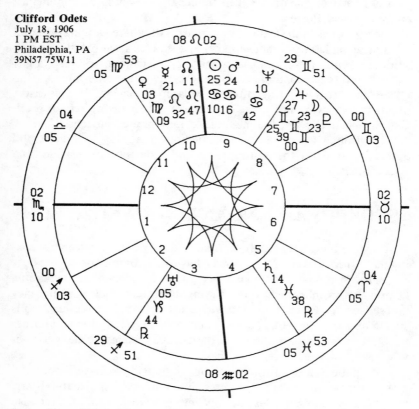

Source: Blanca Holmes (C)

Your self interest, so typical of Scorpio rising, is strong but usually kept well covered up. At times you may appear almost shy and fearful, especially with the Sun or Ascendant in the retiring Pisces decanate, but you always achieve your aims and rarely show your hand. What you call subtle diplomacy in yourself, you tend to see as manipulation in others.

Acutely sensitive to shifts of feeling and atmosphere, you are also perceptibly aware of high spiritual values. As you mature, this understanding transforms self-interest into real outgoingness for the best interests of others. You are capable of developing true healing powers in medicine, religion or the occult. For deep personal satisfaction, growth and the best development of your emotional sensitivity and aspiring self, some form of religious or spiritual interest seems to be a necessity and should be cultivated.

By plumbing the depths of your emotions, you can be a force for positive transformation of yourself as well as the rest of the world.

SCORPIO ASCENDANT — LEO SUN

If you were born between July 23rd and August 23rd between approximately 1 PM and 3 PM, you may have this combination.

Dynamic, forceful, magnetic; your urge is to rise to a position of authority. Your drive is to get to and stay on the top. You value your prestige in direct proportion to your independence and without either one you can be difficult, if not impossible, to deal with. You are aspiring and eventually your faith in yourself brings its own rewards and you can be the image of propriety, honor and dignity. Your emotions and ego need control and handling, but basically your ardor, constancy and capacity for hard work make you an admirable individual.

Proud, autocratic and sure of yourself, with a 9th house Sun or the Sun in the Sagittarius decanate, you are frequently deeply religious or interested in the occult or metaphysics. These areas of investigation are easy for you if either the Pisces or Scorpio decanate is rising, emphasizing intuition. You are honest, hopeful and think in large terms, but with a decidedly personal coloration. Once you're doing your own thing, your intensity of belief, both in yourself and in the idea of the moment, your capacity for self-dramatization and your emotional force and idealism provide you with tremendous magnetism. A good case in point is Jacqueline Kennedy Onassis.

You are capable of being a real leader as well as a popular figure. Your emotions are powerful, but when tied to your purpose they enhance and deepen it and gain you the added respect you crave. You want to be noticed and you actually covet esteem. This is not always an easy combination as Leo and Scorpio are naturally square to each other. If you do not channel your power drive positively (into sports, business, games), life may feel like a constant battle for control. Benito Mussolini, the Italian dictator is an excellent example of this combination applied in a negative way. His Sun in the Leo decanate emphasized his obstinate dedication to his ego-serving goals.

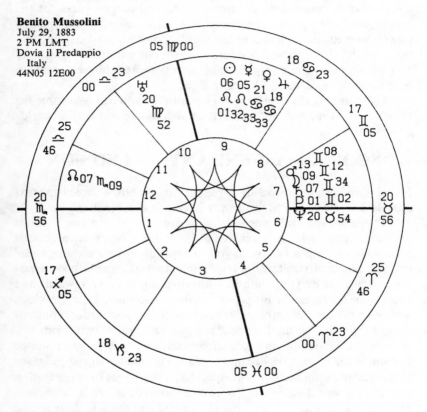

Benito Mussolini
July 29, 1883
2 PM LMT
Dovia il Predappio
Italy
44N05 12E00

Source: Gauquelin #1745 Vol. 5 (A)

    Your elevated Leo Sun in either the 9th or 10th house indicates that you can hardly help but shine, whether you are a politician, minister or teacher. This placement highlights the preservation of law and order and personal dignity, especially if the Sun is in the self-oriented Aries decanate or the conservative Cancer decanate rises. Though completely faithful and loyal, you are no compromiser with necessity. You will stubbornly and sullenly refuse to do what you feel is not your job. While your goals may seem unattainable to others and even at times to you,

you persist in your own inimitable way. Though it goes against your grain, if you need help, you'll take it as your due.

Once you have learned to harness the tremendous energy indicated by this pairing, no force on earth can keep you from attaining your goals.

SCORPIO ASCENDANT — VIRGO SUN

If you were born between August 23rd and September 23rd between approximately 11 AM and 1 PM, you may have this combination.

You can be a wonderfully caring friend, intensely loyal and gracious in the most lowly of services, particularly if you are appreciated, but even when you are not. Then your acute wit and sharp tongue make the situation known. If deep down you think your aid is needed, you'll keep on giving it because your Scorpio-Virgo combination is reforming, often educational or advisory and given to good works. This blend has marvelous organizational skills, thoroughness and a penchant for detail.

With the Scorpio decanate rising or the Sun in the Taurus decanate, you are a practical, astute and factual person whose ability for immediate understanding and calling the turn on people and events should take you far. You know how to keep your own counsel but can still be forthright and uncompromising about what is going on. People take your direct approach and like it. If your Sun is in the Virgo decanate, detachment is your keyword. But watch out that you don't become smug and be sure to apply your perfectionistic standards to yourself as well as others. The Sun in the 10th house or Capricorn decanate is suited to the professions of teaching, nursing and medicine — any job that demands painstaking care even to the point of fussiness.

Quite a variety of prominent people fall into this classification: Werner Erhardt, founder of EST, Jose Feliciano, the blind singer and guitarist, Belgian poet and dramatist Maurice Maeterlinck and authors Grace Metalious and Upton Sinclair as well as Johann Wolfgang von Goethe, the famous German poet.

Although you are essentially a mental and analytical type, there's a passionate forcefulness to your makeup that's strongly emotional and it not only colors your ideas but your personal relationships as well. A 9th house Sun may symbolize literary ability in many fields: poetry, playwriting and philosophy as well as prose. This is especially likely if Mercury is in dramatic Leo, lucid Virgo or the imaginative Pisces or Cancer decanate (tuned to public desires) is rising. If Mercury is in

Libra you are quite sociable and communicative so you could be an excellent salesperson. On another level you can be a printer, publisher, editor or typesetter. Most acquaintances think you "nice," and you have many casual friends. However, you show your deep feelings to only a few, and with those few you go all the way.

Johann von Goethe
August 28, 1749 NS
Noon LMT
Frankfort am Main,
  Germany
50N07 8E41

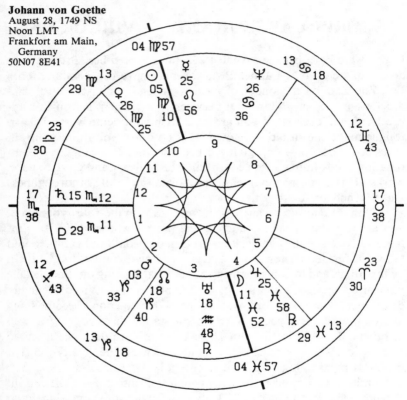

Source: Ebertin (C)

Your quiet intensity may sometimes be overlooked, but once someone knows you well, your capability is deeply appreciated and put to good use.

SCORPIO ASCENDANT — LIBRA SUN

If you were born between September 23rd and October 24th between approximately 9 AM and 11 AM, you may have this combination.

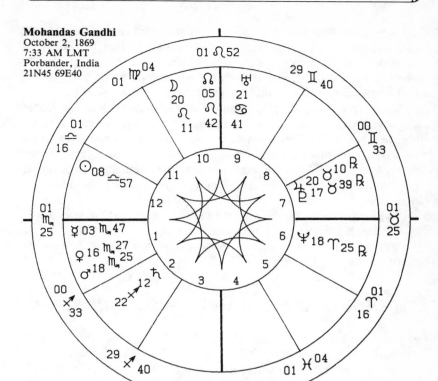

Mohandas Gandhi
October 2, 1869
7:33 AM LMT
Porbander, India
21N45 69E40

Source: *Sabian Symbols* #369 (DD)

You are a person of definite effectiveness and few situations find you wanting. You come by your diplomacy naturally; Libra is the sign of tact and Scorpio always looks before it leaps. You're a born intriguer and finagler and you can phrase your criticism in such a way that others are appreciative rather than offended. You are critical because you are an idealist interested in people and their affairs. Scorpio's ability to face facts unblinkingly plus the perfection and harmony-seeking of the discriminating Libra Sun reveal you as a penetrating and constructively critical observer. Mental if not emotional detachment and poise add to your seemingly unruffled view of the world.

Your native cleverness and subtlety work just as much for your self-interest as they do for group interest. It all depends on which path you choose. Most of the time you choose positively because you're ambitious and want to nail down your place in the sun. This is especially true when the Sun is in the Libra decanate accentuating your desire to move in the "best circles." With the Sun in the 11th house or Aquarius decanate, you'll naturally gravitate toward group activity where Libran social talent and charm work wonders. If your Sun is in the 12th house or the Pisces decanate is on the Ascendant you'd still rather work with others than alone, but in a more behind the scenes way. With your incisive mental ability and the Scorpio talent for probing, you would do well as a detective, researcher, insurance investigator or working in some capacity for the CIA or the FBI, especially if the Sun is in the curious Gemini decanate or the probing Scorpio decanate rises. With the Cancer decanate rising you are often attracted to a job that provides the chance to visit and socialize.

Mohandas Gandhi, the great Hindu nationalist and spiritual leader is a prime example of this combination working at its best.

Your enthusiasm and sheer persuasiveness, charm and magnetism carry others along with you.

SCORPIO ASCENDANT — SCORPIO SUN

If you were born between October 24th and November 23rd between approximately 7 AM and 9 AM, you may have this combination.

You have tremendous charisma and fortitude and when you live your life on a self-controlled plane, you win favor through sheer magnetism of personality. This same power sustains you through any misfortune. You can plow your way through and come up strong in situations that would totally devastate others. Yours is a potent force; exceptional in extremes for good or evil.

You are what you are and there's no denying it. No one could possibly fail to understand you or be unaware of you thanks to your pervasive intensity. You put your all into everything you do and have little compassion or understanding of those who are not as energetic, vigorous and dynamic as you are. A truly remarkable personage, you are unique in that you are so particularly your own person, especially if the Sun or Ascendant are in the Scorpio decanate.

If either the Ascendant or Sun is in the Cancer decanate, you don't come on quite as strong. Much depends on the quality of your family background, education and training. Your forcefulness may need containment and your rampant individualism some restraint. Your greatest need is work so satisfying that you become a part of it; at least as much as you can become a part of anything and forget yourself. You are intensely creative and can give everything you do a creative touch if you are not wasting your forces. This artistic bent is particularly likely if the Sun or Ascendant is in the Pisces decanate.

With the Sun in the 1st house, you are capable of executive ability and formidable energy which at times may have to be toned down or others may find your directness and plain speech hard to cope with. With a 12th house Sun, you are just as powerful, but it is more the "iron fist in the velvet glove" type of strength — more restrained and politic, but there nonetheless. Either of these placements is excellent for the probing surgeon, the dedicated healer, the meticulous meatcutter or the powerful evangelist.

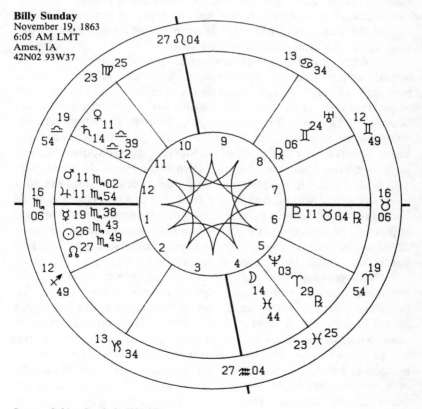

Billy Sunday
November 19, 1863
6:05 AM LMT
Ames, IA
42N02 93W37

Source: *Sabian Symbols* #881 (C)

American evangelist Billy Sunday and French composer Georges Bizet both had this combination.

Your drive is awesome, but usually controlled. When you make up your mind and start any project, it's full steam ahead — no holds barred — until completion.

SCORPIO ASCENDANT — SAGITTARIUS SUN

If you were born between November 23rd and December 22nd between approximately 5 AM and 7 AM, you may have this combination.

The universal perspective and natural gregariousness of Sagittarius combined with the intensity and passion of Scorpio can be a highly influential combination. You are often very magnetic and people respond to you. When things go well and you can feel that you're the power behind the scenes, you're the best of people to be around even though you are always your own individual self.

This combination generally indicates a great deal of ambition with considerable emphasis on the acquisition of money and material power especially with a 2nd house Sun. You speak in the broad philosophical Sagittarian way. In most instances Sagittarius' outgoingness outshines Scorpio's reticence and you are friendly, humane and approachable, going out of your way for others and willingly imparting what you know. This is especially true when the Sun is in the Sagittarius decanate giving a double Sagittarius theme, or when the Pisces decanate rises.

With the Sun in the 1st house or the Leo decanate, you are your own person and will do well in any field you choose. The Sun in the 2nd house or the Scorpio decanate rising often symbolizes involvement in banking or related areas such as escrow service or real estate loans. A 3rd house Sun, especially with the Cancer decanate rising may find you in sales, teaching or counseling and doing a bang-up job.

Your weakness, and it is a weakness in spite of your excellent organizational and planning powers, is your handling of setbacks. Somehow your easygoing Sagittarian philosophical outlook does not always jibe with the Scorpio iron within. When the chips are down you want to lead or you won't play. You rarely give up trying to have your way or prove you're right. Because you are generally well liked, you're excused and helped more and longer than most, but people can tire of your incessant leadership and break away. With the Sun in the energetic Aries decanate you may never give up.

Some very well known people have this dynamic pairing: Benjamin Disraeli the English statesman, Henri Toulouse Lautrec the French artist, Noel Coward the British playwright and Mark Twain, American author and humorist, just to mention a few.

Your intense Scorpio nature is tempered by your sunny Sagittarian disposition and you can be the kindest and most thoughtful person in the whole world as well as an incredibly ambitious soul and a potent influence in other people's lives.

Mark Twain
November 30, 1835
4:45 AM LMT
Florida, MO
39N30 91W46

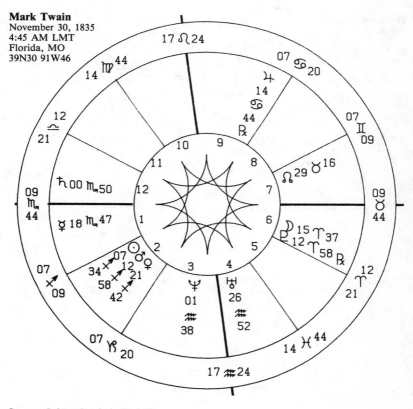

Source: *Sabian Symbols* #914 (C)

SCORPIO ASCENDANT — CAPRICORN SUN

If you were born between December 22nd and January 21st between approximately 3 AM and 5 AM, you may have this combination.

Whatever you do, you do it well. Shrewd, capable, proud and ambitious you take hard work for granted, pride yourself on your accomplishments, seek worldly recognition and usually spend your life trying to better yourself. You're an excellent student and frequently develop fine manual skills especially when the Sun is in the 3rd house and Mercury is in Aquarius. Paul Cezanne, the great French painter is a good example.

Dr. Tom Dooley
January 17, 1727
2:30 AM CST
St. Louis, MO
38N38 90W12

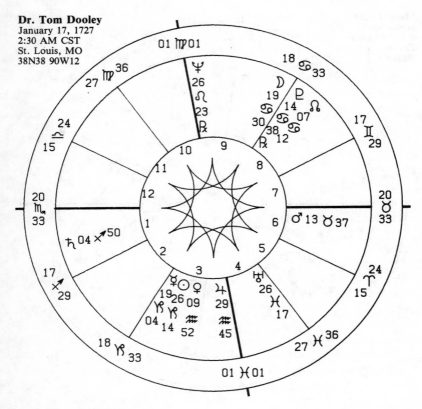

Source: Doris Chase Doane (C)

Faithful, conservative, loyal and sometimes thrifty to extremes, you believe in buying the best because it lasts longer, especially when the Sun is in the 2nd house or in the pragmatic Capricorn decanate. This penchant for the finest things in life is also likely with the possessive Scorpio decanate rising. You can be the businessperson *par excellence*, whose sense of timing allows you to always be in the right place at the right time. If the shy Cancer decanate is rising or the Sun is in the unassuming Virgo decanate, you won't usually pick a fight, but you are a devoted defender of your own beliefs. When your interest is aroused, you can be a champion of the rights of others. Dr. Tom

Dooley, the founder of Medico, the international medical aid mission epitomizes this combination working at its best.

Not usually impulsive, spontaneously outgoing or receptive to new ideas or people, you are an enthusiastic and staunch supporter once you are convinced of their worth. The Sun in the affectionate Taurus decanate or the Ascendant in the sensitive Pisces decanate suggests more warmth in what is essentially a rather cool and calculating combination. Women with this pairing are marvelous traditional wives: family comes first and loyalty and devotion are given unquestioningly. Your greatest asset is an abundance of everyday common sense virtues; your weakness is a tendency to narrow, set and dogmatic views and a consistently materialistic outlook that denies what it can't conceive or believe. You are inclined to view life from a limited perspective, but are willing to consider alternatives if an appeal is made to your logic or common sense. Basically, you support the scientific method of proof for any hypotheses.

Enterprising and self-respecting, you are willing to carry more than your share of the load and others look to your quiet and self-assured leadership.

SCORPIO ASCENDANT — AQUARIUS SUN

If you were born between January 21st and February 20th between approximately 1 AM and 3 AM, you may have this combination.

A hard, efficient worker, you are dependable and don't like to do or be less than your best. Loyalty to family and hereditary tradition is marked and you have high potential for mental and spiritual development. You need a full active life with plenty of human contacts, sustaining effective support. You do best in professions that allow for personal expression.

With the Sun in the 3rd house or Gemini decanate, you may be drawn to the arts or a communication field. With a 4th house Sun, estate management and planning or real estate sales may well be your metier. Either position lends itself to the study and teaching of astrology. You're a warmhearted person with real concern for the welfare of your fellowman, so you might go into politics like ex-actor, president Ronald Reagan or invent things to elevate everyone's life style like Thomas Edison.

When others do something you disapprove of, you try to rise above prejudice even though your outlook can be judgmental and at times, even unyielding. Perhaps you recognize your own tendency toward dogmatic opinions and try to squelch them. You're naturally aspiring and try to constantly live on a high level, though there is a bit of the gypsy in your makeup, especially if your Sun is in the free-wheeling Aquarian decanate or the self-willed Scorpio decanate is on the Ascendant.

Ronald Reagan
February 6, 1911
2:04 AM CST
Tampico, IL
41N38 89W48

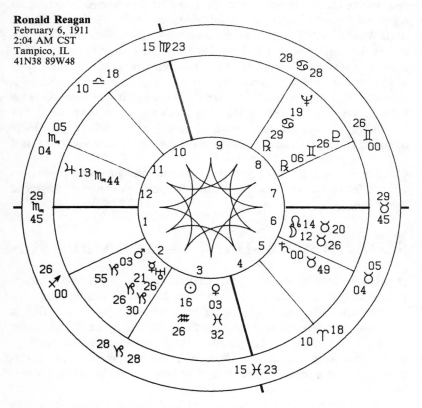

Source: rectified by author (DD)

When you fail, you are aware of it and you are your own strongest accuser. Unfortunately this doesn't mean that you don't repeat your mistakes. Although you like to be liked and are usually outgoing, gregarious and popular, what counts most with you is your own good opinion of yourself. You are your own judge and jury, especially with the Sun in the Libra decanate and you will live and die by your own standards. At the same time you are very sensitive to affection particularly if the Pisces decanate is rising. While not overly demonstrative unless the Ascendant is in the Cancer decanate and the Moon is in a fire sign, you are at your best with those who take your best for granted. You can take any amount of reasonable criticism but bitterly resent what you consider to be unfairness. This is one of the rare Aquarius Sun placements that will harbor resentment when they feel mistreated.

Basically you present a dedicated big brother or sister attitude and really fulfill your best intentions by helping others.

SCORPIO ASCENDANT — PISCES SUN

If you were born between February 20th and March 21st between approximately 11 PM and 1 AM, you may have this combination.

Sensitive and emotional, your feelings run deep and are not usually revealed on the surface. You tend to be a more "right brain" than a "left brain" type and often can use your perceptions in artistic creativity. You are capable of deep emotional attachments and tremendous empathy: "tuning in" to people. Often you lose yourself by trying to "swallow it whole" — understanding in a global (right brain) fashion rather than breaking it into (left brain) pieces. Making lists and dealing with life in a 1-2-3 fashion can help minimize confusion.

When you feel it is in your best interest there isn't anything you can't learn. You are capable of applying yourself with a painstaking steadiness that gets you through to everyone's surprise but your own. Often this can lead to great creative potential and this combination has produced some excellent and sensitive writers like Victor Hugo. His creativity and sensitivity were emphasized by the Sun in the Pisces decanate and the Scorpio decanate rising indicated his dedication to his craft.

Your intuition is so keen that you are apt to rely on it to the exclusion of all else and this can be devastating. You may leap to conclusions that have nothing to do with intuition or reason and then stick to them like glue, especially with the Pisces decanate rising. Sometimes you are inarticulate and confused in self-expression and you confuse others who give up trying to understand you or make you understand them. Neither you nor anyone else can communicate everything at once; keep your information "bite-size" and you are less likely to lose others and/or yourself. Your Scorpio Ascendant indicates the powers of logic and so can Mercury in Aquarius. You need to know when to detach from your Pisces feelings. Otherwise, your one and one often do not add up to two. Since it is rare that anyone can convince you of this, you may go merrily on your way.

You are not essentially ambitious (one of the few Scorpio placements that isn't) except in fits and starts to maintain what you consider your place in the world and there you cling with dogged determination. You tend to live within yourself (especially with a 4th house Sun) and are given to periods of isolation in which you want to be left strictly alone to probe your inner depths and analyze your own psyche. Self-analysis and self-control are particularly important themes when the Sun is in the Scorpio decanate.

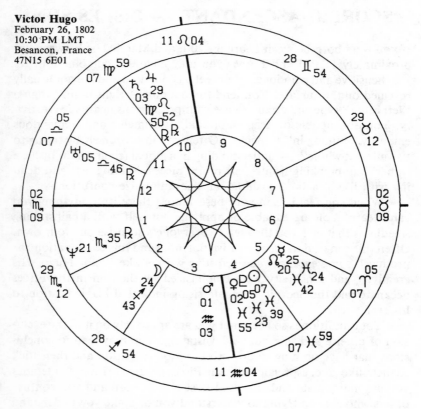

Victor Hugo
February 26, 1802
10:30 PM LMT
Besancon, France
47N15 6E01

Source: Gauquelin #423 Vol. 6 (A)

If the Sun is in the 5th house, fields such as teaching, nursery school attendant, swimming coach or amusement park director may appeal to you. Whatever field you choose, a good education and consistent self-discipline are required not only for success but for good health. A 4th house Sun or the Cancer decanate involved with either the

Ascendant or Sun may find you interested in geology, mining or archaeology — anything that requires digging into the past.

What you need to develop is a factual approach to life and a detached, realistic viewpoint toward yourself. Despite all your sensitivity, in your passive way you can be quite ruthless, ruling through weakness. You may have trouble relating to constructive criticism and tend to look for excuses for yourself. Yet, you're surprised and react with dramatic self pity when the same treatment is handed out to you. Use your wonderful dramatic instincts in sales, promotion or advertising where your skillful playing on people's emotions is highly useful.

The probing sensitivity and responsiveness displayed in this pairing can lead you to great understanding and concern for others. With a positive direction for your intuition and perception, you'll amaze yourself and others with what you can achieve.

CHAPTER NINE

SAGITTARIUS ASCENDANT

Sagittarius rising is the mark of friendliness and companionship. Whatever your inner characteristics as denoted by your Sun sign, this Ascendant camouflages and sometimes totally eclipses the Sun's personality with the simple friendliness of a puppy. Your response is spontaneous and open. Even when seeming superficial, you are nonetheless sincere and well meaning. Forthright, just and candid; occasionally tactless and blunt, your outlook is usually philosophical and your instincts humanitarian. However, your breadth of vision is often more theoretical and theatrical than practical.

You're a born promoter, much better at organization and administration than at routine unless other factors in your chart symbolize this quality. Unless your Sun sign suggests patience, you are apt to feel bogged down by a mire of details and it is easy for you to develop a tendency to let things slide. You tend to spread yourself too thin, take on too much and then find yourself too hampered by details for the quick followthrough that is your stock in trade. Inspirational and stimulating, you can instill confidence in others, and are a super salesperson.

Others may be surprised by your strong religious streak. If not actively involved with churches and dogma, you are at least very philosophical and interested in new thought, new ideas and new ways of doing things. Independent and often rebellious, you do not stand confinement well and therefore you may wait until you're very sure before you leap into matrimony. There is something childlike in your naivete as you resolutely refuse to accept the seriousness of life. Your gambling tendencies may unwittingly betray you. You are willing to take a chance on anything — especially with money. You can push your luck too far with a blind confidence that may be disastrous, particularly if your chart has the fire element strongly emphasized.

Generally fearless, fortunate, usually fond of animals and the great outdoors, you are very restless, much like your opposite sign, Gemini and you hate to sit or stand still for any length of time. Warm and sociable, you have a lot of loyal friends who love you and will go out on a limb for you just as you will for them. When you say you'll do something for someone, you don't just say it, you do it. But in your own good time. Your one inherent fault is procrastination. The tendency is to have a lot of great ideas, but you may put off getting the show on the road. Probably because you are a little overwhelmed by your own grandiose schemes. Though easygoing, you can be quite quarrelsome, enjoying argument just for the sake of arguing.

In appearance, you are usually quite tall and slender with round shoulders or an inclination to stoop, maybe because you grew quickly. You generally have long arms, legs, hands and feet and your toes may turn inward when you sit down. Frequently large-boned, both men and women have a wide hip structure and a hipswinging walk with a tendency to shuffle or stamp the feet.

You often have a long, oval face, much like Libra, but not as curvy or dimpled unless Venus is prominent in your chart. Your face is long from nose to jaw and you may have a protruding, full chin or lantern jaw; a so-called horse or hatchetface. There may be a hump in the bridge of your nose. Your hair is usually abundant and wavy, but the men, like all the fire signs tend to bald early in a long streak on top, which they comb the remaining hair over. Often your lashes and brows are darker than your hair; remaining black or very dark brown even after your hair has grayed. Sagittarius rising can and often does have the largest hands and feet of all the signs and sometimes the largest nose. In the Caucasian race, this is known as the blue-eyed sign and your eyes are usually small, bright, alert and farsighted. Your two front teeth may be rather large, adding to your somewhat horsey look. Of all the signs, you have the most unusual, attention-getting laugh, like a horse's whinny or a chicken's cackle or a low, throaty chuckle. You talk much and fast — so fast at times, that you seem to stutter. Very often the women with this Ascendant have red hair; if not naturally, with a little help from their beautician.

Healthwise, your sensitive areas are the hips and liver and you are prone to rushing headlong into action. You may have a tendency to both overeat and overindulge your fondness for the grape. You rarely give in to illness, usually operating on the theory that if you think positively, and you certainly do, that all things will work to your advantage. Surprisingly, you're frequently right. Your faith and trust in the universe do afford some protection.

Always active, the life of any party, you never hesitate to go out on a verbal limb. A past master of the social gaffe, it has been said of you that you only open your mouth to change feet. But your *faux pas* are hardly intentional; you're just being "honest" and when you try to repair the damage you've done with your verbal goofs, you may only get yourself in deeper. You can also be the most entertaining of guests, utilizing your quick wit in skilled repartee.

You have an innate sense of inner worth and so you are genuinely resentful and surprised when you are taken to task and asked to explain your grandiloquent gestures and bold statements. You feel that if you say something, that makes it so and others shouldn't question. You're most suited to vocations large in scope that move quickly, allow mobility and where you have the authority to work alone.

Your faith, zest and enthusiasm can inspire others and urge them on to higher accomplishments.

SAGITTARIUS ASCENDANT — ARIES SUN

If you were born between March 21st and April 20th between approximately 9 PM and 11 PM, you may have this combination.

Positive and forceful, your response to life is instantaneous and personal. No one could ever doubt your meaning since you rarely engage in double talk and you usually find this difficult to deal with in others. You do not indulge in abstractions or contemplations but at the same time you passionately and literally believe in and dedicate yourself to truth, honor, justice and patriotism. When you offer your opinion, that's it and you rarely permit argument or contradiction. Yet you will often flatly contradict others because you are so sure of your own concept of right and wrong.

You're naturally pleasure-loving, naive and youthful in outlook, but you must take care not to let pleasure seeking become a way of life, especially if the Sagittarius decanate is on the Ascendant or occupied by the Sun. Dedicate yourself to higher goals. The pitfall of careless hedonism is easier to avoid with a 4th house Sun, because it indicates some of the security minded qualities of Cancer to supplement the self-reliance and courage of the Aries/Sagittarius. With this placement, some sensitivity to the needs of others is suggested, softening your otherwise rather unfeeling attitude toward people. Although this appears to be callousness, it is more an unawareness of others having likes and dislikes separate and apart from yours. It is hard for you to realize that anyone can react to a given situation differently from the way you would.

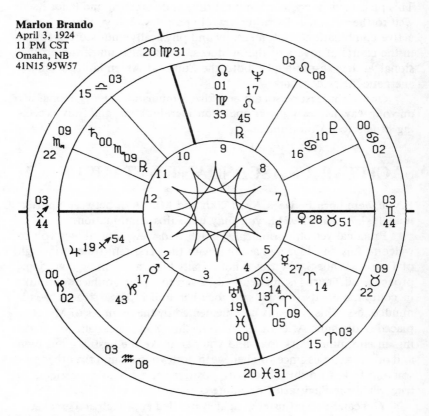

Marlon Brando
April 3, 1924
11 PM CST
Omaha, NB
41N15 95W57

Source: Doris Chase Doane (C)

Your creative urge is strong and self-expression is sought in many avenues — music, composer-conductor Henry Mancini with a 4th house Sun; acting, perennial leading lady Gloria Swanson with the Sun in the 3rd house; actor-activist Marlon Brando with a 5th house Sun; writing, French novelist Emile Zola with a 3rd house Sun.

A 5th house Sun or in the Leo decanate or that decanate rising suggests self-expression through invention, fine craftsmanship or a hobby. This placement also indicates a natural gambler and risk taker and therefore you may find fulfillment in fields like flying, race car driving or anything that suits your adventurous spirit.

Often you are a great theorist, pioneering a new or an ancient field, providing insights and visualization like erudite astrologer Dane Rudhyar, especially if you have the Sun in the 3rd house, as he does. This placement suggests mental courage and foresight and lends itself well to the pursuits of writing, travel and sales ability. This is a very active combination, both mentally and physically and is often found in the charts of lovers of the outdoors. It may also mark the professional athlete, especially if both the Sun and Ascendant are in the energetic Aries decanate.

One of the least personally sensitive combinations, you go blissfully on your way, achieving your not inconsiderable goals and fully expecting others to do the same.

SAGITTARIUS ASCENDANT — TAURUS SUN

If you were born between April 20th and May 20th between approximately 7 PM and 9 PM, you may have this combination.

Practical yet philosophical, your broad viewpoint allows you to welcome any new idea and adapt it with the persistent follow through of Taurus. While Sagittarius is not usually known for an organized approach, and Taurus is not generally given to a philosophical outlook, in combination they work well together indicating a steady broad-mindedness. This is greatly complemented by the qualities of Mercury placed in dynamic Aries or flexible Gemini. You are capable of carrying an enormous work load and you can make the best of your own and others abilities since you believe in both yourself and the other person and follow up this belief with positive action. This is particularly true when the Sagittarius decanate is rising.

You can be an adjuster with an unruffled approach and great sensitivity to the needs of others especially if the Sun is in the Capricorn decanate. Patient with details (like no other Sagittarius Ascendant), you are able to see the end result of most situations. Sometimes the idealism symbolized by Jupiter can lead you to pursue illusory ends with as much determination as real ones. Because of this tendency, you may trip occasionally before you learn the difference, especially on the emotional level.

With the Sun in the 5th house or the Leo decanate rising, you are frequently artistically creative like Florentine painter and sculptor, Leonardo da Vinci and English poet Robert Browning. You definitely need an emotional outlet for your exuberant good spirits.

With the Sun in the 4th house or the Taurus decanate, you have a natural bent for real estate sales, surveying, estate management and the home loan or escrow services. If the Sun is in the 6th house or the Virgo decanate, your Taurus patience and Sagittarian adaptability suggest that you can be an excellent secretary, travel agent or hairdresser.

Robert Browning
May 7, 1812
10 PM LMT
London, England
51N30 0W06

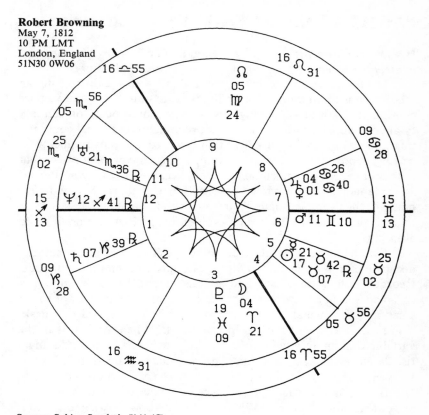

Source: *Sabian Symbols* #141 (C)

Ardent, loyal and deeply loving, you usually consider life barren and boring without a strong reciprocal affection, especially when the Aries decanate rises. You are usually very money conscious and may have exceptional good luck at times. Prodigality, both emotional and financial is also likely. If you are inclined in this direction, you don't care whose money you spend as long as you can do the spending. When you develop your personality to be fully responsive, depend upon yourself rather than luck and use your Sagittarian flair productively, then you're at your best and you'll attract genuine good fortune gratifying your Taurus soul.

Practical and persevering as well as inspirational and uplifting, you can ground your grandiose schemes in very real achievement.

SAGITTARIUS ASCENDANT — GEMINI SUN

If you were born between May 20th and June 21st between approximately 5 PM and 7 PM, you may have this combination.

The friendliest person in the world, that's you — enjoying human relationships of all kinds. Your mind is always on the go and you are continually learning something new — in school or out. You can talk to anyone about anything. This is a predominantly mental combination and you do well in any field that is varied and moves quickly — writing, reporting, teaching, speaking, selling, travel. You prefer that it doesn't require too much physical toil, because like many Sagittarius Ascendants, you are somewhat physically lazy. With the Sun in the 7th house or the Libra decanate, your airy mentality makes it easy for you to deal with others in fields such as sales, psychology, counseling and even law.

Your ambition is readily apparent with a 6th house Sun or the Aries decanate on the Ascendant. You'll work hard to achieve like botanist George Washington Carver and architect Frank Lloyd Wright.

The Sun in either the 6th or 7th house must take care not to get stuck in some menial type service job that keeps you tied to a desk. You need freedom of motion in your work. When the Sun is in the variable Gemini decanate or the freedom-loving Sagittarian decanate rises, your restlessness is even more pronounced and unless there is some fixity in your chart, you may always seem to be two feet off the ground.

If the Sun is in the Aquarius decanate, your foresight is every bit as good as your hindsight. When the Leo decanate rises and the Sun is in the 6th house, your ego needs are great and not always easily handled. You certainly want to be someone and you will make every effort to achieve, but you would prefer it if you could gain the recognition you seek without too much personal effort. You can be quite an opportunist, even the super con man, always ready to tell any kind of story to make a buck. If mental agility, ingenuity, keenness and friendliness were awarded prizes, you'd take first place, hands down. But your restlessness, changeableness and glibness can get you into trouble. The same qualities that make you popular can lead you down the garden path if you don't cultivate some continuity of purpose and set high goals for yourself.

Frank Lloyd Wright
June 8, 1867
8 PM LMT
Richland Center, WI
43N20 90W22

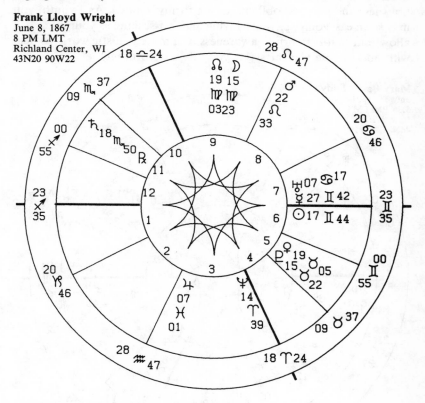

Source: Penfield quotes mother's papers (C)

You can be the most inspired and inspiring of communicators, a natural teacher and a lifelong student of everything the world has to offer.

SAGITTARIUS ASCENDANT — CANCER SUN

If you were born between June 22nd and July 23rd between approximately 3 PM and 5 PM, you may have this combination.

Ambitious, sensitive and self-aware, you combine true friendliness and caring for others with an equal amount of self-interest. You may appear adventurous and may even be venturesome, but you rarely

wander far from the status quo. You need acceptance. Family influence
is strong and even when restrictive, the familial pattern, conscientiousness and parental obligations are firmly imbued. As a youth, you
may seem easygoing, pleasure-loving and self-seeking as your purse will
allow, but maturity brings awareness of a more realistic world to deal
with and in true Cancer style, you adapt accordingly.

Mary Baker Eddy
July 16, 1821
5:38 PM LMT
Bow, NH
44N21 71W19

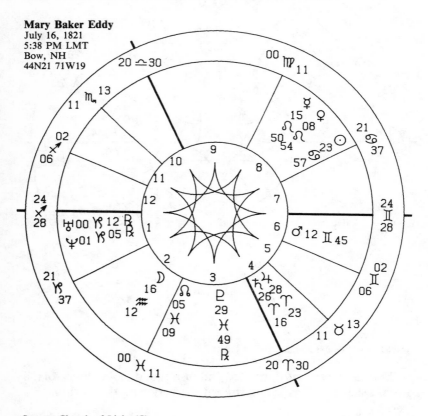

Source: Church of Light (C)

Occasionally your deep-seated pride causes you to overvalue
yourself and your contributions and you adopt a "holier than thou"
attitude, but at the same time you're so "nice" that you're forgiven
your naive conceit just as you forgive others. This is particularly emphasized when the Leo decanate is on the Ascendant. You are one of
the few Cancers unlikely to hold a grudge, but you are touchy and sensitive, though it is sometimes hard for others to know what it is that

you're hurt about. Though you talk a lot, you rarely reveal what you really feel and it is important for you to learn to share your inner experiences with those you care for. Sentimental and sweet, rather than deeply emotional, you gain your knowledge and awareness of other's feelings from an innate knowing, not from any first hand experience. You try to avoid depth of passion or heartfelt emotion as well as any situation that would deprive you of life's niceties or pitch you into any high spirited turmoil.

Strongly religious and/or philosophical or metaphysical (Mary Baker Eddy, the founder of Christian Science had this combination), you seek at all times to make the best of your resources and develop them as you feel necessary. A religious streak is strongly evident if the Sagittarian decanate rises and the Sun is in the Pisces decanate. With the Sun in the 8th house or the Scorpio decanate, your theological interest may be more in the direction of the occult or mystical.

With a 7th house Sun or the Sagittarius decanate rising, you may be attracted to politics, writing, the educational field or law. When the Sun is in the Cancer decanate, there may be an opportunity to live away from the country of your birth. If the Aries decanate rises, you evidence surprising energy and the desire to be constantly on the move. The Leo decanate on the Ascendant symbolizes a great deal of natural charisma and ability to sway others emotionally.

You prefer that your life run smoothly and to your best advantage and you usually achieve this without too much struggle. This combination is one of the most farseeing, sensitive, prophetic and psychic in the zodiac.

SAGITTARIUS ASCENDANT — LEO SUN

If you were born between July 23rd and August 23rd between approximately 1 PM and 3 PM, you may have this combination.

Beyond a shadow of a doubt, you are the most self-assured person in the world. You may seem modest, even humble but nothing could be farther from the truth. Your self opinion is so good that you don't have to broadcast it. Just knowing it inside yourself is enough; and truly, at your best, you're quite a person — loyal, ardent, high-minded and philosophical; even deeply religious in a personal, unorthodox fashion if the Sagittarian decanate is prominent in the Ascendant or Sun. You have keen insight, your creative touch is strong and sure and sometimes prolific, showing itself in various ways: writing, music, teaching, science, the occult, to name a few.

You take it for granted that people will look up to you and you are helpful, encouraging and inspirational, while expecting the best of others. You live by your own code, especially with a 9th house Sun; however this placement used negatively can indicate problems with the law. If the Sun or Ascendant is in the Aries decanate, you have a strong love-nature that usually permits romantic variation. While you are devoted to and provide for spouse and family, the tendency to wander is strongly pronounced in both sexes unless Venus happens to be in Virgo. Then, you may be a bit more circumspect, believing in the proprieties.

Bernard Baruch
August 19, 1870
1:50 PM LMT
Camden, SC
34N14 80W36

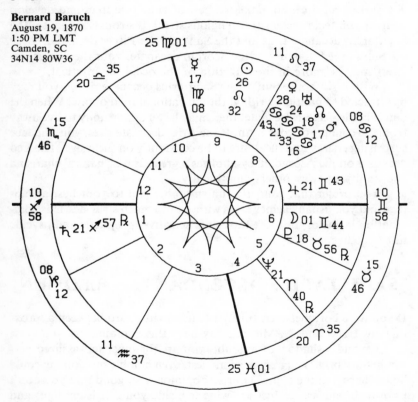

Source: Church of Light (C)

You make no excuses. You take freedom for granted and are always honorable to your own code. As you mature, obligations grow heavier and of necessity you settle down a bit, but your innate dash, ardor and adventurous nature all guarantee that for you the romantic

Leo Sun will always shine. This is doubly emphasized if either the Sun or Ascendant is in the Leo decanate. Youthful and idealistic, the worst that can be said of you, is that in religion you sometimes tend toward bigotry.

With the Sun in the 8th house, you may be drawn to financial fields like consummate financier, Bernard Baruch. Sometimes you are attracted to medicine, but only if other placements in the chart verify this. This combination often suggests an aptitude for the jewelry trades as designer, diamond cutter, stonesetter, etc.

Dramatic and flamboyant, you are rarely daunted by circumstances, conditions or obligations, taking life in your stride and overriding all obstacles and minor annoyances with good grace.

SAGITTARIUS ASCENDANT — VIRGO SUN

If you were born between August 23rd and September 23rd between approximately 11 AM and 1 PM, you may have this combination.

Devoted, zealous and often self-sacrificing, you are a great friend who will excuse your friends' faults if you think they are doing the best they can in any given set of circumstances. The meticulous and painstaking Virgo side holds the Sagittarian tendency to braggadocio and bombast somewhat in check. You tend to stay on the sidelines until you're sure of acceptance especially if the Sun is in the Virgo decanate. Your flair for arrangement and fixing things makes you long on advice, sometimes to the point of being a busybody. But since you are seldom self-seeking, are intellectually detached and so practical, your advice is usually the best around. Also, you generally set a good example by your own actions.

With the Sun in either the 8th or 9th houses or the Sagittarius decanate rising, the professions — literary, editorial, religious, occult, educational — or crafts are right up your alley. If one isn't your vocation, another will surely be your avocation. Jackie Cooper, the child actor who went on to become a TV producer and director has this combination. His Ascendant in the Aries decanate emphasized his drive while the Sun in the Taurus decanate illustrates the tenacity to hang in there and achieve.

Ambitious, practical, active, painstaking and alert, you are a doer with the Sagittarian broad view of things that adds scope and flourish to your Virgo fussiness. Your range is so wide that you don't like to think you've left a single stone unturned in your search for unrestricted knowledge. You take details in stride and are a good manager, adaptable and fluent with a sure touch especially if the Sun is in the capable Capricorn decanate. Though sensitive and artistic, you try to hide these qualities and thus at times, appear a bit brusque and unfeeling. You have considerable creative and imaginative flair especially in business fields when the Sun is in the 10th house or the Leo decanate rises.

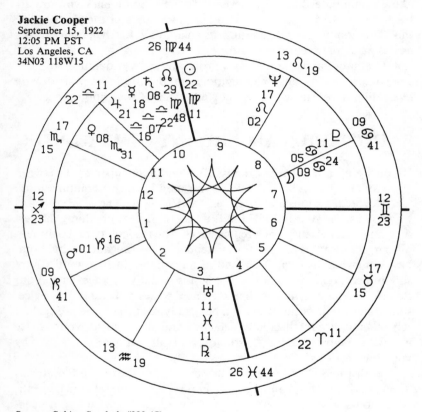

Jackie Cooper
September 15, 1922
12:05 PM PST
Los Angeles, CA
34N03 118W15

Source: *Sabian Symbols* #222 (C)

Open and approachable as well as orderly and neat, your Virgo practicality can ground Sagittarian visions and grandeur into a productive outlet.

SAGITTARIUS ASCENDANT — LIBRA SUN

If you were born between September 23rd and October 24th between approximately 9 AM and 11 AM, you may have this combination.

This is a delicate, refined and aspiring blend and is sometimes the mark of the dilettante. Here Libra symbolizes an airiness and charm to add to the outgoing and sometimes blustering Sagittarian personality. Your innate good taste makes you the perfect hostess or host. Your native tact, enlivened by Sagittarian humor, insures that everyone will have a good time.

Some prominent people with this combination are first lady Eleanor Roosevelt, composer George Gershwin, German philosopher and poet Friedrich Neitzsche and Italian physicist Enrico Fermi.

Eleanor Roosevelt
October 11, 1884
10 AM EST
New York, NY
40N45 73W57

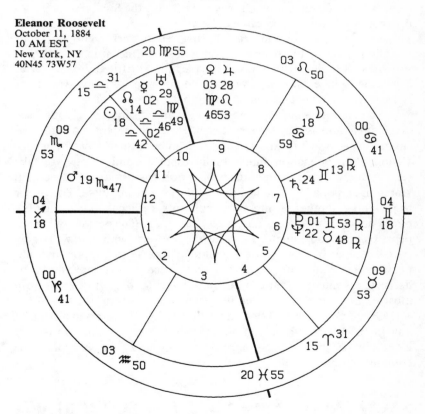

Source: Isabel Hickey (C)

Your social attitude is pleasant and cheerful even if not profound. You are interested in everyone at their own evaluation and this adds to your popularity. It is hard for you to make an enemy. Who could be affronted at your agreeability and genuine need to please and be accepted? With the Sun in the 11th house or Aquarian decanate, you are well suited to the social sciences and any field where diplomacy and tact play a key role: working for the government in the role of embassy employee, for instance. With the Sun in the 10th house or the Aries decanate rising, politics and law may attract you. If the Sun is in the 9th house or the Sagittarius decanate is on the Ascendant, a double Sagittarius theme, you would be a great cruise director, pilot, or flight attendant. Anything that allows you to move around, be charming and that doesn't require that you get your hands dirty is appropriate. Charm and a search for ease are emphasized if the Sun is in the Libra decanate or if the Leo decanate rises.

Your naturally optimistic, extroverted temperament and your socially sensitive and dreamy Libran soul sometimes find stark reality too difficult to deal with and you escape into a drifting, dream world. Everyone comments on your talents and potential — if you would only exert yourself — and that's a very big "if."

You are very magnetic, appear quite amorous in spite of your basic detachment and usually have many romantic encounters. You are dutiful, more because it is expected of you than because of any strong convictions about obligation. Intellectually responsive and curious, you take readily and naturally to philosophic concepts without any deep soul searching, especially when the Sun is in the Gemini decanate. You prefer to pick up a number of interesting concepts, rather than investigating one in depth. When things do not go your way, which occasionally happens, you can come unglued and turn on those around you with unexpected temper because you are genuinely unable to see how it could possibly be your fault. Your greatest need is the cultivation of decisiveness and persistence. You are, strangely enough, protected from most of life's adversities, due in part to your faith in the universe.

Gracious and tactful (which is not usually a Sagittarian attribute) you fit in well anywhere you go and are a welcome addition to any gathering because of your approachability and your penchant for communication.

SAGITTARIUS ASCENDANT — SCORPIO SUN

If you were born between October 24th and November 23rd between approximately 7 AM and 9 AM, you may have this combination.

This is a very individualistic combination — magnetic, helpful, capable of hard work and even self-sacrifice to attain a goal and/or perfection. You aim high, are aspiring in an idealistic way, philosophical in outlook and very stern and uncompromising in your views of right and wrong. Intellectually oriented, your rather broad scope of understanding makes you appear tolerant, but you are more fixed in your opinions (Scorpio) than you appear to be on the surface (Sagittarius). It is easy for you to zero in on others who are slick, shrewd or even crooked, probably because you understand where they are coming from and can head them off at the pass. Even though you are aware of such possibilities, it is rare that you use them. You don't even always protect yourself, and can be victimized. The Sun in the Cancer decanate indicates you might be susceptible to appeals to your nurturing instinct.

Bob Mathias
November 17, 1930
7:47 AM PST
Tulare, CA
36N13 119W21

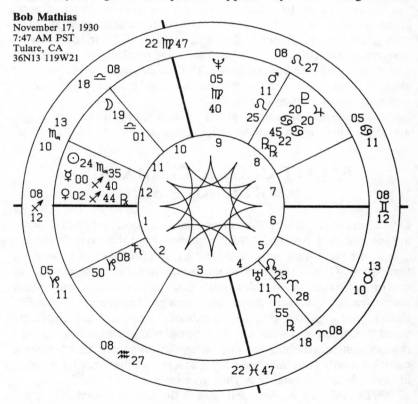

Source: *Contemporary Sidereal Horoscopes* (A)

Two great athletes have this winning combination — baseball great Stan Musial and Olympics decathlon champion and congressman Bob Mathias.

In spite of a certain gullibility, you're no pantywaist. With Scorpio iron and Sagittarian self-assertion, you're capable of considerable ruthlessness in your own defense, especially if the Sun is in the relentless Scorpio decanate. But with typical Sagittarian clumsiness, you sometimes lash out at the wrong person at the wrong time. At your best, you're the most faithful, loyal and loving of friends and spouses, especially with the Sun in the 11th house and you will put yourself out for others endlessly.

What you need most is to decide early in life on an attainable goal that does not require too much support from others and then stick to it. With the Sun in the 12th house or in the Pisces decanate, this goal may be realized in the fields of medicine, research or entertainment. If the Sun is in the 11th house or the Aries or Sagittarius decanate rises, your goals may be oriented to the outdoor service fields in some way — forestry, paramedics or the like. Teaching, particularly history and philosophy may well be your forte. With the Leo decanate rising, your flair for drama comes in handy here. But aim at what you can reach and hold on to it once you attain it.

Outgoing and exceedingly affable, people who don't know you well are often surprised at your underlying discernment and incisiveness.

SAGITTARIUS ASCENDANT — SAGITTARIUS SUN

If you were born between November 23rd and December 22nd between approximately 5 AM and 7 AM, you may have this combination.

You have a high sense of adventure and the energy to carry out your quest. Only a tendency to go to extremes has to be curbed, as overoptimism can be your downfall. You start out like a house afire, are the teacher's pet, win scholarships, are a good athlete or cheerleader, head school organizations, have loads of friends and are invariably voted "most likely to succeed." You go right from school to a "good" position. Intense, dashing and inspirational, your superb self-confidence carries not only you, but others along in a mind-blowing, cliff-hanging lifestyle. Your personality is your greatest wealth.

When things are going well, you're the perfect companion, partner and boss: hardworking and persistent, seeking new and better ways of doing things. While you believe in your own ethics and philosophy, you are nevertheless tolerant and don't foist your beliefs on others. If you choose a profession or business where you encounter no reversals, obstacles or serious setbacks, you will have a fairly fortunate and successful life. Some fields that may appeal to you are trucking, construction, sports, coaching, fire fighting or on another level, the law or ministry. Much is indicated by the sign and house Jupiter is in.

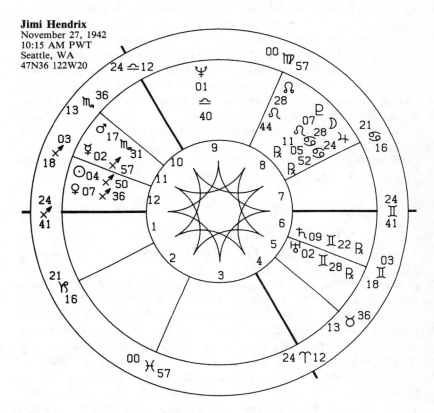

Jimi Hendrix
November 27, 1942
10:15 AM PWT
Seattle, WA
47N36 122W20

Source: Chester Kemp in *American Astrology* (C)

When things go awry, it is difficult for you to see how it could possibly be your fault. This shortsightedness is most noticeable when the Aries decanate is involved with either the Sun or Ascendant. Generally criticism passes over you lightly, but when it does penetrate (and this is especially true of the Sun in 12th house), you may have difficulty and tend to come apart at the the seams. Then all your ego and arrogance come into play and you seem like two different people. With a 1st house Sun (or with the Sun or Ascendant in the Leo decanate), when under stress you may blow up over the most trivial issues and create havoc at home, in business and among your friends.

When you reach this stage, any means justifies your ends: continual self-assertion. Sports can help channel your fiery energy. Winning on the playing field is usually more constructive than always "winning" arguments at work or at home. And fighting for a worthy cause is a better use of your energy than putting friends down.

When the Sagittarian decanate is rising or if the Sun is there, you are a born reformer and organizer. In business you work best alone, such as in a one-person shop or at the head of your own enterprise, especially if the Leo decanate rises. Sometimes you are a super salesperson, particularly when selling and promoting a new concept or item. With the Sun in the 2nd house this can be a combination for great financial success. Rock star Jimi Hendrix's chart illustrates the sudden flare of fame and acclaim which double fire can reach.

Fun-loving, restless and ever on the go, your enthusiasm carries you far and helps you reach your goals.

SAGITTARIUS ASCENDANT — CAPRICORN SUN

If you were born between December 22nd and January 21st between approximately 3 AM and 5 AM, you may have this combination.

The Sagittarian flair for philosophical and idealistic exploration plus the matter-of-fact Capricorn ingenuity and efficiency show you are in a class by yourself. Your Sagittarian personality tends to be interested in a myriad variety of subjects, but your Capricorn soul follows through on each one until you master it. You are ambitious, a good leader and generally sympathetic to others. It is not easy to fool you, but you are subject to considerable emotional ups and downs while young and you remain intense long after the fire in others has died down so you are surprisingly youthful. The combination of Sagittarian farsightedness and Capricorn earthiness tunes you in to others and you instinctively know what appeals to the public as well as the individual. Consistent stability could well be the key to your personality.

You are a natural money maker. If the Sun is in the 2nd house or the Taurus decanate, financial fields like banking, management and big business may attract you. With a 1st house Sun or the Aries decanate rising, you are often the self-made man like hotel czar Conrad Hilton. You like the good things in life and you must beware of overindulgence and wasting your considerable talents like American writer and poet Edgar Allan Poe.

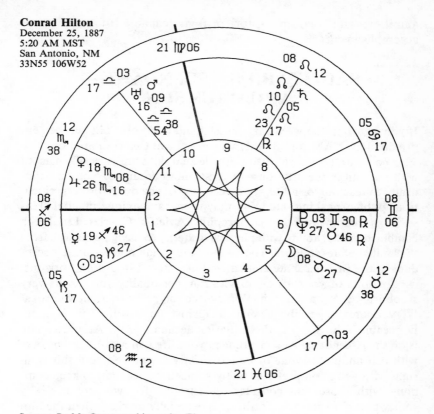

Conrad Hilton
December 25, 1887
5:20 AM MST
San Antonio, NM
33N55 106W52

Source: *Be My Guest* autobiography (B)

If the Ascendant is in the Sagittarius decanate, you may show a tendency to moralizing and sometimes set your ideals so high they seem impossible to fulfill for anyone but you. If you fall into perfectionistic standards, you may become critical of yourself or others who show human shortcomings. You are capable of much; give yourself time, patience and reasonable goals. Capable, practical, broad in your thinking processes and dynamic in action, you can combine idealism and down-to-earthiness with mental ability and shrewd know-how, especially when the Sun is in the efficient Capricorn or hardworking Virgo decanate. You can be extraordinarily gifted and outshine yourself in any or all of the arts (especially when the Leo decanate rises), the occult, science and public speaking. Whatever your field, you are a competent and sensible businessperson.

This combination of idealism and broad vision (Sagittarius) with ambition and realism (Capricorn) is capable of truly great accomplishments.

SAGITTARIUS ASCENDANT — AQUARIUS SUN

If you were born between January 21st and February 20th between approximately 1 AM and 3 AM, you may have this combination.

You are a born idea person. Intellectual skills are especially marked with the Sun in the 3rd house or the Gemini decanate. You take naturally to teaching or a literary career, one of the dramatic arts, elocution, public speaking, etc. You may even have unique manual skills such as mapmaking or calligraphy. Aviator Charles Lindbergh combined mental ability with physical dexterity to navigate his way from the United States to Paris. The double Sagittarian note with the Ascendant in the first decanate emphasized his interest in distant horizons.

In spite of your affable Sagittarian personality you can be very stubborn, an Aquarian trait. While often too polite to argue vigorously, you are not easily persuaded against your will. This is more noticeable if the Sun is in the Aquarian decanate or the Aries decanate is on the Ascendant. At some time in your life you may be on the outs with just about everyone or be left strictly to yourself. But this is all right with you. You prefer to be by yourself rather than to keep company with those you consider undesirable, for you are basically somewhat of a snob. This attitude is especially marked when the Sun is in the 2nd house, where you may feel that yours is the only viable value system. At your best, you are open and tolerant, viewing everyone and anything as a potential learning experience.

Practical when it comes to pursuing a career, you could care less about domestic chores although you do live up to what is expected of you. Your children may skip breakfast and lunch on junk foods, but this doesn't bother you as much as the idea that their mental concepts may suffer. You generally find someone to do the menial jobs and you somehow seem protected from adversity. Above all, this is an intellectual combination and you are not always appreciated by those who live on a more physical level. If the Leo decanate rises or if the Sun is in the Libra decanate, you may tend to overdramatize yourself and your ideas. You are a great abstract thinker and theoretician. Drawn toward the future, you are often involved with new technology.

Your reforming concepts are so broad that you sometimes appear inconsiderate when it comes to current issues. Your air of innate refinement and idealism can put others off and give you the appearance of having a superiority complex. This is particularly true when you are at your best, revealing your comprehensive knowledge of any and every field. But you are capable of getting along with anyone when you choose.

Charles Lindbergh
February 4, 1902
2:30 AM CST
Detroit, MI
42N20 83W03

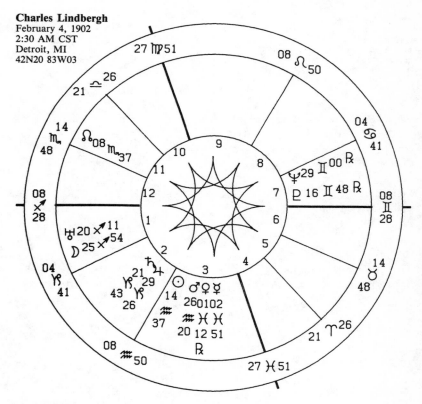

Source: *Sabian Symbols* #581 (C)

Friendly and outgoing, you are always willing to share your abundant knowledge and have a willingness to help others in any way possible.

SAGITTARIUS ASCENDANT — PISCES SUN

If you were born between February 20th and March 21st between approximately 11 PM and 1 AM, you may have this combination.

No matter what your vocation, you are a true idealist and humanitarian: genuinely charitable, philosophical and emotional. You feel the woes of the world keenly and often leap to the aid of the underdog; you may be found working with the underprivileged or the institutionalized. You are also drawn to the philanthropic fields.

Jackie Gleason
February 26, 1916
2:13 AM EST
New York, NY
40N45 73W57

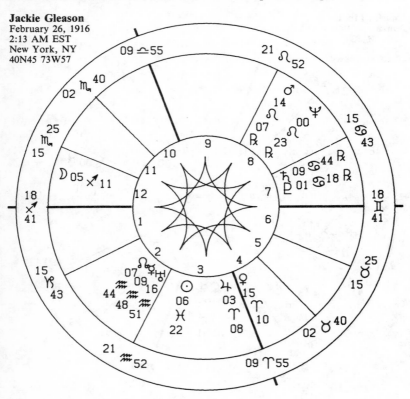

Source: Horoscope Magazine (C)

You think in broad terms and generally act without pettiness and self-seeking. Though you may often be impractical in your viewpoint, others react to you on your own terms because they can sense your good intentions. You bring out and stimulate the best in your fellow human. You relate to the basics of life and have exceptional insight along with real vision and breadth. This is usually more apparent when the Sagittarius decanate rises. If the Sun is in the Scorpio decanate or the Aries decanate is rising, you may show a decided ability for sports especially of the water variety.

This is the combination that can designate the clown or comedian especially if the Sun is in the 3rd house or Pisces decanate or if the Leo decanate rises. There seems to be a need to play the buffoon. Television comedians Jerry Lewis and Jackie Gleason are good examples of this pairing. You tend to exaggerate things and events out of all proportion to their importance and then have a hard time handling the situation you have created. Your exaggerative tendencies make great comedy but are less useful when taken seriously by others. Remember to keep your sense of humor along with your idealism.

With a 4th house Sun or if it is in the Cancer decanate, your tendency is to be contemplative and withdrawn, so you seem more Piscean than Sagittarian. You can be a natural healer, whether it is occult, medical or religious. A most generous judge of others you are emotionally perceptive, but still a sucker for a sob story. Both humble and noble, and sometimes melancholy in outlook, you may at intervals tend to lead a lonely introverted life — but not for long. Your Sagittarian optimism sends you back out into the world where you belong.

Open and genuinely kindhearted, you have the ability to make everyone appreciate that you are their friend.

CHAPTER TEN

CAPRICORN ASCENDANT

Your Capricorn Ascendant adds a conservative note to any Sun sign. Serious, ambitious and surprisingly social, you are naturally efficient, don't like loose ends and when working under stress, you are at your most productive. Often aspiring and enterprising, you are an essentially practical person. Sometimes you are not so much anxious to get ahead as you are afraid of being an also-ran or just plain being left out. Seemingly timid and nonaggressive, you nevertheless, with patience and an air of self-deprecation win out in most situations, especially business.

The commercial world of dog-eat-dog is where you shine. Your perseverance plus your ability to subtly maneuver bring great reward. You value prestige and accomplishment and your sense of duty is strong. You give service sometimes with, but often without, affection or genuine sympathy. In your quiet and unassuming way, you achieve all your goals and then some. When you do things with love, your sense of dignity and loyalty tie you to others with unending self-sacrifice and devotion.

You often seem to have a faint aura of melancholy around you, a nagging self-doubt that denies you an optimistic and happy-go-lucky personality. A fire sign Sun can brighten up your Capricorn personality but it may only be an intermittent spontaneity. Enhancing your self-esteem and lessening your self-criticism can help. Remember to count your assets as well as your flaws.

You have great respect for law, order and authority and you really want a position for yourself. After all, your symbol is the mountain goat who can climb to heights that no other animal can reach. You honor heredity and tradition and are basically a shy and conservative person, who is always willing to give others their due, if in your view, it is deserved.

It is said of Capricorn that they are old when young and seem younger as they grow old. You identify with work, accomplishment and productivity. As a young person you may be frustrated and ill because you have nowhere to channel that drive for fulfillment. Once you find satisfying work, you are usually healthy unless you retire completely. Children with Capricorn rising should be given responsibilities (at their level) so they can gain a sense of contributing to society (or family) even when quite young. You have such a potential for survival that it is very possible you will live to celebrate your hundredth birthday.

Your most sensitive areas are your knees and skin. With your inherent ability to get stronger as you get older, one would think you would avoid hospitals and doctors. But this is not necessarily so because you often worry or work yourself sick. Extremely cautious and fearful of almost everything, it is necessary for you to develop a more positive outlook if you would achieve good health and a harmonious life. This may not be easy for Capricorn because of your "doom and gloom" attitude. Your teeth may give problems and your sometimes rigid and unbending outlook can contribute to arthritic and rheumatic difficulties. Reasonable responsibilities (not too much, not too little) make teeth problems, arthritis, etc. less likely.

There are two distinctly different looking Capricorn Ascendants. Both types are identifiable by their very distinctive walk, which is akin to a strut. One is of small stature, slender, narrow chested with a thin neck, bony hands, feet and knees and a small sharp nose with a downward point. Often this type appears knock-kneed. Your skull is bony and the skin is taut; you have a high square forehead with rather small features placed very close together in the middle of your face. Your hair is thin and sparse, your eyes small and sometimes peering, your mouth is thin lipped and you may have a rather sad or grim expression. Your ears are small, close to your head and lobeless and you have a strong, narrow chin.

The second type of Capricorn Ascendant resembles your opposite sign, Cancer. You have a rather broad flat face with very prominent cheekbones and sometimes large, beautiful eyes. You are large boned, often have prominent knuckles and a rangy look. There may be a lantern type jaw and a pronounced underbite.

Like the other earth signs, Taurus and Virgo, you are very concerned with facts and figures and are very good at any kind of detail work. Your greatest gift is your resourcefulness and a certain dry or saturnine wit. Often you are strongly opinionated but necessity can transform you into the smoothest of diplomats. You make an excellent organizer and manager and are generally endowed with remarkable executive ability. It is rare that you let your emotions blind you to facts and so it is said that you often marry for money or social position. This is not necessarily true. Once given, your affection is loyal and lasting. But it must have been a Capricorn who said, "It is just as easy to fall in love with a rich person as a poor one."

CAPRICORN ASCENDANT — ARIES SUN

If you were born between March 21st and April 20th between approximately 11 PM and 1 AM, you may have this combination.

You are a force to be reckoned with. Clever, capable and dominating, you are busy with everything and everyone. You are a "take charge" person and are willing to take on much more than your share. Usually you are physically strong with great endurance and the ability to outlast your competition. Your drive and ambition generally propel you to the top of your field. But you may decide, "If I can't do it **my** way, I won't play!" and give up completely.

At your worst, you can be downright bossy and officious. You certainly speak your mind and rarely put up with any contradiction. While what you say is to the point and sensible, more people would listen and heed your words, if you could tone down your strident delivery. Your tendency to override others is hard for people to cope with even though they recognize that your observations are accurate and to the point. It would be expedient for you to remember that "it is easier to catch flies with honey than vinegar." But your answer to that would probably be that you're not interested in catching flies.

Accomplishment is your keyword and you get things done by moving fast and directly and making others step to your pattern especially if the energetic Aries decanate is occupied by the Sun. However, as you surely can appreciate, this is not a method guaranteed to stimulate and further friendly relations. So you act somewhat as a loner, never fully realizing just why it is that people are put off by your direct and rather brusque approach. Working within a structure (such as a business organization) often helps you channel your assertion in socially acceptable ways.

With a 3rd house Sun or in the Sagittarian decanate, you would do well in the travel fields, invention, science and any area where your inquiring mind could be stimulated to explore new avenues. With the

Sun in the 4th house or the Capricorn decanate rising, you may well be attracted to archaeology, mining, farming, geology and other earth related fields. But whatever career you choose you can undoubtedly rise to the top and make a name for yourself with the dynamic drive of Aries and the untiring ambition of Capricorn. If the Taurus decanate rises, banking, accounting or escrow services are career possibilities. If the Sun is in the Leo decanate, sports or recreational activities could be areas of endeavor.

Arturo Toscanini
March 25, 1867
2:18 AM LMT
Parma, Italy
44N48 10E10

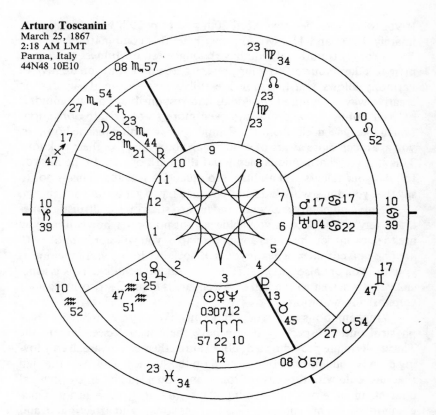

Source: Church of Light (C)

You are both skeptical and practical, especially if the Virgo decanate is on the Ascendant. Although like most fire signs you are susceptible to flattery, your head is not easily turned. You can be blindly indifferent to other people's needs and may walk over others without a thought. What you need to develop most is an awareness of others and their outlooks. Some well-known people with this combination are conductor Arturo Toscanini, magician Harry Houdini and basketball star Jerry Lucas.

With Aries drive and Capricorn tenacity, you are capable, competent, productive and able to achieve your ambitions.

CAPRICORN ASCENDANT — TAURUS SUN

If you were born between April 20th and May 20th between approximately 9 PM and 11 PM, you may have this combination.

Strongly traditional, you have enough resourcefulness and enterprise to adapt yourself to your present needs and your innate love of harmony allows you to enjoy life fully. You frequently express in creative ways. Dignified, reserved, and responsible, you are mindful of your public P's and Q's and even more so of private obligations (much like Queen Elizabeth II). Behind your charming facade however, you are much more aware of others than you would like them to know. This is a very harmonious blend and this harmony could incline you to take your talents and abilities too much for granted. This is not to say that you don't work hard but you may try to get by on your charm.

Simple humanity and your tendency to stick up for altruistic issues aid in any public success you achieve. But no matter how willing you are to stick up for the underdog in principle, you will not hobnob with anyone you consider beneath yourself socially. Polite and gracious as you are, you are also rather stiff, formal and unbending. This is especially true when either the Sun or Ascendant is in the Capricorn decanate emphasizing ambition.

Your emotions are strong and you, like most Taureans, need a physical outlet, especially if you have the Sun or Ascendant in the Taurus decanate providing a double Taurus theme. You are deeply loving even if you appear a bit reserved on the surface. Taurus is the sign that has to do with the sense of touch and you need and enjoy physical contact, in spite of your seemingly austere Capricorn exterior. Once committed, you are endlessly faithful, passionate and affectionate and the staunchest of friends. You may take emotional setbacks very badly, retreating within yourself in a sometimes unhealthy way. Often you are inclined to hide your amorous side, especially if the Virgo decanate is prominent in either the Ascendant or Sun. If you truly value yourself, someone else's rejection will not devastate you. You need to practice self-appreciation and tone down self-criticism.

A 4th house Sun may find you interested in the earth sciences, real estate, mining or the housing trades. With the Sun in the 3rd house, you are very good at dealing with the public and understanding its tastes and needs, even though they may be quite unlike your own. Music (both pianist Liberace and violinist Yehudi Menuhin have this combination) and dancing are fields that you will find challenging, if not as a vocation, at least as an avocation.

Queen Elizabeth II
April 21, 1926
1:43 AM GMT
London, England
51N30 0W06

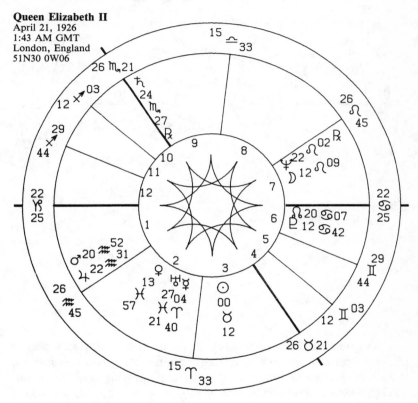

Source: American Federation of Astrologers (C)

Good taste, a flair for entertaining and a genuine liking for people mark you as a person helpful to associates and enjoyable to friends.

CAPRICORN ASCENDANT — GEMINI SUN

If you were born between May 20th and June 21st between approximately 7 PM and 9 PM, you may have this combination.

Robert Schumann
June 8, 1810
9:10 PM LMT
Zwickau, Germany
50N43 12E30

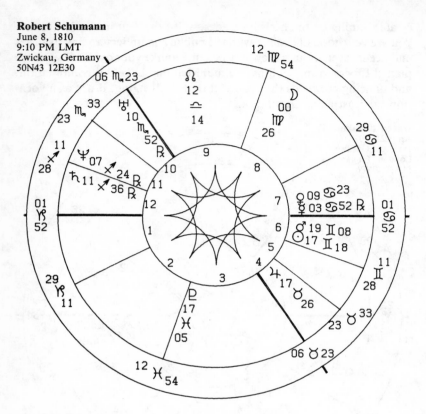

Source: AFA 3/57 (C)

At your best you have real feeling for others, putting each person in the proper relationship, adjusting working conditions and seldom, if ever, asking for favors. You do well when applying your not inconsiderable gifts to a new goal — mentally setting up and then physically pursuing it to a meaningful outcome, particularly with the Sun in the Aquarius decanate. You cope easily with many problems that others find difficult if not downright impossible because your decisions are made with reason and the reservation that your opponent has a right to a different opinion. This is an excellent mental combination and shows an unerring eye for pertinent detail, discrimination in its use and an executive flair that can leave others gasping. The acute administrative ability of Capricorn blends well with the quick Gemini mental capacity and enables you to accomplish much with minimum effort.

When thwarted ambitions get the best of you, you are capable of a subtle maneuvering of others, just to stir up trouble and justify your own viewpoint. Innately you want recognition, whether it is openly administered or wielded quietly behind the scenes. But for you to feel fulfilled, power is what you must have. Most of the time you earn it because you are a persistently hard, self-driven worker with a fertile, ingenious and subtle intellect, especially marked when the Sun is in the versatile Gemini decanate.

With the Sun in the 6th house or the painstaking Virgo decanate on the Ascendant, you have a fine eye for detail and make a great bookkeeper, accountant or bank teller. With the Sun in the 5th house or the Capricorn decanate rising, music may well be your metier and you would do very well in any area of the arts, as a teacher if not an actual performer. You may also be the type of corporate lawyer whose work is carefully prepared, presented at the right time and before the right judge. You leave nothing to chance and are dependable, faithful and the most dutiful of people.

With the Sun in the Libra decanate, pleasure comes from getting things done and helping others as much if not more than being rewarded yourself. When the Taurus decanate is on the Ascendant, management or financial areas may attract you. Robert Schumann, the German composer had this intellectual and sometimes brilliant combination.

The dexterity and mental energy (symbolized by your Gemini Sun) added to the inherent need for perfection (symbolized by your Capricorn Ascendant) can make you a person to be reckoned with both in the business and social world.

CAPRICORN ASCENDANT — CANCER SUN

If you were born between June 22nd and July 23rd between approximately 5 PM and 7 PM, you may have this combination.

You often innately know how to relate to the public and like a true Cancer, are able to keep your finger on the public pulse and put this ability to work furthering your own career. You are eager and materially minded because both Cancer and Capricorn crave security and power backed by worldly acquisition. This is even more pronounced if either the possessive Taurus or ambitious Capricorn decanate is on the Ascendant. Not for you a home by the side of the road. You need and want recognition and often you seek it in the administrative and executive fields where your canniness and acuity flourish well. Your viewpoint is worldly without being hard and your broad outlook favors the wide, rather than the particular in scope, unless the Ascendant is in the exacting Virgo decanate or the Sun is in the obsessive Scorpio decanate. Keenness and depth of perception frequently color this blending which decidedly suggests the professions, particularly those dealing with people en masse.

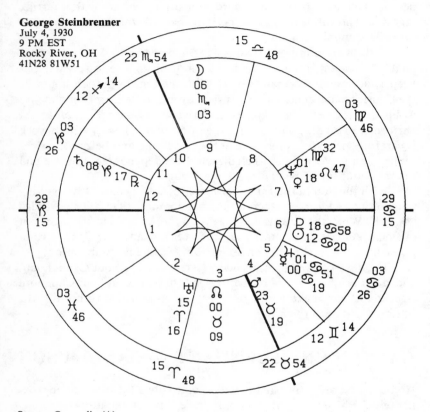

George Steinbrenner
July 4, 1930
9 PM EST
Rocky River, OH
41N28 81W51

Source: Gauquelin (A)

The Capricorn Ascendant indicates self-discipline in an otherwise timid and overly sensitive nature. You are able to bear hardship with greater endurance than the average Cancer. You may call yourself lazy and excuse yourself for not doing more than you do, but in your diffident way, you seldom lose sight of your goals. Ambition and self-directedness are the core of your nature. With Cancer indirectness but Capricorn undeviating persistence, you get where you're going. At your best you are an appeaser among others, seeing everything in the large context or relating everything to every other thing so that nothing stands alone. This placement represents the universality of Cancer at its very best. You are tolerant of other people, peacefully giving up outwardly to maintain the status quo, though you hug your inner vision of yourself to yourself and try not to let anyone else know just where you are coming from.

With the Sun in the 7th house or in the Cancer decanate, you may do well in the social services, home decorating, advertising, foreign affairs and trade. The Sun in the 6th house suggests the retail or hotel business. If the Sun is in the Pisces decanate or the Ascendant is in the Virgo decanate, nursing or animal husbandry may attract you. Whatever your field, you are an achiever and handle your chosen career with an air of conciliation and propriety.

George Steinbrenner, the sports entrepreneur who owns the New York Yankees baseball team has this pairing.

Home, family and tradition are usually important to you. Generally you take your responsibilities as a parent very seriously. Patriotic, somewhat conservative; you support the status quo.

Careful, seeking emotional and physical security, you patiently follow society's rules and expect to reap the benefits.

CAPRICORN ASCENDANT — LEO SUN

If you were born between July 23rd and August 23rd between approximately 3 PM and 5 PM, you may have this combination.

To the self-assurance of Leo is added a conservative Capricorn note, coming across as modesty, which every Leo can use a little of. Faithful and ever loving, you'll do almost anything for love, working yourself to the bone and often asking little but the acceptance of your generosity in service, thought and material support. But this doesn't mean that you are a namby-pamby or Mr. Milquetoast. Far from it. You have an innate sense of yourself and rarely yield to coercion. When you do, you bitterly resent it and vow, "Never again." But you do want acceptance and so sometimes you give in to others against your better judgment. However, most of the time you're strongly individualistic, go your own way and seldom listen to anyone else's advice.

Overly tolerant of those you love and trust, you reserve judgement endlessly, especially if the Ascendant is in the affectionate Taurus decanate. But outside that small but exclusive circle of those close to you, you can be intolerant, critical, and even rigidly unforgiving of anyone who doesn't meet your approval or who doesn't live up to your rather strict code. Your internal "shoulds" and "shouldn'ts" are more emphasized when the Virgo decanate rises, indicating firm principles.

This is often the pairing of those who pull themselves up by their bootstraps. You remain loyal to the people and environment of your beginnings especially if the Capricorn decanate is on the Ascendant. You'll do anything to get ahead and rarely deviate from your announced goal, once you decide what it is. With the Sun in the 7th house or in the Leo decanate, this may be the entertainment business like actor Dustin Hoffman or in government employ where you can deal diplomatically with others.

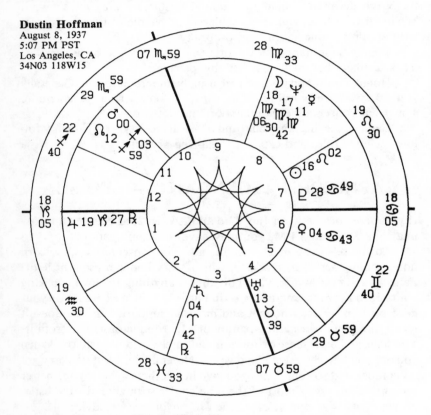

Dustin Hoffman
August 8, 1937
5:07 PM PST
Los Angeles, CA
34N03 118W15

Source: Lockhart quotes Birth Certificate (A)

If the Sun is in the 8th house or if it is in the Aries decanate, you may be attracted to the medical field, or on another level, butchering or meatcutting. But whatever field you choose, you want the good things in life and are willing to work hard for them and then usually share generously with all in your circle, especially when the Sun is in the expansive Sagittarius decanate.

Sometimes this combination is exceptionally charitable, but always in a personal fashion. This is one of the few Capricorn Ascendants who do better in the professions than in business. You need to give your Leo Sun a chance to shine in a personal way.

Likeable, affable and pleasing, your warmth coupled with your practicality and dedication make you a popular as well as a productive person.

CAPRICORN ASCENDANT — VIRGO SUN

If you were born between August 23rd and September 23rd between approximately 1 PM and 3 PM, you may have this combination.

Cautious, thorough, exacting and hardworking, you believe in going "by the book." You pay your dues and expect an earned reward eventually. Your natural reserve and a disinclination to defy conventional standards may obscure your need for emotional satisfaction and you must take care not to pass up your romantic opportunities. You, more than most Virgos, like the good things in life and strive persistently to have them. It is seldom that you marry below your station or without good material prospects and even then you would encourage your mate and use every ability at your command to help him or her achieve desired goals.

This combination can symbolize a large scale operation which demands both the conscientiousness of your Virgo Sun and the resourcefulness of your Capricorn Ascendant. It is an excellent pairing for both business and the arts — especially writing and music. You are patient with detail, practical in planning and outlook and executive in scope, especially if the Taurus decanate is involved with either the Sun or Ascendant.

You have the innate ability to keep yourself in the swing of current ideas by constant reorientation into new contexts. You are able to use and make over the old through practical insight and thus keep yourself and others abreast of the times. If both the Sun and Ascendant are in the analytical Virgo decanate there may be a tendency to pay so much attention to the trees that you can't see the forest. But by and large, this is a great combination for material accomplishment.

Actors Sean Connery and Sophia Loren both have this pairing and it seems to indicate a certain physical attractiveness and magnetism.

Sophia Loren
September 20, 1934
2:10 PM MET
Rome, Italy
41N54 12E29

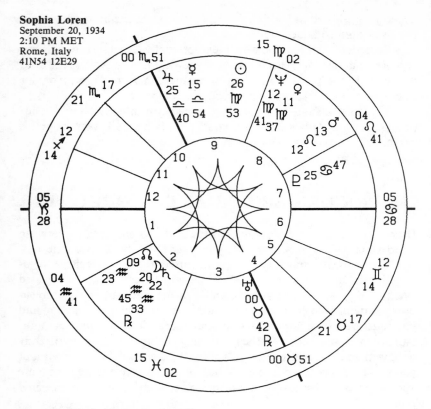

Source: Astrological Assn., London (C)

With an 8th house Sun you do well in any field where you can transform or rejuvenate things, such as furniture refinishing, restoration of old paintings or antiques. In fact, your ability for detail and hard work qualify you well for the role of museum curator, financial manager or advisor. With the Sun in the 9th house, politics, law and any area that deals with travel may attract you. You are able to bring others together in a spirit of cooperation and responsibility, so you are a natural for any field where you can coordinate and grease the corporate wheels.

Conscientious and dutiful, you will always do more than your share, but you prefer not to be in total control of any given situation. You are much more at home as the second in command unless the Capricorn decanate is involved with either the Ascendant or Sun. You are unwilling to put up with anyone who will not carry their share of the load.

You tend to have a calm and steadying influence on others and they often rely on your good judgment in both business and personal affairs.

CAPRICORN ASCENDANT — LIBRA SUN

If you were born between September 23rd and October 24th between approximately 11 AM and 1 PM, you may have this combination.

There is an intense mental sharpness with this combination. You can be extremely logical, figuring out the most rewarding path to follow. You are not as conservative as you appear on the surface, but still value material worth. Sometimes indecisive, you are always amenable to reason, as you value intellect. A doer, you are ambitious like all Capricorns, but your Libran affability allows you to come across as gracious, sociable and polite. Tact and diplomacy could be your keywords.

You are very restless and really happy only when in motion, especially when the Sun is in the changeable Gemini decanate. You are at your best when what you do entails responsibility and your greatest effort. When nothing is expected of you, you tend to slide by in true Libran fashion and this can develop into a bad habit. You're a perfectionist, never interested in second best. But this sometimes keeps you from making the best of what you have; you yearn for the unattainable while possibilities that are under your nose are ignored. This seems to be especially obvious when the Sun is in the Libra decanate or the self-critical Capricorn decanate rises. Learn to cherish your mistakes; they indicate growth. If you did it right the first time, you haven't learned anything.

You have executive capabilities like most Capricorn Ascendants, and do things with dispatch and precision. You do what is expected of you, are faithful and often fulfill obligations well beyond the call of duty. You are sustained by the hope that others will recognize your worth and you can be bitterly disappointed when acknowledgment is not forthcoming. You tend to bury the disappointment within, as you're usually not aggressive. But once you're aroused, you have to have your say; sometimes in the wrong words and at the wrong time. Timing is not one of your better qualities, unless the sensible Virgo decanate is on the Ascendant, and even then you may have lapses. The natural poise and charm of Libra needs to be harmonized with the worrisome astuteness of Capricorn.

You are fair, detached and theoretically — if not personally — sympathetic. Your objectivity is even more highlighted when the Sun is in the Aquarius decanate. However, you may not be strong on the warm, human touch or the ability to put yourself across congenially. Your real kindness and generosity may go unappreciated — probably because it is so difficult for you to reveal your deepest self to another. You may protect your deeper feelings with a cool exterior.

Maury Wills
October 2, 1932
1:46 PM EST
Washington, DC
38N55 77W04

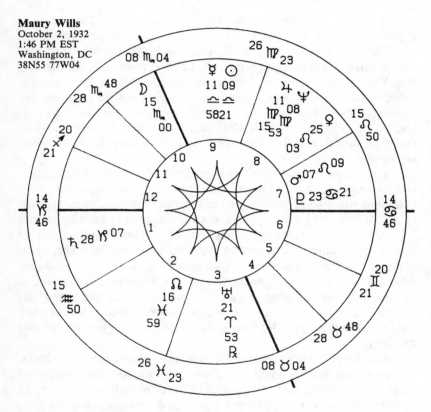

Source: From him personally (A)

When the Ascendant is in the Taurus decanate, your opinions are sometimes based on labels rather than real worth, but you are capable of much support and assistance to others. Your detachment plus your social poise make you the best of "front" men. You certainly know how to do the honors and you love being up in front of a crowd and doing and saying all the right things. For this reason, you do well in the political arena whether your Sun is in the 9th or 10th house. You may need to cultivate clear-cut decisiveness and real tolerance for standards other than your own. Maury Wills, the great Dodger base stealer has this combination.

Companionable, congenial and very socially oriented, you can be the life of the party, communicating your ideas and making everyone feel a part of the festivities.

CAPRICORN ASCENDANT — SCORPIO SUN

If you were born between October 24th and November 23rd between approximately 9 AM and 11 AM, you may have this combination.

Though you appear restrained and self-disciplined, you are really highly emotional and only your strength of will prevents you from letting others see your underlying intensity. Secretive, but not necessarily furtive, you are self-repressive rather than cautious and far more purposeful and driving than you like to let on. Vital, ambitious and forceful, you have a fair amount of social awareness and even talent. You are subtle, smart and often very intuitive and perceptive with a fine sense of the ridiculous that draws others to you. You are quite gregarious especially with an 11th house Sun and you don't spend too much time alone unless you have to. This can be the combination of the top level executive or administrator whose sense of timing is exquisite. Timing seems to be a key here, particularly when either the Capricorn or Virgo decanate rises.

Your assessments of other people are usually right on and this enhances your business ability. At times your personal bias may make you reverse yourself and go against your instincts, but most of the time you're humane, sympathetic and fair-minded. With the Sun in the Scorpio decanate or the Taurus decanate rising, a serious attitude and depth of personality usually develop with maturity and you are well suited to almost any profession that demands administrative forcefulness, innate understanding of public needs and solid business ability.

A 9th house Sun generally finds you with an interest in foreign affairs and often you are someone to be reckoned with in international matters like Chiang Kai Shek, the Chinese general and statesman. With the Sun in the 10th house or the Cancer decanate, the military could be your forte as it was for Erwin Rommel, Germany's "Desert Fox."

If the Sun is in the Pisces or in the Scorpio decanate, you could have a decided aptitude for medicine. You need to develop warmth in your personal affairs or others may avoid close encounters with you because of your seeming austerity. Take care not to come across as grasping and opportunistic. Instead use your inherent drive and ambition to aid and abet others in their daily affairs.

Erwin Rommel
November 15, 1891
12:00 CET
Heidenhein,
  Germany
48N42 10E09

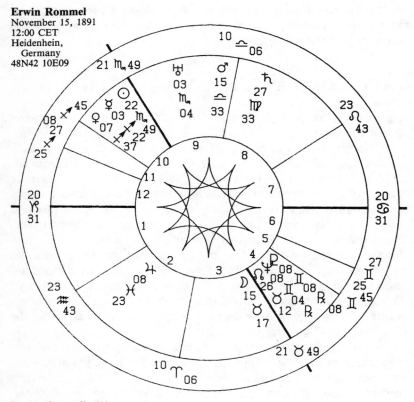

Source: Gauquelin (A)

Driving, ambitious and perspicacious, you are willing to strive long and hard to achieve the top in whatever your life circumstances.

CAPRICORN ASCENDANT — SAGITTARIUS SUN

If you were born between November 23rd and December 22nd between approximately 7 AM and 9 AM, you may have this combination.
Your demeanor is serious and you place emphasis on worthwhile

accomplishment rather than spectacular results. Capricorn suggests a dignified bearing and depth of interest and Sagittarius emphasizes diplomacy and a humane and humorous outlook, indicating your well balanced personality. You think on a broad plane and are very practical in every day affairs. This blend suggests a vast array of vocational possibilities. Generally quite talented, you are very independent but you don't force this on others so you are not met with resentment. Often this combination is the mark of the self-made person, one who is willing to work behind the scenes to achieve goals.

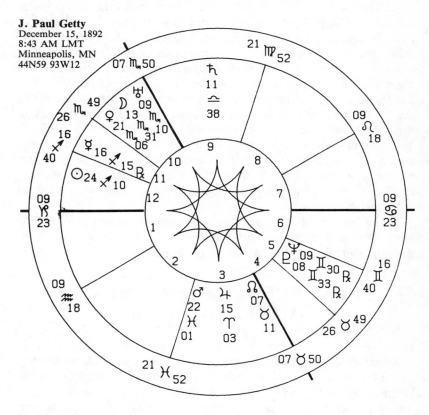

J. Paul Getty
December 15, 1892
8:43 AM LMT
Minneapolis, MN
44N59 93W12

Source: AFA 7/63 (C)

With the cautious Capricorn or stable Taurus decanate rising you can put on a sober air of learning. Your foresight allows you to make the most of your education and put it to the best use. You are usually both altruistic and conservative in your methods. You are solid in outlook and practical in approach often with good financial ability.

With the Sun in the 11th house, you can be quite the philosopher, humane with a broad outlook that suggests you are a leader among your friends and acquaintances. If the Sun is in the 12th house, you are more seemingly self-effacing and your interests are quite subtle and varied, ranging from shipping to medicine and philanthropy. This is a good combination for business in any capacity. J. Paul Getty, the millionaire oilman had this powerful pairing. His Sun was in the Leo decanate so he was able to deal dramatically from behind the scenes.

This combination can indicate a very high-strung temperament especially if Mercury is also in Sagittarius or the Sun is in the active Aries or restless Sagittarius decanate. You keep going constantly and may have two serious occupations going side by side, not to speak of a bunch of hobbies that you feel need your continued attention. If the Virgo decanate rises once you establish a personal relationship, you can be surprisingly detached, going your own way without disturbing the emotional tie. Work may take precedence over relationships. You are a financially and morally responsible person, so once committed, you generally remain quite faithful, at least outwardly. You do best with a tolerant, nonpossessive mate and mental compatibility is your number one requirement. Your greatest need is to develop the warmth of Sagittarius and apply the practicality of Capricorn to all your relationships.

This is an excellent combination for business as you can combine your Capricorn astuteness with your extensive Sagittarian outlook to develop a breadth of vision second to none.

CAPRICORN ASCENDANT — CAPRICORN SUN

If you were born between December 22nd and January 21st between approximately 5 AM and 7 AM, you may have this combination.

You're all business. When you start out on a course of action, nothing distracts you and you will follow through to the bitter end. You are a hard taskmaster to yourself, but usually very fair in your dealings with others. With both your Sun and Ascendant in achieving Capricorn, all Saturnian qualities are doubly emphasized: thoroughness, realism, thrift, responsibility and hard work. Your ambition is pronounced as is your thirst for authority and prestige. You do things with speed and precision and are often impatient with those who don't. Conventional and conservative by nature, you can be severe and exacting, but you are strong in your loyalties and constructive in your thinking.

J. Edgar Hoover
January 1, 1895
7 AM EST
Washington, DC
38N53 77W01

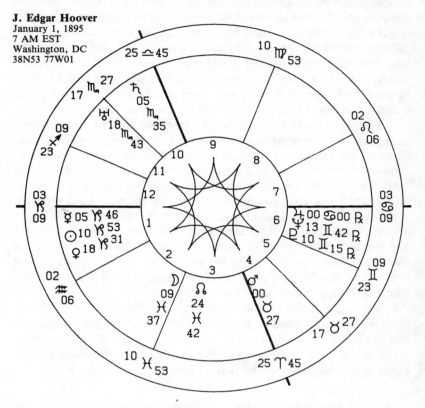

Source: Church of Light (C)

If the Sun is in the 12th house, you can very easily be the power behind the throne — the manipulator, *par excellence.* On another level, you may be a mystic or seer, knowing instinctively the reactions of others. With a 1st house Sun, you are often a perfect "take charge" person for any large business or organization that needs a firm hand. You are very success oriented and not above using others to gain your own ends, especially if the Taurus decanate is involved with either the Ascendant or Sun. A Taurus note symbolizes the desire for money and possessions. If misdirected, this can expressed as excessively self-centered, rather than comfortable and pleasure-oriented.

Executive and administrative ability is your outstanding asset. You'll work just as faithfully for another — through whom you can see your way to advancement — as you will for yourself, especially if either the Sun or Ascendant is in the dedicated Virgo decanate. If given an inch, you'll usually take a foot. Awareness of other people's rights is not your strongest quality. Emotions need to be considered as well as "the bottom line." This may not be easy for you and could inhibit your personal life. Your need to feel in charge of your life often makes you appear more aloof than you are; people sometimes find it hard to warm up to you. If Saturn, your ruler is in Leo or Libra, indicating a desire for emotional ties, you may be more demonstrative.

You are able to control all of your reactions and opinions if it suits your purpose. Your aim is consistent self-advancement. You are generally incredibly efficient, accomplishing exactly what you set out to do. Emotion may color your judgment occasionally, but usually serves your ambitions. People tend to see you as pretty cold and even on some occasions — heartless. You rarely look beyond the main issue and what you can get out of it. Though your aim is to be just and equable, your practical viewpoint can obscure a depth of vision; material gains are not the only values in life. When the Sun or Ascendant is in the Capricorn decanate, this pragmatic emphasis is a repeated theme. Be sure you want what you go after. If you drive too harshly to the top, you may find it lonely and unrewarding.

Some prominent people with this combination are J. Edgar Hoover, long time head of the FBI; mystic Swami Vivekananda and Russian dictator, Josef Stalin.

Since you are so dependable and indefatigable, if someone wants a job well done, you are the perfect person to ask to do it.

CAPRICORN ASCENDANT — AQUARIUS SUN

If you were born between January 21st and February 20th between approximately 3 AM and 5 AM, you may have this combination.

You have a genuine feeling for others and a common sense outlook plus a very idealistic nature. Your gregarious Aquarian instinct added to the subtlety of Capricorn works out as a need to make everyone happy. You're a born compromiser: adjusting, reorganizing, smoothing things out here and there until you're the most popular and genuinely well liked person in your environment. This social acceptance is very necessary for your sense of well being. You seem to be subconsciously motivated to use your resources to create a warm spot in everyone's heart. You earn it because you seldom begrudge anyone your services and are an efficient and industrious worker.

Your warm, simple friendliness usually attracts the same response from others. When the Ascendant is in the Capricorn decanate you are cautious and prudent in handling your affairs. Your mind is so agile that you startle others by coming up with ideas which appear extremely revolutionary and though you seem at times to be radical and impulsive, you remain faithful to your strong principles.

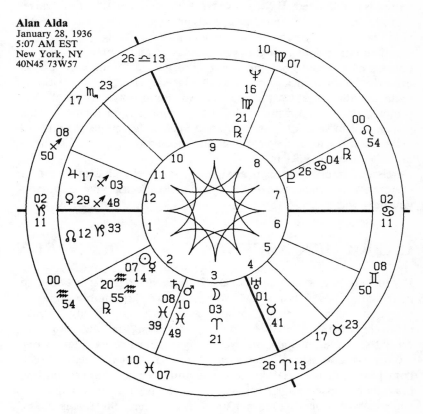

Alan Alda
January 28, 1936
5:07 AM EST
New York, NY
40N45 73W57

Source: Phillip Sedgewick (C)

With a Sun in the 1st house or in the Aquarian decanate, you may be in the entertainment field with an emphasis on comedy, wit or satire like comedian Jack Benny, actor Alan Alda and ventriloquist Edgar Bergen.

Administration in the aircraft industry or the computer business may attract you. With the Sun in the 2nd house or the Taurus decanate on the Ascendant, your values may be somewhat unusual and you may have a unique way of earning a living ranging all the way from soliciting sales routes to repairing slot machines. With the Sun in the Libra decanate, you can be philosophically expedient — the here and now which includes all the goodies of life, suffices. Pleasure is your goal. With the Sun in the Gemini decanate or the Virgo decanate rising, the emphasis is on Mercury. If it is in Capricorn, the serious side of your nature is emphasized. If Mercury is in Aquarius, you may be attracted more to the new and unusual. If Mercury is in Pisces, you are probably emotional, susceptible and ardent.

Though in your thoughts you are daring and romantic, in action you are quite traditional and conventional. You combine the best of orthodox Capricorn and eccentric Aquarius. You aim to raise your social standing or at least maintain it, so you usually marry well. You want the best of everything and may base your judgment on labels and prices. But in spite of that, you are a keen judge of people and will value them for what they truly are and not by their social distinction or the clothes they wear.

Broad-minded, though analytical, you seem able to blend the customary with the unconventional and make it acceptable to everyone you deal with.

CAPRICORN ASCENDANT — PISCES SUN

If you were born between February 20th and March 21st between approximately 1 AM and 3 AM, you may have this combination.

Your mind is deep, philosophic and you're consistently helpful, using this quality in an everyday way of helping the underdog. You do not seek the limelight, but your single-mindedness brings its own recognition. Occasionally the officiousness of your Capricorn Ascendant plus the emotional but self-determined Pisces Sun can indicate that you overassert yourself, interfering in a busybody way with others while fiercely resenting any personal interference. But this is the exception rather than the rule.

A 2nd house Sun or the Ascendant in the Taurus decanate may find you in consumer affairs, the advertising business, nursing of the practical kind or you may be musically or poetically gifted. A 3rd house Sun could symbolize an attraction to politics, writing, the mail order business or the transportation field, especially involving travel over water. With the hygienic Virgo decanate rising or the Sun in the Scorpio decanate, you may find the medical field interesting.

You appear to be prudent and methodical but underneath your businesslike Ascendant lurks the soul of a pussycat. If the Capricorn decanate is rising, the pussycat has claws. You are a sensitive individual who is given to fits of temperament, sometimes letting your emotions run rampant especially when the Sun is in the Pisces decanate. Though warmly interested in others you are not a carefree, social butterfly and really are not interested in social activities as such. You try to avoid trouble and help the less fortunate. Sometimes you attempt to be liked by creating a harmonious and social atmosphere.

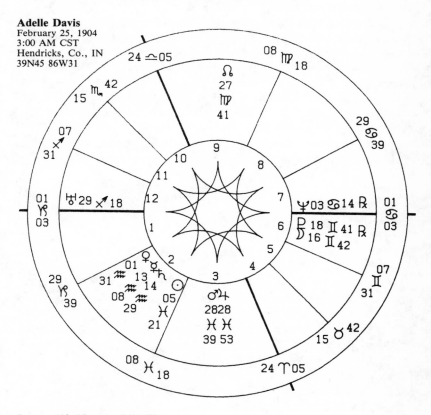

Adelle Davis
February 25, 1904
3:00 AM CST
Hendricks, Co., IN
39N45 86W31

Source: *Life Magazine* 5/71 (B)

If the Sun is in the Cancer decanate, you act as your brother's keeper basically because you cannot help yourself. You have genuine sympathy for his plight and a strong sense of responsibility for your fellow human being that keeps you actively occupied with helping others whether it is through your profession or just in a neighborly, friendly way.

This bent plus your innate Capricorn administrative talent suggests that you are a natural for philanthropic and social service work. Adelle Davis, the nutritionist, was one person who embodied the qualities of Capricorn and Pisces in caring about what happens to others.

Your blend of compassion with calculated logic reveals a personable soul who is vitally concerned for the other people in your environment.

CHAPTER ELEVEN

AQUARIUS ASCENDANT

This Ascendant indicates an idealistic outlook and broad approach in addition to whatever qualities your Sun sign symbolizes. Essentially a realist, you are able to see events in an overall concept that is bigger than personal immediacy or necessity. Your orientation is toward the future; your perspective is long-range. Extremely objective, you can understand why others might consider you eccentric, unpredictable and, at times, even contrary. You can be an extreme individualist, priding yourself on not being like anyone else. Your freedom is very important to you and you resist being confined, tied down to relationships or categorized. Though you enjoy defying public opinion, and even like to shock others on occasion, no one is more kindhearted than you are when the chips are down. You will go out of your way for others at the drop of a hat. Aquarius denotes an easy friendliness even with the least outgoing Sun signs such as Virgo, Cancer and Pisces. When combined with the fire signs, you may be a dynamo of drive and energy and are capable of bowling people over if you're not careful.

The word "prejudice" is not in your vocabulary, because you rarely view others as anything but individuals. In your eyes they have no color or creed. You judge them solely on performance and personality. When you attain professional and/or social advancement through your many talents: musical, literary, scientific, artistic, humanitarian and business, you can be the finest of people, unpretentious and modest. But you need to keep a careful rein on your social aggressiveness.

It is said of Aquarius that they are always willing to help others, whether or not the person wants or needs help. You need to feel needed,

but most of the time it has to be on your own terms. You express genuine concern for your brother (and in your frame of reference, everyone
is your brother) and you will go out on a limb to defend those in whom
you take an interest — and that can be almost everybody. You can
become totally involved with others, pumping them for a reaction, often
out of sheer curiosity. At your worst you like to draw blood and you
certainly do draw resentment at times. You love to give advice and arrange other people's lives, but seldom heed advice, even when you ask
for it. No one had better try to arrange your affairs. "Do what I say
and not what I do" could sometimes be your motto. You can be
unbelievably kind or overbearingly arrogant and both qualities may
manifest at the same time.

At your best, you keep alive the bonds of interest and friendship
on many levels over long periods of time and infrequent contact. People refer to you as friendly and Aquarius has a reputation for being
altruistic and humane. However, what others often fail to realize is that
your gregariousness and friendliness is generally from arm's length and
on your terms. Basically you are a loner, even shy, but you cover up
your insecurity with an overt refusal to conform that makes others think
of you as a clown, rebel, show-off or agitator. You may not have many
intimates but you do cultivate quantity rather than quality in your many
acquaintances. Your love of independence doesn't allow many intense
emotional commitments. But when you do break down and take on
an emotional obligation you are usually very faithful and abidingly
loyal.

Your herd interest propels you toward group activity, but usually
you are found at the head of the group. In other words, if you can't
lead, you do not want to play. When you utilize this group activity to
push yourself ahead, people have the feeling that you are using them
and often this is resented. You can be an excellent group facilitator
but must remember the group's goals are not always your goals.

People cannot understand your feeling of having outgrown a situation or person and your ability to detach when this point is reached.
You can rationalize almost anything and retreat from feelings into intellect. You are often so far ahead of your time in your thinking and
approach that others cannot possibly catch up with your advanced viewpoint, so they feel left out and annoyed. You are more at home with
abstract concepts and new technology than feelings anyway.

You rarely fight fiercely for a cause. It is said of you that you stir
others up, start the revolution and go home and watch it on TV. You
respect the truth and will not back down on your convictions. It's just
that you don't hang around and fight. Observant, coldly practical,

funny, perverse and independent, you can also be gentle and diplomatic when the occasion demands it. But no one should ever take you for granted.

Any illnesses you suffer are usually connected with the circulatory system. You may freeze in winter and die of the heat in the summer. To Aquarius rising, 65 degrees is often too cold and anything over 75 degrees is most certainly too hot. You may be susceptible to varicose veins, hardening of the arteries and rheumatic and arthritic complaints as you age, unless you watch your diet very carefully, which you are not usually inclined to do. All of these afflictions may be avoided if you learn to adapt. Aquarius is a fixed sign and it may not be easy to cultivate flexibility in your mental attitudes. But if you will, your health will show it. Of all the signs, you can get by on the least amount of sleep but you need plenty of fresh air and you should watch your salt intake. You have a tendency to retain fluids and may therefore have problems with your weight. You are usually not very active physically; your activity tends more to the mental. Make an effort to get plenty of exercise to keep your circulation going.

Being one of the fixed signs, you generally have a large body, deep chest and are usually big boned with a decidedly square look. Broad of shoulder and hip, you are usually well proportioned and moderately tall. You have regular, chiseled features, a handsome open expression and a high, square forehead. Aquarius rising is easy to spot because they often have a square look from the front or in profile and the back of the head is often flat, as is the derriere. There is a spade-like look to your jaw; it tends to jut forward. You have thin lips, a rather compressed look about the mouth and a brilliant smile. Your eyes are large, with an open, fearless look and large lids. There is a broad delta between your eyes and often the corners tilt up. You have square hands, with long fingers and square, rather spatulate nails. Often you are a nail biter, cuticle chewer or hair twister. Next to Aries, you have the loudest voice in the zodiac and next to Leo, the largest head.

Extremely bright, original and innovative, you help shake people up and can propel them into change. Your mind is your best tool and you constantly seek more knowledge and understanding about world issues and future patterns.

AQUARIUS ASCENDANT — ARIES SUN

If you were born between March 21st and April 20th between approximately 1 AM and 3 AM, you may have this combination.

You are able to take a very objective attitude toward life and thus you generally direct your energies to humanitarian ideals and seek a broad application for your principles. Your self-assurance is so deep rooted as to be automatic and you have a direct, approachable manner. You are unpretentious, your composure stemming from a deep certainty that you are right about all your beliefs. If your Mercury is in Pisces, your ingenuousness may come from an attempt to cover up your insecurities or a spiritual conviction. You expect to be taken at your own evaluation and usually are, because you call your own tune as far as behavior is concerned You seem so self-contained that others rarely argue with or question your motives.

Your slant is usually mental and you can be very touchy when you don't live up to what you know you are capable of on the intellectual level. Others had better not step on your toes in this area, because you are so sure you're right that you might haul off verbally or even physically to let them know where you're coming from. At your best, you know your weaknesses and in typical Aries fashion rarely display them. Your courage is of the invincible "head in the lion's mouth" variety and your mentality is keen and productive. Highly restless, you usually need thorough training for real accomplishment. Sometimes your insatiable curiosity impels you toward a wide variety of studies and you are often self, but well taught. Thomas Jefferson, the third president of the United States, a very erudite and knowledgeable student of the humanities had this blend. His Sun in the Sagittarian decanate symbolized his broad interests: science, agriculture, philosophy, diplomacy and law.

With the Sun in the 1st or 3rd house, in the Aries decanate or with the Gemini decanate rising, you may have genuine humanitarian and charitable interests reflected in your daily life. As a rule you will go out of your way for others, therefore you do well in the social sciences and welfare fields. A 2nd house Sun seems to indicate financial areas as a useful focus: big business, the stock market and working for the federal reserve in some capacity. But whatever house your Sun is in, you maintain your Aquarian detachment and tend to avoid those who do not agree with your good opinion of yourself, especially if the Libran decanate rises. With the Aquarian decanate on the Ascendant or the Sun in the Leo decanate, you're an individualist, first, last and always and your self-will may blind you to your best interests, especially when you allow your conceit to take over. Man or woman, you live and die by your own code which is liberal in romance and sexual matters as well as social and political. With all your capabilities and talents, it sometimes seems that you make life unnecessarily hard for yourself by not developing your follow through.

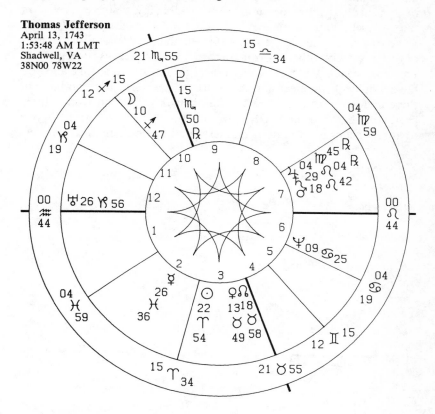

Thomas Jefferson
April 13, 1743
1:53:48 AM LMT
Shadwell, VA
38N00 78W22

Source: Doris Chase Doane (C)

Assertive, positive and mentally oriented, you like to be "in the know" and are always willing to share your knowledge with the world.

AQUARIUS ASCENDANT — TAURUS SUN

If you were born between April 20th and May 20th between approximately 11 PM and 1 AM, you may have this combination.

Basically conservative in spite of your Aquarius Ascendant, you are somewhat of a contradiction. Your personality (Ascendant) and soul (Sun) can engage in a tug-of-war between your inherent Taurus need for security and your detached Aquarian attitude. Magnanimous and romantic, you see the world with broad vision and then attempt to translate it into fundamental terms and this is not always easy. You face yourself, your weaknesses and aspirations squarely, generally know what you want and plunge unswervingly ahead. You are just as candidly honest with others as you are with yourself, because deceit is just not in your make-up. Sometimes others find this hard to take and you have a difficult time earning the approval you seek. But you hang in there and when you see the need for change, you make it and others eventually come around. Of all the Taurus Suns, it is easier for you to make changes in your personality and outlook than any other.

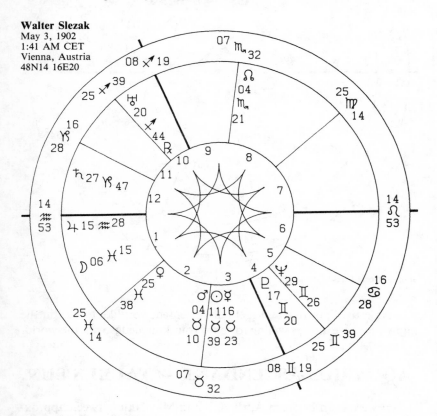

Walter Slezak
May 3, 1902
1:41 AM CET
Vienna, Austria
48N14 16E20

Source: Autobiography (B)

You take criticism well even if it hurts, provided that you feel it is constructive. You are seldom mercenary, but you do like the good things in life as do all Taureans.

A 2nd house Sun, or in the Taurus decanate, finds you very concerned with values and self-worth. Because Taurus is the natural sign for this house, you may be caught up in supplying the needs of others in the catering, clothing or commodities fields. This is also noticeable when the Sun is in the Virgo decanate symbolizing the need to serve. If the Sun is in the 3rd house or the Gemini decanate rises, you may be very creative and have a fertile imagination, so you often find self-expression through writing, acting or sales. You can be the teacher who awards a scholarship, not because the child is outstandingly musical, but because s/he's bright, willing and tries hard. Artistic fields are a potential when the Libra decanate rises. You are likely to have an unusual approach to fashion, design, music, photography or other aesthetic areas. With the Sun in the Capricorn decanate, you rarely lose your heart to romance, because you are so sure that some day you'll realize your dream; and more often than not, you do. Individuality, inventiveness and uniqueness are central to your identity, especially with the Aquarian decanate rising.

Those with this combination tend to decide early in life on a goal, whether career or marriage or both, because they combine high hopes with faith in success and hard work — an almost unbeatable combination. You believe that virtue is its own reward. This may be the combination of genius. Many prominent people have this effective pairing, among them: German political philosopher Karl Marx, French revolutionist Robespierre, actor Walter Slezak and French composer Jules Massenet.

Tenacious and far seeing, your vision is practical so it is easy for you to achieve tangible results.

AQUARIUS ASCENDANT — GEMINI SUN

If you were born between May 20th and June 21st between approximately 9 PM and 11 PM, you may have this combination.

You are the eternal idealist, the reformer who does away with all the outworn and outmoded mores of society and takes the trouble to listen to all sides of every issue. Your aspirations are varied and broad in scope and your basic restlessness keeps you moving: mentally, creatively and physically. Intellectually oriented, genuinely humane and sympathetic, you are eager to lend a hand or a dollar, as the case may be.

You're a born romantic and will usually have many amorous experiences. Your acts, through misplaced sympathy and unthinking haste, are not always a reflection of your highest ideals. This is a scientific and literary combination, and you may fall short careerwise, because you are in such a hurry to get on with life that you miss the educational boat. With the Sun or Ascendant in the Libra decanate, socially you are much in demand because of your charm and flexibility, but you may be lacking where patience and stick-to-it-iveness are concerned. Your greatest need is to make a decision and then follow it faithfully.

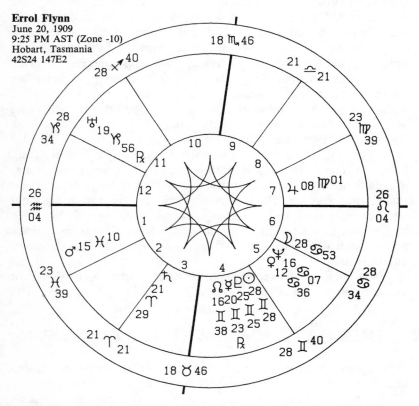

Errol Flynn
June 20, 1909
9:25 PM AST (Zone -10)
Hobart, Tasmania
42S24 147E2

Source: Church of Light (DD)

If your Sun is in the 3rd or 5th house or if it or the Ascendant is in the Gemini decanate, the sports arena may attract you because it blends activity with stimulation and it moves fast. Newspaper reporting, sports car and yacht racing, auto mechanics and any sales field are good areas for you. With a 4th house Sun, your basic restlessness, even though toned down by the Cancer theme, may find you developing an interest in boating, flying or diving for buried treasure. Errol Flynn, the swashbuckling movie star of the 1930s and 1940s is a perfect example of this combination.

Fickle, devil-may-care, your aim is to live life to the fullest — as you see it. Persistence is not your long suit unless the Sun or Ascendant is in the Aquarian decanate indicating more fixity. It is generally hard for you to sustain interest in any one thing for any length of time. But if there is a new cause somewhere, you're right in the vanguard and you lure others to follow you. Surely the Pied Piper of Hamelin had this combination.

You favor anything that arouses your quick, enthusiastic response, anything that you can jump into and out of and go on to the next adventure. Your interest in life is in its variety — and pleasure is your keyword.

AQUARIUS ASCENDANT — CANCER SUN

If you were born between June 22nd and July 23rd between approximately 7 PM and 9 PM, you may have this combination.

Your Aquarian Ascendant tends to broaden clannish Cancer's horizons and your primary interest is human issues. You are attracted to new and unusual ideas and may even give the appearance of being a swinger, but you are usually more comfortable sticking to your home base and a more conventional approach to life. If the Moon is also in Aquarius, or for that matter, in Aries or Sagittarius, you may be more what you appear and a little less Cancerian. But you will rarely leave your safe, little world to pursue your humanitarian ideal. Whatever you do, your sense of balance is intact as is your well thought out value system. When you make a decision, you've considered all the pros and cons and then you stick to your premise. A visionary on the large issues, in everyday practical affairs, you are a realist, cagey and self-protective as are most Cancers. You are not selfish, generally considering the other person and you are known for your philanthropic generosity and honest concern for others.

With the Sun in the 5th house, or the Libra decanate rising, you're ambitious and your field could be music, writing or childcare. A 6th house Sun is just as ambitious but may be willing to forego some of the limelight. If the Sun is in the Scorpio decanate, your areas of interest could be nursing or the computer field. You go your proper way, always being yourself, respectful of other's whims and caprices and respected for your own.

With the Sun in either the Pisces or Cancer decanate, you are perceptive, have a sharp mentality and often seem able to read another's mind and even finish their sentences, especially if your Mercury is also in Cancer. You are a great companion because you listen well and others appreciate your attention. Not long on small talk, what you say is direct and to the point unless the Gemini decanate is rising. Then you may talk for the pure pleasure of talking.

George Sand (Aurore Dupin)
July 1, 1804
10:15 PM LMT
Paris, France
48N50 2E20

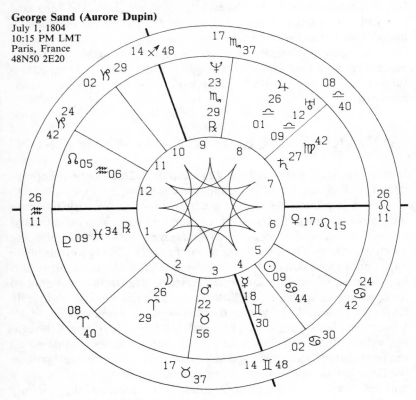

Source: Starr in *AA* 2/69 (C)

You disseminate your creative gifts with aplomb and are appreciated for your discrimination. You are rarely, if ever, taken in by shoddy performance or seeming bargain prices so you would do well in the fields of buying and consumer relations. An exception is when the Aquarian decanate rises. That suggests you may be too impatient to comparison shop, but you have tremendous inventiveness and the ability to cope with almost any situation.

George Sand, French writer and consort of Chopin had this combination with a 5th house Sun, which fits her unconventional behavior and writing talent.

Your extensive Aquarian outlook and caring Cancer nature allows you to nurture your whole world.

AQUARIUS ASCENDANT — LEO SUN

If you were born between July 23rd and August 23rd between approximately 5 PM and 7 PM, you may have this combination.

You have a genuinely warm feeling for others, often going out of your way to help them in their endeavors with kindness and service. You seem to love the whole world and though self-dramatizing, this feeling is genuine and comes from your heart. Often musically and/or artistically gifted, you take your not inconsiderable talents for granted and may not achieve the heights to which you could aspire. You need to make peace between your desire for stardom (Sun) and your appreciation of equality (Ascendant). Once you accept that it is okay to be special (i.e. "better than") in some areas, you can achieve your vast potential.

The Sun in sign opposition to the Ascendant may put you at cross purposes. As much as you love adulation, you often sublimate your ego to mundane service rendered from behind the scenes. This is particularly true of the Sun in the 6th house, where it takes on a deferential Virgo coloring. There is some conflict between Leo's innate desire to cling to fixed opinions and the Aquarian tendency to progressive thinking, but when you work this out, you can be absolutely brilliant. Once you choose your way and settle down to pursuing it, you are painstaking and persistent especially with the Sun in the Aries decanate. The same thing is true romantically. You are outgoing and impressionable, ardent but loyal. Once you find your loved one, you will pursue your romantic goal tenaciously especially if the Libra decanate is rising.

With the Aquarius decanate rising or the Sun in the Sagittarian decanate, you are ideally suited to philanthropic or organizational work where your ambition to be someone is recognized and your talents utilized. If the Sun is in the 7th house, you may be involved in politics, sales or some kind of counseling. Since the Sun rules the 7th house, any field where you can deal with people on either a one-to-one basis or with the public in general is a natural for you. The Gemini decanate rising symbolizes great verbal facility. You have a way with words and can be witty and entertaining as well as informative in a number of fields.

At your best, you forget Leo's inherent self-love and operate more on the selfless love level of Aquarius; working on the humanitarian plane, warmly demonstrating your creative expression with caring and sincerity. At your worst you are capable of running away with yourself romantically and may have many affairs as well as many occupations, rarely settling down in any one area with any one partner. This is especially noted when the Sun is in the Leo decanate. You need a positive outlet for your desire to be special. However, your basic loyalty and fixity of nature usually show up after a rather flamboyant and errant youth. Then you make the best of spouses and are an unusually fine parent — probably because you understand your offspring's need to sow their own wild oats.

Jill St. John
August 19, 1940
6:21 PM PST
Los Angeles, CA
34N03 118W15

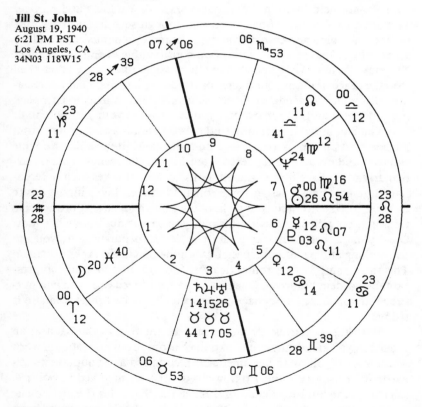

Source: Church of Light (C)

A very attractive lady from the movies has this stimulating combination: Jill St. John.

The warmth of your Leo Sun is diversified through your universal Aquarian Ascendant and you bask in the good will and cordiality of the whole world.

AQUARIUS ASCENDANT — VIRGO SUN

If you were born between August 23rd and September 23rd between approximately 3 PM and 5 PM, you may have this combination.

This is a pairing that combines broad vision with dutifulness, a flair for detail and unselfish service to others. You could well be a scientific inventor with all the analytical qualities (Virgo) and awareness of future needs (Aquarius) to achieve conspicuous success. You are frequently the outstanding nurse, doctor or hospital attendant and are undoubtedly suited to rehabilitative work especially if the Sun is in the 8th house or the Virgo decanate. You know that you are good, but this knowledge, rather than expressing as conceit, only makes you determined to do a better job. Your quiet self-confidence opens many doors and you earn and frequently receive promotion and preferment. Conscientious and unsparing of yourself down to the last detail, your personal needs rarely interfere with your sense of duty, especially when the Sun occupies the scrupulous Capricorn decanate.

With a 7th house Sun or the Libra decanate rising, you work well with others in fields such as psychological counseling or psychiatry. You are tolerant and very interested in others in a general sense; but romantically you're picky and choosy and certainly not always easy to please. Women with this pairing expect (and usually get) the most chivalrous treatment without making an issue of it, because their idealism is so readily apparent. Men are idealistically devoted but prudent. You tend to delay marriage and often don't seem inclined to take a partner until you find your ideal mate. This is more marked when the Aquarian decanate rises, symbolizing a desire for independence. But you do keep on looking for a potential partner. Basic unwillingness to take chances reflects in your romantic attitude, which at best is very self-protective. Because you have so much to offer, you might try to loosen up a bit in this area.

You can feel pulled in two directions: the theoretical and abstract versus the practical and applied mind. Since both Aquarius and Virgo are mentally oriented, you usually seek mental rather than physical fulfillment. You are unstintingly loyal, affectionate and trusting in friendship, but strangely hesitant in any relationship that demands strong emotions. Your Virgo attention to detail and need to gather facts combined with the broad Aquarian interest in everything and anything could lead you into the research field like the English sociological writer and historian, H. G. Wells. The Gemini decanate on the Ascendant emphasized his need to communicate and the Sun in the Taurus decanate indicated his ability to bring his values to the reading public.

H.G. Wells
September 21, 1866
4:30 PM LMT
Bromley, England
51N25 0E01

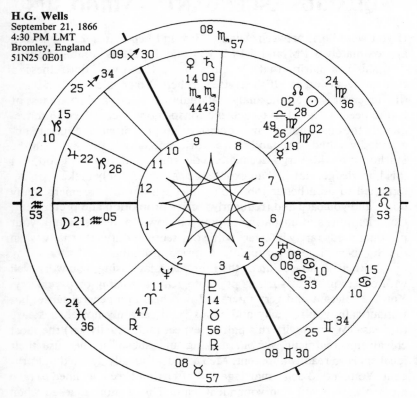

Source: *H.G. Wells* by MacKenzie (B)

The discriminative capability symbolized by your Sun is enhanced by the intellectual interests indicated by your Ascendant; you may be a discerning technician in any number of fields.

AQUARIUS ASCENDANT — LIBRA SUN

If you were born between September 23rd and October 24th between approximately 1 PM and 3 PM, you may have this combination.

You are one of the zodiac's outstandingly idealistic and romantic combinations with quite a variety of high-flown visionary concepts that would be wonderful if you could only apply them practically. You often act unconventionally, especially if the Ascendant or Sun is in the free-wheeling Aquarius decanate, and are attracted to the unusual. Despite appearances, you weigh very carefully the consequences of your premeditated action and rarely throw caution to the winds. Basically an individualist, you are usually unselfish and your idealism seems to surround you like an aura that attracts others to you in a magnetic way.

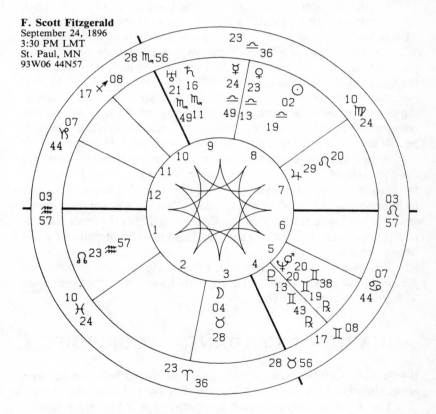

F. Scott Fitzgerald
September 24, 1896
3:30 PM LMT
St. Paul, MN
93W06 44N57

Source: *Exiles From Paradise* (B)

Sometimes you are an introvert who tends to dream your life away, but your social poise and charm are business and professional assets. When you pull yourself together realistically, you can go far as a "front office" person in a semi-social business such as hotel and apartment management or restaurant host or hostess. However, the professions fit your creative flair much better and you would make a good lawyer or teacher of philosophical subjects. Literature, the fine and decorative arts and music are all within your grasp. A good education is a fine asset but even without it, you are inclined to self-education, if you feel stimulated enough to get off your duff and achieve. A perfect example of this pairing is dilettante writer of the 1920s, F. Scott Fitzgerald. His Sun in the Libra decanate symbolized his social proclivity and the Aquarius decanate rising emphasized his free thinking spirit.

If either the Sun or Ascendant is in the Libra decanate, your search for the best — philosophical or romantic — can cover a lot of territory. You're impressionable, warm-hearted and sympathetic and above all, you mean well. Yet you have an elusive quality and are very hard to pin down to any practical cause if the restless Gemini decanate is on the Sun or Ascendant. There is a childlike innocence that overlays your personality so others are willing to forgive you any transgression. Aquarius indicates a certain gregariousness and Libra symbolizes responsiveness to others, so your presence is always welcome wherever people gather and you willingly play the role of the "life of the party."

With a 9th house Sun you may have a natural religious bent, are fond of travel and get along famously with those of different backgrounds than your own. If the Sun is in the 8th house, you may be interested in the occult or metaphysics. You like form and ceremony and take readily to religious conversion; not only for the inner inspiration it may bring, but also for the ritual and pomp that make you feel important and focused.

Self-assured yet receptive, your appeal is to all ages, because you genuinely like other people and are able to draw them out of their shell with your sincerity and vitality.

AQUARIUS ASCENDANT — SCORPIO SUN

If you were born between October 24th and November 23rd between approximately 11 AM and 1 PM, you may have this combination.

This is the combination that marks the gypsy. You are magnetic and powerful and often distinguished by a dominating personality. Realism (Scorpio) and idealism (Aquarius) blend well here and your intuition, insight and penetration enable you to see through others instantly; so it is rare that anyone can pull the wool over your eyes. You have an innate faculty for anticipating what another person is going to say and do.

Deeply emotional, passionate, affectionate and loyal, your persistent Aquarian optimism is decidedly tempered by your Scorpio side. Your moods while sharp, are not usually long lasting and you snap back resolutely. If the Sun is in the Scorpio decanate, the woes of the world may weigh heavily upon your shoulders and you seem mature when quite young. In spite of the fact that you are so strongly fixed, you are a wanderer, especially if you have a 9th house Sun or the mobile Gemini decanate rises. It is hard for you to tie yourself down to any one main interest until you have gotten the wanderlust out of your system.

Robert Louis Stevenson
November 13, 1850
1:30 PM LMT
Edinburgh, Scotland
55N55 3W10

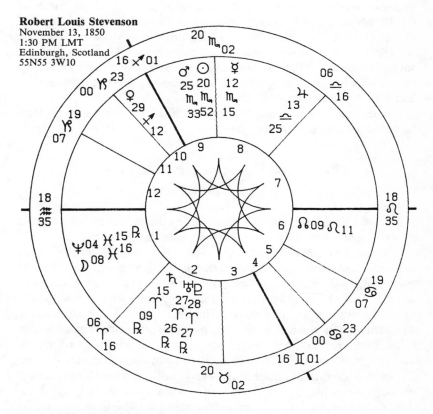

Source: *Sabian Symbols* #869 (C)

Children with this pairing are frequently leaned upon at home or treated as adults because of their sensibility and grown-up attitudes.

Your sympathy extends toward humanity in general, particularly to the underdog. The Sun in the sensitive Pisces or nurturing Cancer decanate highlights this altruistic theme. You are apt to be the most important person in your home; you are certainly noticed in a crowd. Though you are generally popular, you are not aware that you are frequently the center of attention, unless the Aquarius decanate is on the Ascendant. If the Libra decanate rises, your social graces are quite apparent.

Your mental outlook is both noble and profound and you have a distinct leaning toward abstract studies: religious (though not always orthodox), occult and even astrological. With the Sun in the 9th house, you may be drawn to space travel, psychiatry or any field that requires application of your analytical and diagnostic abilities. If the Sun is in the 10th house, you have a real and natural expertise for self expression in the fields of art, music, dancing or poetry. Whatever you do, on whatever level, once you've passed the point of taking your abilities for granted and put them to work, you will be a person of consequence and leave your mark. Robert Louis Stevenson, the great Scottish author had this dynamic combination.

The vigor and intensity that you generate can be an inspiration to all who come in contact with you.

AQUARIUS ASCENDANT —
SAGITTARIUS SUN

If you were born between November 23rd and December 22nd between approximately 9 AM and 11 AM, you may have this combination.

Though you may appear unorthodox, good judgment precedes your every move and you are a born philosopher, seeking the best in everything and everyone. When you don't carry your generalization too far, your viewpoint anchored in the largest frame of reference possible, is a definite asset. You try to maintain a practical attitude in every day affairs, but when the friendly, overexpansive Sagittarian Sun is teamed up with the unconventional, attention-craving Aquarian personality, you may bite off more than you can chew. You want to be involved in everything, understand everyone, and have an opinion on or judge everything.

You're talented, clever and independent, forthright in speech and act and are totally loyal to an idea, cause or person. Your romantic idealism rarely says die. Even if you're its only supporter, you still carry your banner high and come "hell or high water," you will not let your cause down. This is a most precarious position you place yourself in and often you find it hard, if not impossible, to extricate yourself. The ascendant in the socially aware Libra decanate may help to soften your flamboyance.

Vital, positive, enthusiastic, you act with the stamp of authority and no one dares contradict you. Therefore other people find it hard to cope. You may wonder why, since you're so friendly, others are giving you a wide berth. It is just that they cannot quite handle your larger than life personality. Try to tone it down a little and give them a chance to offer their opinions. You don't really have to listen; just act like you do.

Helen Gahagan Douglas
November 25, 1900
12 PM EST
Boonton, NJ
40N54 74W25

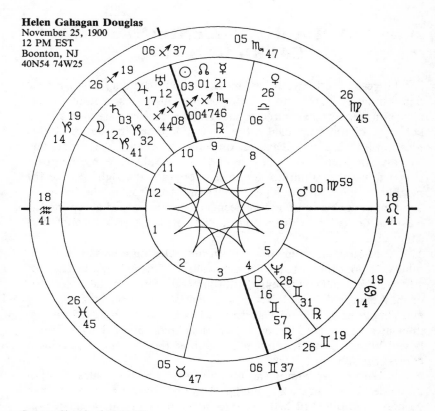

Source: Church of Light (C)

If the Aquarius decanate is rising you may find politics your metier. If the Sun is in the Leo decanate, acting may afford an opportunity to express your striking individuality. You are often attracted to the law and promotion fields whether your Sun is in the 10th or 11th house and especially if it is in the Aries or Sagittarius decanate. You pour all your talents into whatever you do and when lit by your creative fire, there is nothing you can't accomplish. At your best, you are perennially youthful without being naive, especially when the Gemini decanate is on the Ascendant. You have a zest for life that expects the best with every chance of getting it. Helen Gahagan Douglas, actress and politician had this sometimes autocratic combination.

Your sheer enthusiam and good spirits are contagious and others always look forward to your company.

AQUARIUS ASCENDANT — CAPRICORN SUN

If you were born between December 22nd and January 21st between approximately 7 AM and 9 AM, you may have this combination.

You display an acquired spontaneity because you are basically inclined to be self-contained rather than outgoing. In you, Aquarian idealism finds a practical expression while your Capricorn realism and worldly ambition doesn't lose sight of larger values. You are not inclined toward straining to get to the top with the right people for neighbors. Your Aquarian personality isn't free from deliberate social climbing, but this combination seems to incline toward accepting the world at face value with an urge to know its better side through personal effort.

Your sometimes unconventional and reforming ideas may be at odds with your innate prudence and caution. This may not be easy for you to handle and could cause irritation. If the Sun is in the 11th house or the Aquarius decanate rises, your Aquarian nature tends to take over and people who think of Capricorn Suns as stodgy and stick-in-the-mud are a bit surprised by your, at times, unpredictable behavior. Usually sensible and modest, you take for granted the fact that achievement comes through hard work.

Often with the Sun in the 11th house or with the restless Gemini decanate rising, you are attracted to risky and adventurous careers like pioneer pilot, Billy Mitchell. His Ascendant in the Libran decanate suggests his later legal problems while the Sun in the Capricorn decanate emphasized his businesslike attitude toward flying. (The Libran decanate can also indicate the importance of a partner.)

On another level, you work well in routine type jobs, often for the government or a large business organization, especially if the Sun is in the dedicated Virgo decanate. A stickler for detail, you would never try to ''get away'' with anything just because of your position. Very uncompromising in your ideas of right and wrong, you will not consider questionable short cuts and you stick undeviatingly to your own concepts. With a 12th house Sun, service is your keyword and you often work uncomplainingly and tirelessly in jobs that others find boring and inconsequential. But your sense of values is so well balanced, that you know your own worth and you take your dependability for granted. This is one combination where you really like and respect yourself, especially with the Sun in the comfortable Taurus decanate.

Billy Mitchell
December 29, 1879
10 AM LMT
Nice, France
43N42 7E17

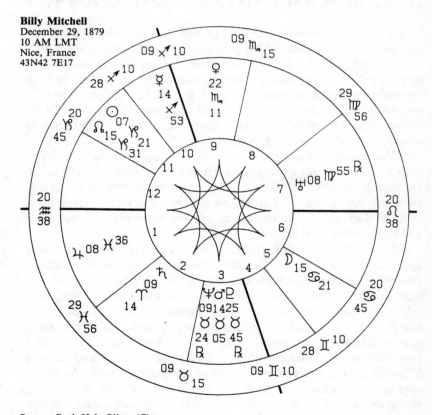

Source: Ruth Hale Oliver (C)

Children with this placement are often a strong support at home and generally the favorite with the grandparents. You are suited to professions where your authoritative personality and clear-cut standards make you one of the masses yet not involved with them. In business, common sense, ethical conduct and humane instincts point your way to the success you are willing to work for. You take a rational and practical approach to all matters, so others respond to you on that level and know that they can count on you to always be in the right place at the right time.

Following the rules in your own unique way leads you to practical as well as humane achievements.

AQUARIUS ASCENDANT — AQUARIUS SUN

If you were born between January 21st and February 20th between approximately 5 AM and 7 AM, you may have this combination.

Though faithful, affectionate and often deeply loving, you are not an easy person in any emotional relationship because you are seeking constantly to relate to your ideal and it is hard for any one person to live up to your image of them. Indeed, it is hard for you to live up to your ideal of yourself. Intensely idealistic, you are the progressive thinker personified and a law unto yourself.

You usually want your relationships on your terms. If you feel your freedom is being infringed, you may protect yourself by criticism (of others), intellectual detachment or just plain leaving the scene. Generally you have a good mind; capable, exacting and efficient, especially if Mercury is in Aquarius, and you are a completely dependable and responsible worker.

In you, the Aquarian affability shows up in your simple, friendly approach to everyone, but basically you seem to need no one with the possible exception of your chosen partner. This is especially true if the Sun, ruler of the 7th, is in the 1st house. Your air of detachment holds others off even when that is not your intention. Your ideas of people and your observance of their behavior are sometimes more interesting to you than the actual person. You seem to say, "Hold still while I examine you," and then you casually dismiss them. This is a more likely behavior pattern when either the Sun or Ascendant is in the Aquarian decanate, reinforcing the Aquarian detachment. You're not unkind, unless deliberately, but your attitude sometimes seems cold and can turn others off. You may have to consciously try to generate warmth; it does not always come naturally to you.

Your defenders stand by you faithfully, but your detractors are just as resolute. You seem to have all your eggs in the same basket with both the soul (Sun) and the personality (Ascendant) in individualistic, dogmatic and arbitrary Aquarius. It may be hard for you to move away from yourself and you can be high-strung and nervously irritable. You might be subject to health problems that are difficult to diagnose, relating as they do to your nervous system, especially with the Sun or Ascendant in the restive Gemini decanate. When you feel confined, hemmed in or frustrated, your health may react. Keep your options open. If either the Sun or Ascendant is in the sociable Libra decanate, you are better able to reach out to others and evidence the concern that you seem determined to keep hidden.

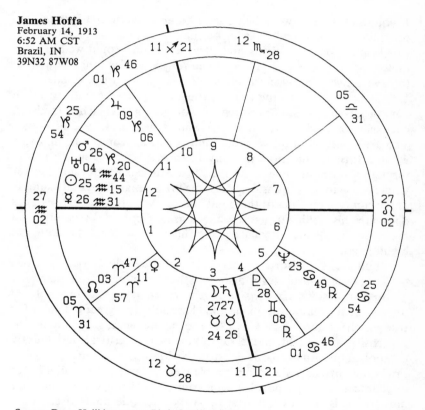

James Hoffa
February 14, 1913
6:52 AM CST
Brazil, IN
39N32 87W08

Source: Dana Holliday quotes Birth Certificate (A)

With a 12th house Sun, writing of the detective, scientific or research variety may attract you. If your Sun is in the 1st house, you could be drawn to any field where individualistic self-expression is an asset. You are so self-determined and self-motivated that it may be hard for you to relax, take it easy and just be one of the crowd. Some well known double Aquarians are opera star Leontyne Price, English scientist Havelock Ellis, union organizer Jimmy Hoffa and actresses Merle Oberon and Kim Novak.

Intent on marching to your own internal tune, your openness and originality can lead to innovations in your own and other people's lives.

AQUARIUS ASCENDANT — PISCES SUN

If you were born between February 20th and March 21st between approximately 3 AM and 5 AM, you may have this combination.

Life to you is for living and "try, try again" could well be your motto, as you rarely let anything get you down for long. You seem to have a mystic belief in the credo "Life is great, life is wonderful." You live up to this to the best of your ability, trying hard to instill your beliefs in others. For this reason, you are a good teacher, minister, counselor or advisor whether your Sun is in the 1st or 2nd house. You are a part of all the world around you and seem to tune in, often without formal education, to many arts and sciences. You learn more through absorption than direct teaching. Music is a natural outlet for your deep emotions. So is comedy. Shelley Berman is a good example of the comedic qualities of this combination. With the Sun in the Pisces decanate, his ability to assume the mask of comedy is emphasized and with the Gemini decanate rising, his wit and quick thinking are highlighted.

You are, surprisingly, a perfectionist, especially if your Sun has the 2nd house/Taurus flavoring or is in the Cancer or Scorpio decanate. To do your best is your aim. You are a free thinker, both original and unorthodox; genuinely humane and charitable with great potential for true unselfish goodness. This expresses as patience, helpfulness and generosity in thought and action. You can be critical and bluntly outspoken but usually along constructive lines. Others realize this and rarely take offense. You are a people watcher and a discerning judge of character, seldom fooled when it comes to pegging others and their motives. This is especially true when the Libra decanate rises.

You provide inspiration for others, urging them on to great accomplishment, not always by example, but sometimes by belittling and prodding. But whatever your method, you succeed admirably. You are really bighearted, merciful and tolerant like most Pisces, but you often try to hide these traits under the impartial attitude of your Aquarian personality. This is most relevant when the Aquarius decanate rises.

Your biggest fault is your susceptibility and gullibility. A sucker for a sob story, you can be an easy mark for anyone who approaches you on the emotional level. Even the objectivity of an Aquarian Ascendant may not save your Pisces side from emotional pliancy. You tend to marry young and if you feel well mated, you are very faithful. However, if your choice is not suitable, you tend to roam and try many different relationships, perhaps none of them too satisfactory. But you are so basically easygoing and pleasant that your circle of friends, lovers and acquaintances is ever widening.

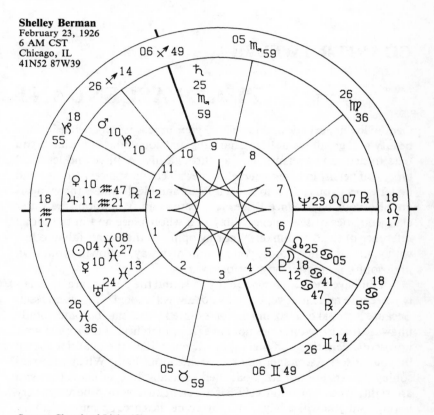

Shelley Berman
February 23, 1926
6 AM CST
Chicago, IL
41N52 87W39

Source: Church of Light (C)

Idealistic and romantic, you do your best to leave life and other people better off than before you arrived.

CHAPTER TWELVE

PISCES ASCENDANT

Gentle, loving, artistic and idealistic, your urge is to experience infinite beauty and goodness in life. Charming and sometimes a bit lazy, you tend to drift and dream your way through life. A "live and let live" type, you persist in being yourself under all circumstances. No one had better expect you to live up to their ideas and ideals unless those ideals are also your own. Since Pisces is a water sign, you adopt the water characteristics of seeing everything in a whole piece and in the broad reference of the free thinker, ignoring opinions that don't fall into line with yours. In other words, you go your own way, following your own philosophy no matter how visionary it is.

You have the 12th house ability to sound the depths, are unusually perceptive and intuitive, but may not always recognize this as an asset. Because you take it so much for granted, you can become totally unaware that everyone does not have this capability. If the rest of your horoscope denotes good mental proficiency, then the qualities shown by your Pisces Ascendant can be a tremendous help. When your reasoning powers are not so good, then your absolute sureness that you are right, when not intuitively based, can cause you to be very, very wrong. But you will rarely admit this to be the case, because your sensitivity (some might call it touchiness) can lead you into stubbornness. This is not a trait usually associated with Pisces, but all the water signs have a certain amount of obstinacy in their makeup. When their emotional security is threatened, water people can retreat into inflexibility.

You really would like to look at the world through rose-colored glasses and unless your Sun sign indicates some acuity and depth, you are in danger of escaping from reality and living in your own warm and wonderful little world, where there are few demands on you to live up to your potential. You do have considerable potential, including a surprising ability to consolidate and organize, to think conceptually and an overriding sense of humor that can help get you out of ticklish situations. You are often drawn to art, creating a more beautiful world, or to the helping professions, creating a more ideal world.

There can be a wide gap between your theory and your practice because your basic motivations are so deep that they may be unclear to you. You just feel your way through events and circumstances and more often than not, your feelings are right on target. There is an emotional self-awareness that is associated with a Pisces Ascendant. Other factors in the chart may symbolize strength and objectivity. When not counterbalanced, emotionalism can be a lifelong problem. This can be particularly dangerous because you are usually the last person to be aware of it.

Since Pisces is a water sign, people with a Pisces Ascendant are often noticeable because of their constant need for liquid intake. This doesn't mean that they are all alcoholics, although some are and this could be an area that needs attention. One young man with Pisces rising is rarely seen without a can of Dr. Pepper. A housewife keeps the coffee pot plugged in at all times and has been known to drink twenty-five or thirty cups a day.

You are a clown at heart and very often joke and make fun of situations to cover up your innate insecurity. Emotionally vulnerable, sometimes you avoid emotional commitment just because becoming involved would reveal your softness and caring. However, once you give your heart, you are very faithful, thoughtful and sincere. At your best you are kind, warmhearted, humane and even selfless. At your worst you think you have all these qualities, but your desire for emotional security results in cold self-centeredness that fools no one but you.

You may not take very good care of yourself physically and sometimes have to be prodded to see the dentist or doctor, even when you know you should. This probably goes back to your inherent laziness or a feeling that if you ignore the problem, it will go away. Facing facts about diet, exercise and physical needs will help tremendously in maintaining good health. Poor eating habits can contribute to liver and digestive ailments. You generally have a slow metabolism and thus often have to fight a tendency to put on weight. Exercise is a good antidote. Accidents to your feet, hips and hands are common and you seem to be highly susceptible to colds and flu. Pisces rules the feet; fallen arches, as well as bunions and corns may plague you. All of this may be alleviated if you work on understanding yourself in relation to others, doing what you can, and having a sense of faith in something higher to do the rest.

In appearance you can be one of the most beautiful people in the world, with large, liquid eyes and long, thick, curly lashes. Pisces rising tends to be short, stocky and fleshy unless of course, the Sun is in one of the tall, lean and lanky signs. But regardless, you have a certain roundness that adds a soft, pleasant look. Women tend to have a wide hip structure like the rest of the mutable signs. Your hands and feet are usually small, but wide and drop-shaped. Your face is large and you may have a rather pale complexion. Your eyes are your outstanding feature; they are large and sometimes protruding with sleepy looking lids. They never seem to be very alert, but seldom miss anything. Your brows are arched with a down drooping line at the corner, and you often have a very soulful expression.

Your nose is short, small and flat and may give the appearance of not having much of a bridge. Your chin is round and even if you are thin, you appear to have a double and sometimes triple chin. Your hair is usually plentiful and often untidy. Most Pisces Ascendants are not very concerned with appearance unless Venus is very strongly placed or the Sun is in Taurus or Libra. Your legs are quite short, even when you have a long torso, so sometimes you appear to be out of proportion. Your walk is a kind of saunter, slow and dreamy and you are often a good dancer. Pisces rising is the mark of the actor though not necessarily on the professional level. Like Leo, you are always on stage, not in such a show-offy way, but more as a cover-up to your true personality.

Many times you show talent in more than one field and therefore have difficulty in settling down to one area. This can create problems. Parents of Pisces rising children should point them in a constructive direction early or they may have a tendency to flounder around aimlessly and waste their considerable talent. Your urge is to create the beautiful dream on earth and you need a channel of expression for your almost mystical idealism.

PISCES ASCENDANT — ARIES SUN

If you were born between March 21st and April 20th between approximately 3 AM and 5 AM, you may have this combination.

The delicate perception of Pisces and the dynamic and outgoing exuberance of Aries can denote a person whose insight and energies work harmoniously to good purpose. There is a cohesiveness about this combination that makes it potentially competent and enables you to present a solid front to the world. It can also show one who is torn between making the self a vital part of life or running away from the world. The choice is yours. Pisces demands broad impersonal participation in life, while Aries operates on a much more personal level, one that brings recognition of the ego. This ego need is highlighted if the Sun is in the assertive Aries or expressive Leo decanate.

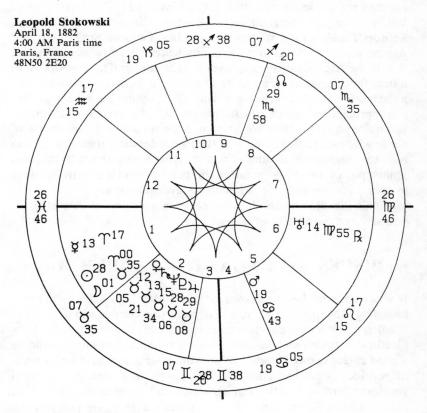

Leopold Stokowski
April 18, 1882
4:00 AM Paris time
Paris, France
48N50 2E20

Source: Church of Light (C)

The Pisces Ascendant indicates that you are self-protective and sensitive, and sometimes this comes across as overaggressiveness, a kind of compensatory reaction. But you don't really like to quarrel and you function best in a harmonious atmosphere, letting your aggression express in business enterprise. Ardent in love and friendship, you are generous, aspiring and generally a tireless, creative worker. Usually ambitious, you are not afraid to achieve and you want very much to be "someone."

With a 1st house Sun, you are often a dynamic businessperson with the drive and persistence to get ahead in the cold, cruel world. A 2nd house Sun inclines you to such fields as business management, banking or commodities trading. Whatever field you choose, the more your outlook can rise above the personal (Aries), the more you are able to use the broader, more sympathetic qualities of your Pisces Ascendant. Warren Beatty, the versatile actor, producer, director has this pairing. So does flamboyant symphony conductor, Leopold Stokowski. The Ascendant in the Scorpio decanate indicates his drive and intensity.

If the Ascendant is in the Cancer decanate, you may be drawn to a field that demands an understanding of public needs and this is like a sixth sense for you. You are usually very popular because your simple approach and desire to wind up on top of every situation makes you quite powerful. You are a strong competitor and generally a winner in whatever game you play. If the Pisces decanate rises and the Sun is in the Sagittarian decanate, you may have an interest in religion, philosophy or metaphysics. Often this combination is heavily involved in sports competition, vocationally or avocationally.

This blending symbolizes the gentle giant. You are aspiring for yourself but thoughtful of others.

PISCES ASCENDANT — TAURUS SUN

If you were born between April 20th and May 20th between approximately 1 AM and 3 AM, you may have this combination.

Persistent and sensitive, you are both ardent and affectionate, truly idealistic, intuitive and beauty loving. Art, dancing or music could be a good career choice for you. Often your charm and dashing, romantic good looks can cause trouble for you with the opposite sex, until you learn how to handle your charisma and magnetism. This blend seems to draw Taurus out of its sometimes stodgy image and you can appear as a very glamorous person.

When the Sun is in the Taurus decanate or the Scorpio decanate is rising, you project a submissive and impressionable image, but in reality you have a good idea of what you want out of life and where you are going. Cautious by nature, you are also steadfast and loyal. You have enough objectivity to recognize the overemotional pull of Pisces. When your enduring Taurus feelings are aroused, control of your feelings can be a challenge.

Basically your outlook is simple and you feel that the world is good, and "being good" is the answer to all difficulties. If the Ascendant is in the Cancer or Pisces decanate you may be plunged into emotional frustration when your too trusting attitude is invalidated. As imaginative as you are temperamental, you are often found in the creative arts, interested in many varied subjects, yet leading a full social life. Domestic stability is essential for good mental as well as physical health and you must take care not to overindulge your fondness for food and drink. Everything in moderation should be your motto.

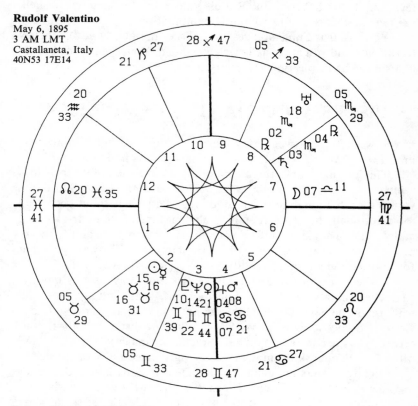

Rudolf Valentino
May 6, 1895
3 AM LMT
Castallaneta, Italy
40N53 17E14

Source: *Valentino* by Tajiri (B)

You need someone to love and do for. If the Sun is in the conscientious Capricorn decanate, your full development requires attaining mature responsibility. You tend to lose yourself in a broad philosophical outlook which must be tempered with Taurus practicality if you really want to achieve recognition. Regular habits, high goals and work that provides creative satisfaction are your greatest needs especially if the Sun is in the productive Virgo decanate.

A home in the country or a place to do some gardening will help both your physical and mental outlook. When your love is returned, you ask little else of the world. But when you lack a recipient for your affection, you can wallow in self-pity. One of the things you need to learn is discrimination in love affairs. You are often "in love with love" and this attitude may lead you down the garden path. Margot Fonteyn, the British ballerina and Rudolf Valentino, the silent screen sheik are two examples of this romantic combination.

Your Taurus Sun stabilizes your Pisces mutability and tendency to vacillate and you are usually well grounded. Your feeling for beauty is a source of inspiration for yourself and others.

PISCES ASCENDANT — GEMINI SUN

If you were born between May 20th and June 21st between approximately 11 PM and 1 AM, you may have this combination.

This pairing marks the mediator; you have the ability to lend a sympathetic Pisces ear to another's troubles, but your Gemini Sun allows you to detach enough to offer good, sound advice without becoming too emotionally involved. You have a talent for human understanding and you like people, therefore your success lies in your ability to appraise any situation coolly and dispassionately. You'll always go to bat for another person more readily than you will for yourself.

If the Pisces or Cancer decanate rises, you may be very moody: gay, cheerful and exuberant one moment, sentimentally blue and withdrawn the next. Despite blowing hot and cold at times, you need a strong domestic base for your life. Where realistic stability is concerned, you are constant. You have practical managerial capability and often fine manual skills, many times being an accomplished musician. Your greatest assets are genuine, humane sympathy and understanding, keen response and mental fertility. Your weakness is variability of the weather-vane type, and sometimes an overdeveloped social sense that covers so much casual ground that you never get around to making any lasting relationships. This is especially noted if the Sun is in the Libra decanate indicating a need for the approval of others.

Since both Gemini and Pisces are mutable signs, you feel a constant need to communicate your ideas to others and have them be a sounding board for your thoughts, particularly if the Sun is in the Gemini decanate. If you allow your dreams to carry you away, you may have a problem separating the actual truth from what you tell yourself is true. When you are young this can create difficulties between you and your parents or peers. As you mature, you can turn this liability into an asset and become a good salesperson or promoter. With the proper education, you can be a talented lawyer — courtroom type rather than corporate, unless the Sun is in the Aquarius decanate or the Scorpio decanate rises.

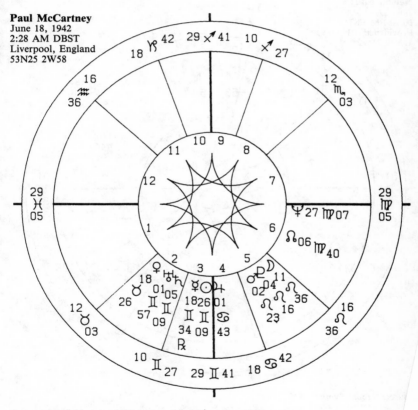

Paul McCartney
June 18, 1942
2:28 AM DBST
Liverpool, England
53N25 2W58

Source: Penfield states 2:30 AM rectified by author (DD)

With the Sun in the 3rd house, you often have writing ability, f⟩ quently in a musical direction like Beatle Paul McCartney. If the S⟩ is in the 4th house, your interests tend more to interior decorating ⟩ writing of a domestic nature such as cookbooks or romantic no⟩

Volatile, versatile and adaptable, you are often a Jack or Jill of all trades, perfectly at home in any metier.

PISCES ASCENDANT — CANCER SUN

If you were born between June 22nd and July 23rd between approximately 9 PM and 11 PM, you may have this combination.

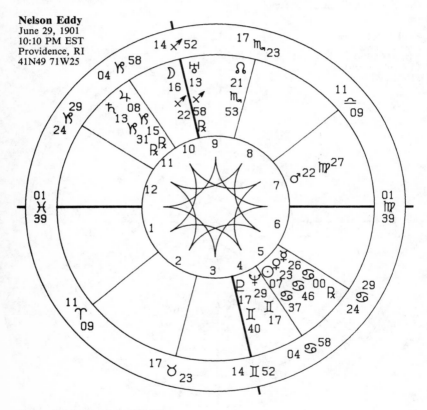

Nelson Eddy
June 29, 1901
10:10 PM EST
Providence, RI
41N49 71W25

Source: *Sabian Symbols* #309 (C)

This is a very watery pairing and what you don't pick up through perception and sensitivity is not worth relating to. You are very kind-hearted and go out of your way to help others, but you are so shrewd that every move you make seems to pay dividends. This is not conscious on your part, just something that invariably happens, especially with either the Sun or Ascendant in the wily Scorpio decanate. You always give the effect of total unarmed resistance and escaping from uncomfortable situations is your way of life. You are naturally and honestly self-protective; you know what hurts you and unconsciously avoid it. By the same token, you go out of your way to protect others.

You have a receptive listening ability that encourages people to tell you things and this is wonderful for legal, marital or astrological counseling. It may also make you a doctor with a great bedside manner. You have a natural soothing effect that suggests medicine as an ideal career especially with a 6th house Sun or the healing Pisces decanate on the Ascendant or occupied by the Sun.

You are a born romantic, usually marry well, are often religious in an orthodox way and can be a pillar of the community. This can be a combination that indicates great beauty, canny foresight and moodiness that must be dealt with before you can achieve recognition and success. Nelson Eddy, the movie baritone and Marcel Cerdan, the French boxer both had this pleasant and impressionable blend.

If your Sun is in the 5th house, you can be an excellent teacher with an innate knowledge of how to reach your students and make them want to learn. With the Sun in the 4th house, in the Cancer decanate or with that decanate rising, your family ties are strong, especially to your mother. Although strong, the tie is not always loving. Clarifying your feelings about your mother will help you deal more comfortably with your deep emotional needs. Though the professions are best for you, your native astuteness is a good business asset and with typical Cancer insight, you know well what the public wants and how to give it to them. Many times this pairing symbolizes fine musicians.

Charismatic, responsive and comforting, others seek you out as a sounding board for their ideas and plans and you are always a considerate audience.

PISCES ASCENDANT — LEO SUN

If you were born between July 23rd and August 23rd between approximately 7 PM and 9 PM, you may have this combination.

You are consistent in the basic affairs of life; express genuine kindliness, sympathy for others and a tolerant outlook. You have great appreciation, many times repaid and never forgotten for any good deed done for you. Your Pisces longing for emotional security plus your Leo affection and ardor makes you the best of lovers, mates and friends. You can show a faithful love for a partner and a passing love for an inamorata, side by side, and carry it off. The funny thing is that in both cases your feelings are true and sincere.

Robert Redford
August 18, 1936
8:02 PM PST
Santa Monica, CA
34N01 118W30

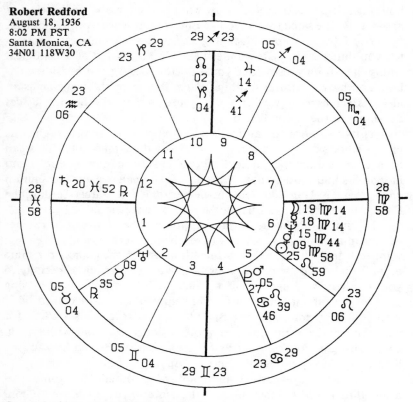

Source: Lockhart quotes Birth Certificate (A)

You may appear to be gullible and easily led, but beneath your seemingly impressionable exterior, you are one whose authority cannot be denied. You are broadminded and truly helpful especially with the Sun in the Sagittarian decanate. Your heart goes out to everyone and you wouldn't hurt a fly, but this attitude may get you into trouble. Your emotional ups and downs are legendary. Even when you are depressed, you try valiantly to cover it up. Your Leo code stresses dignity and self-respect which certainly does not allow you to show any Pisces vulnerability even when it is there. But you may also wear the Pisces mask of controlled sorrow very becomingly and get away with it, while everyone holds your hand and commiserates with you. You are always dramatically self-aware; this is the combination of the consummate actor and you probably enjoy your many changes of mood even if those around you find them hard to cope with.

If your Ascendant is in the pliable Pisces decanate, you are very impressionable, want to be someone and often are, mainly because you pour yourself into things with such abandon. With the nurturing Cancer decanate rising, you are usually very fond of children and can be a sensitive teacher or wonderful nurse for them, particularly if your Sun is in the 6th house. Creative ability in art and literature may be apparent with a 5th house Sun or if it is in the dynamic Leo decanate. You need continual encouragement if you are to achieve your aims and you sometimes lack drive in following through unless the persevering Scorpio decanate is rising. Your Pisces Ascendant depersonalizes your Leo ego and if you keep your goals in sight and your shoulder to the wheel, your emotions will fall into line and you will surprise everyone, including yourself, with your show of strength. This is especially noticeable with the Sun in the Aries decanate. Actor Robert Redford and director Alfred Hitchcock both have this dramatic and pliable pairing.

Bold and dramatic, but caring of other's feelings, you are an extremely tolerant person always ready to give others the benefit of the doubt.

PISCES ASCENDANT — VIRGO SUN

If you were born between August 23rd and September 23rd between approximately 5 PM and 7 PM, you may have this combination.

You are able to combine the intuitive qualities of Pisces with the sound discrimination of Virgo and come up with a viable working policy that makes you genuinely charitable to those who really need. You will help them to the best of your ability. What you do and how you do it is practical, founded in a common sense work-a-day world. You believe that by taking care of the little things, the big issues will resolve themselves. You usually do not get bogged down in detail because your Pisces Ascendant indicates a broad, sympathetic outlook while your Virgo Sun shows that you can find pleasure in the joy of service. Your approach is so simple and humane that no one resents your helpfulness which can be given in an advisory way. This is a big requirement in the philanthropic and social service work for which you are eminently suited.

You are often found working in hospitals, institutions, even jails, or as a probation officer, especially if the Sun is in the law-abiding

Capricorn decanate or the idealistic Pisces decanate rises. On another level you may be a skilled secretary, typist or filing clerk, happy to be doing the exacting work that others may find dull or boring. This is especially true with the Sun in the dedicated Virgo decanate. With the Sun in the 6th house, your service is willingly given in the areas of nursing, rehabilitation or anything that combines practical service with sympathy for the limited and needy. Medical work can also be symbolized by the Scorpio decanate rising. If the Sun is in the 7th house, you may be drawn to newspaper work, teaching, city or government charity and the personnel field.

Hamilton Jordan
September 21, 1944
6:07 PM EWT
Charlotte, NC
35N14 80W51

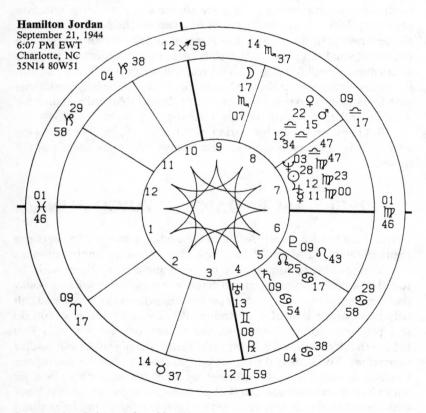

Source: Arlene Robertson from him (A)

On a personal level, you are often pulled in two different directions: your Pisces romantic inclinations at odds with your Virgo need for discrimination in personal relationships. You often marry late, devoting your early years to a demanding career, or on some occasions, to a demanding parental situation. You may be a daydreamer and escapist, seeking solace in the privacy of your illusions and dreams and passing up many opportunities because you are looking inward instead of outward.

This seems to be a pairing that is very fond of cats especially when the Ascendant is in the Cancer decanate. And you are better off nurturing pets or saving people professionally than establishing love relationships with people who need taking care of. The latter is a danger if your romantic idealism and need to serve are not channeled positively. When the Sun occupies the Taurus decanate, you may channel some of your desire for beauty and ease into making useful objects that provide comfort and pleasure in the home.

Hamilton Jordan, who served as an advisor to former President Carter, has this combination.

Your Pisces Ascendant adds a creative and imaginative touch to your neat and orderly Virgo soul.

PISCES ASCENDANT — LIBRA SUN

If you were born between September 23rd and October 24th between approximately 3 PM and 5 PM, you may have this combination.

You are gentle and kind and may allow yourself to be imposed upon rather than break off any relationship suddenly. You are truly concerned that you may hurt another person unnecessarily. You can be fooled by your feelings, becoming involved in affairs and events that you never intended. You are a salesman's favorite customer because you really have difficulty saying "no." People who care about you, and there are many, often feel that you should not be let out without a keeper. That's how ingenuous and open you are.

This combination is very creative, musical, artistic, poetic. You can often go far in any field that requires talent, charm and that makes use of beauty. This could be the decorative arts, hairdressing or interior decorating. If the Sun is in the 8th house or the Ascendant is in the Pisces or Scorpio decanate, you may have a flair for the occult; surely you have an interest. Often with the Pisces theme you make a good researcher or detective.

Carole Lombard, the zany film comedienne of the 1930s is one of the few prominent people who had this combination. It certainly does not seem to be a placement that seeks fame and public life.

Creative, emotionally perceptive and delicately balanced, you can be the most vacillating of people and drive others wild with your in-decisiveness, especially if the Sun is in the Gemini or Libra decanate. You appear to be adaptable to the ideas of others and sometimes hesitate to make a decision. However, you put in a great deal of forethought which keeps you from being as gullible as you appear. To be a real achiever you must deliberately cultivate an objective viewpoint, espe-cially if the Sun is in the 8th house. Otherwise, you may have the tenden-cy to be enmeshed in other people's subjective or hidden values and needs, allowing them to obscure your own emotional motivation.

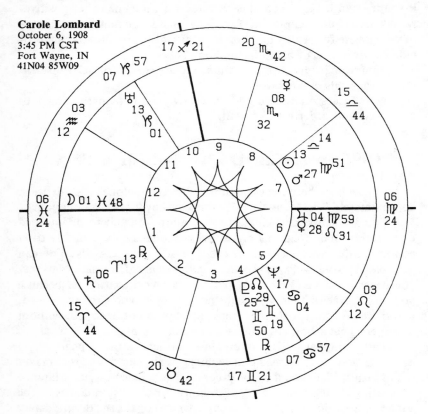

Carole Lombard
October 6, 1908
3:45 PM CST
Fort Wayne, IN
41N04 85W09

Source: *Sabian Symbols* #587 (C)

With either a 7th or 8th house Sun, your will may be directed toward others; your needs are often caught up in their needs and you desperately want to please. For this reason you seem humble and ap-peasing and often are. But no one should take you for granted. Just as sure as they do, your keen judgment, perception and intuition come to the fore and you forge ahead on your own path. You really require no help or assistance from anyone, particularly if the Sun is in the independent Aquarian decanate.

Your biggest fault is a scattering of interests; dabbling a bit here, then dashing off to see what is happening over there. Once you focus your talents and find a satisfying outlet for your energy, you can accomplish a great deal and lead a very social and rewarding life. Many times this pairing symbolizes good salespeople who are enterprisingly creative in their approach to their customers, especially if the Ascendant is in the Cancer decanate. As do all Pisces Ascendants, you have a good sense of humor and with your Libran sociability, you are much in demand on the social circuit.

Sweet and loving, you give much to others and seek to always have life run smoothly and beautifully.

PISCES ASCENDANT — SCORPIO SUN

If you were born between October 24th and November 23rd between approximately 1 PM and 3 PM, you may have this combination.

You give the appearance of being kind, gentle and easily led, but nothing could be further from the truth. You definitely have a mind of your own. Although you are emotional and experience things deeply, you have great strength of will and almost always manage to direct your energies toward goals in keeping with your own personal desires. You are often a perfectionist and have an uncanny instinct for the best. You scorn substitutes, working persistently toward your goals. Others can learn from you the fine art of discrimination. But sometimes you may carry this too far — for perfection is not really an end in itself. Able to look beneath the surface of life and other people, insight and intuition are your greatest assets.

Not always an easy person to live with, you have been called obsessive. Since you are so attuned to hidden feelings, you often ask awkward questions, refusing to accept surface appearances. Sometimes you expect others to almost read your mind — giving them credit for more intuition than they possess. If you criticize others, it not only robs them of the joy of their effort, but does not even give you much satisfaction. When people turn on you, you won't take it and tend to withdraw in self-righteous anger.

You take feelings and emotions seriously and may overreact. You are typical of the water element's self-sufficiency and seldom, if ever, admit defeat, becoming the most stubborn of people once your mind is made up. If either the Sun or Ascendant is in the Pisces decanate, worrying seems to give you pleasure; if you don't have something to worry about, you are not happy. This may sometimes cause you to develop a negative attitude. What you need most is an objective viewpoint. Faith in a divine power can be your bulwark in life. Without faith or objectivity, you may find it difficult to be either mentally or physically well and you could go through life with a series of minor illnesses, chronic in effect. Your deep emotions need recognition and a positive expression in your life.

Jack Haley, Jr.
October 25, 1933
3:21 PM PST
Los Angeles, CA
34N03 118W15

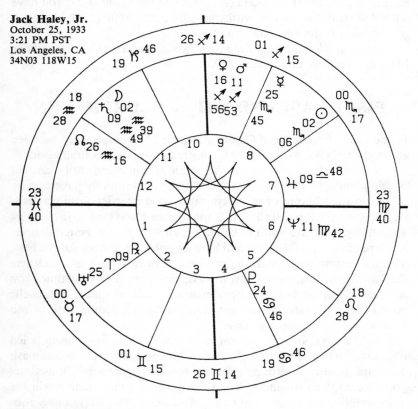

Source: Church of Light (C)

As a child, you need strict, but loving training, systematic discipline and a broad education. Life is not always easy for you as you have the knack of complicating its smallest details for yourself and others.

This is a very occult and creative position with the Sun in the 8th house. With either the Sun or Ascendant in the Scorpio decanate you are often drawn to medical fields, especially those concerned with rehabilitation. On another level, the monetary arena may attract you because of the double Scorpio theme. With the Sun in the Cancer decanate or the Ascendant there, you may have an interest in religion, finding the pomp, rites and ceremony comforting, plus the security of something to trust. If your Sun is in the 9th house, the import-export business could be a good way for you to display your knack for knowing innately what others will or will not be interested in. This position often indicates an interest in the legal field. In either case, once you learn to handle your rather intense, inward personality, there is no reason why you can't enjoy a rich and fulfilling life.

Movie producer Jack Haley, Jr. has this pairing and is a perfect example of its creative fortitude.

Your Scorpio drive is channeled through your idealistic Pisces Ascendant and you are able to winningly persuade others to your viewpoint.

PISCES ASCENDANT — SAGITTARIUS SUN

If you were born between November 23rd and December 22nd between approximately 11 AM and 1 PM, you may have this combination.

You seem to be unworldly and impractical, but this is only on the surface and in small and insignificant matters. You're a born philosopher and idealist, sympathetic, friendly and approachable. You like people individually and in crowds, and you are your best when at the head of some large enterprise that serves many or is very broad in range. History, philosophy, ethics and the social sciences all come naturally to you. You make a fine teacher, good lawyer, outstanding political reformer or a persistent promoter especially when you don't have to worry about the monetary end of your plans. Because of this you should seek a profession with a stable income or a business where money matters are taken care of by a more practical, less visionary person than you are.

Extravagance could well be your keyword. You are extravagant in all you do: from your grandiose ideas, to your exaggerated method of communicating them, and of course, in your profligate attitude toward finances. Unless you tone down your Sagittarian prodigality, you have a tendency to get carried away with yourself. With your naturally sweeping outlook, you tend to bite off more than you can chew. You may be stymied when you can't proceed according to your grand plan and have trouble understanding why the wherewithal is not forthcoming to keep you going. Planets in pragmatic Capricorn or the persistent Scorpio decanate rising show that you have the ability to be very organized, thorough and ground your grandiose ideas with realism.

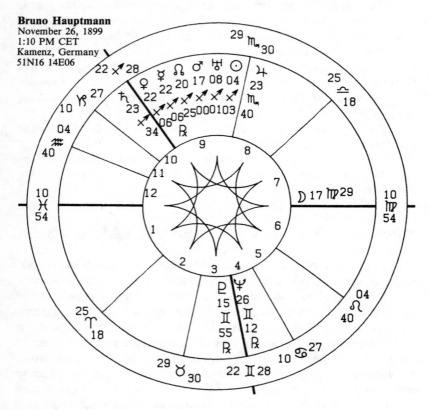

Bruno Hauptmann
November 26, 1899
1:10 PM CET
Kamenz, Germany
51N16 14E06

Source: Lyndoe in *American Astrology* (C)

With the Sun in the 9th house or in the Sagittarian decanate, you may come into contact with the law in some way as did Bruno Hauptmann, the Lindbergh baby kidnapper. With the Ascendant in the Pisces decanate, if you don't apply your energy positively (such as in sales, drama, advertising), you may be marked as a con-man, twisting and exaggerating the truth to gain your own ends.

If the Sun is in the 10th house or the Cancer decanate rises, you may be a natural leader having a sure touch with the public, knowing instinctively what appeals to them. To make the best of your many gifts you should train yourself to pay attention to details and seek out and recognize practical realities, especially if the Sun is in the impulsive Aries decanate. This seems to be a good pairing for sports, especially when the Sun is in the performing Leo decanate. You are unfailingly inspirational and this quality brings you more chances and support than most people ever get. Learn to concentrate your efforts where results and not theories pay off.

The inspired idealist; you are capable of moving masses with your emotional appeal to their dreams.

PISCES ASCENDANT — CAPRICORN SUN

If you were born between December 22nd and January 21st between approximately 9 AM and 11 AM, you may have this combination.

Responsive, you are eager for affection and liking, are very impressionable and never turn down a plea for help. Yet, you are not gullible. Your strong Saturn side curbs that tendency. You understand people. While your own personal standards may be strict and even sometimes chaste, you seldom sit in judgment and are tolerantly humane almost to the point of self-sacrifice. You would be a fine lawyer, the most honest of judges, a dedicated teacher or doctor, and your attitude toward your work is serious and profound. Music may be your hobby and relaxation and you may even make it your career. Dance is another of the arts that attracts you as it did Gwen Verdon. Her Sun in the Virgo decanate indicates her ability for the precise timing and discipline required by a dancer.

Kind, sympathetic and often paternal, especially with the Sun in the Capricorn decanate, you are usually humble and hardworking and aware of practical realities. If the imaginative Pisces decanate is rising you can seem to woolgather for a while. This confounds everyone who knows you with the idea that you will never make up your mind about what you want to do. Then one day you get it all together and there is no stopping you. This is the secret to your success. You pull all the pieces together and have your plans all worked out and then take off.

With your elevated Sun in either the 10th or 11th house, the idea of achievement appeals to you and you forge ahead with great singleness of purpose. This concentration is a repeated theme with the Scorpio decanate rising. You intend to get to the top, but on the way — and even after you arrive — you never lose sight of human values and needs especially if the caring Cancer decanate is on the Ascendant. If the Sun is in the Taurus decanate, you may have a beautiful voice and music will appeal to you — if not as a career, at least for your personal enjoyment. Often your ambitions are tied to the needs of society and therefore you make a good social worker, government employee in some area like the department of HEW or working in a field where you can help others less fortunate than you are. You have a natural ability to get along with older people so some form of geriatrics could appeal to you as an employment opportunity.

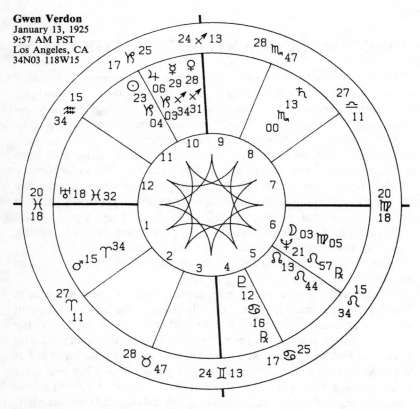

Gwen Verdon
January 13, 1925
9:57 AM PST
Los Angeles, CA
34N03 118W15

Source: Lockhart quotes Birth Certificate (A)

The sure, practical touch of your Capricorn Sun is heightened by the emotional sensitivity of your Pisces Ascendant.

PISCES ASCENDANT — AQUARIUS SUN

If you were born between January 21st and February 20th between approximately 7 AM and 9 AM, you may have this combination.

You have great powers of persuasion, though you often keep your own counsel. When you feel you will not be misunderstood, you have much to say and others are more than willing to listen to your ideas.

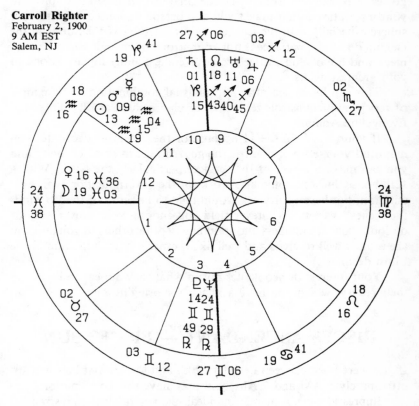

Carroll Righter
February 2, 1900
9 AM EST
Salem, NJ

Source: Celebrity Horoscopes *by Gallo (C)*

You are able to combine the vision of Pisces with the practicality of Aquarius and you accept the here and now and use it in a broad context. If you are a homemaker, you make no secret of the fact that household routine bores you, but you'll do your work efficiently and without fuss and still have time for social, philanthropic and creative interests. Men with this pairing may be up to their necks in business and family responsibilities but still find time for church and fraternal obligations.

If your Ascendant is in the Scorpio decanate, you may be outspoken, somewhat critical, but you always make an effort to be constructive. You love life, with a deeply felt mystical belief in the infinite as a daily part of your existence. Sometimes you are religious, but even if you are not a churchgoer, you have a profound respect for a divine power, especially with the Pisces decanate rising. Infinitely spiritual, your inspirational flair marks you as a person of consequence in your sphere especially with the Cancer decanate rising. If the Sun is in the Gemini decanate, patience is not your strong point, but you are rarely mean and honor and justice are your code. Family loyalty is one of your greatest assets.

This can be an eccentric and unusual combination and a couple of very prominent astrologers have this placement: Carroll Righter and Evangeline Adams.

If your Sun is in the 11th house or the Aquarius decanate, you may find yourself working for the government in some capacity and you can make a career of the service, particularly the Navy. With a 12th house Sun you could also work for the government or a large institution, but here your work would tend to be more of the "behind-the-scenes" variety. Whatever field you choose, your universality of outlook, your friendliness and spontaneity draw others to you and you are usually well received and well liked, especially with the Sun in the Libra decanate.

Your interest in people lies not in what they appear to be but in their reality, which you have a knack for bringing out.

PISCES ASCENDANT — PISCES SUN

If you were born between February 20th and March 21st between approximately 5 AM and 7 AM, you may have this combination.

Impressionable, romantic and idealistic, you rarely meet a stranger. You have a universal quality about you that others respond to without knowing just what it is that attracts them. Emotional, dreamy, receptive and restless, you are the most approachable of people and are unpretentious and friendly. You really get into the swing of things and are usually in touch with all the current modes and fads.

If the Sun is in the 12th house or the Pisces decanate, or if that decanate rises, you can be somewhat reserved and secretive and your deep-rooted need for security might make you quite self-protective. But you still have an innate perception of what makes the other person tick, so people feel that they can confide in you and receive your understanding. Sometimes you don't let your right hand know what your left hand is doing and this ability to dissemble makes you a fine actor or actress. You can make any cause or act appear to be the right one if it suits your purpose. Several very successful politicians have this combination, among them German chancellor Konrad Adenaur.

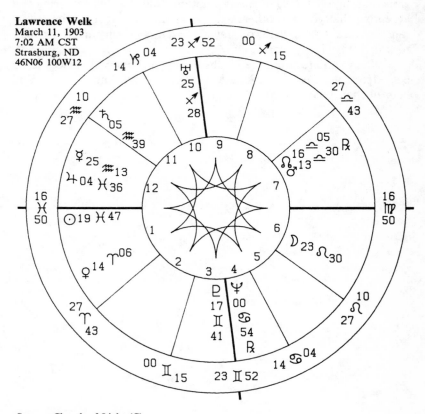

Lawrence Welk
March 11, 1903
7:02 AM CST
Strasburg, ND
46N06 100W12

Source: Church of Light (C)

With the Cancer decanate involved with either the Sun or Ascendant, basically you are kind and charitable, aware of the woes of the world and willing to work to help alleviate them. At least you are always interested, even if you are sometimes too lazy to do much about it. Often you are creative, musical (bandleader Lawrence Welk) and imaginative with a poetic flair for literature, the arts or photography.

You tend to be worrisome and function at your best when you keep busy and do not allow yourself too much time to brood. When things do not go right for you, you may withdraw into a "reality" where everyone but you is wrong. When you are in this state, you try to isolate yourself from everyone and may get along only because those closest to you feel sorry and make an effort to accommodate you. This is especially noted when the Scorpio decanate is on the Ascendant or the Sun is there, symbolizing an intensely emotional nature. Remembering and accepting that you and others are human and the world is limited — and not ideal — will help you stay in consensual reality and not retreat to a private fantasy world.

When you are using the idealism and spirituality of Pisces to its best effect, there is no one kinder, more understanding of others and helpful than you.

APPENDIX 1

HOW TO FIND YOUR ASCENDANT

The Ascendant is calculated according to the time of birth. Below is a simplified illustration (Figure #1) of how this works. As you can see, if you are born between 8 AM and 10 AM, your Sun will most likely be in the 11th house. If you were born between 2 PM and 4 PM, the Sun should be in the 8th house. Naturally, this is an approximation. The farther north or south of the Equator you are born, the more likely there is a distortion. Daylight Savings or War time have to be taken into consideration also. The best way for you to find your Ascendant is to have your chart figured by a computer or a professional astrologer. [See the last page of this book for information on how to order an accurate, computer-calculated chart from Astro Computing Services.] If you do not know what time you were born, try reading the descriptions for your Sun with each different Ascendant. You may find one that fits you.

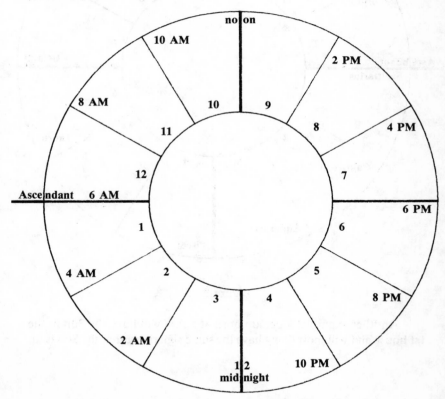

Figure 1: Placement of Sun in Horoscope

The sign the Sun is in and the time of day you are born determine your rising or ascending sign. For example: if you were born on May 1st, you are a Taurus. If you happen to be born at 7 PM, your Sun should be in the 6th house and either Scorpio or Sagittarius will be on the Ascendant. This is quite easily figured out by referring to Figure #2.

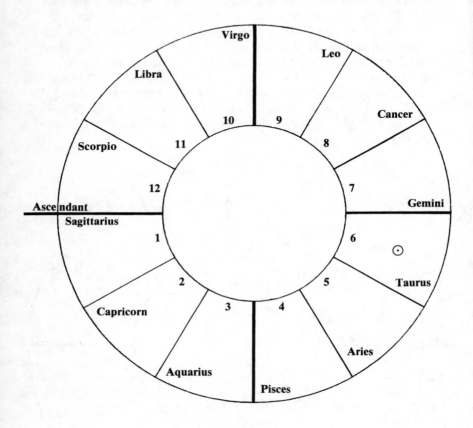

Figure 2

Another example: a person born at 5 AM will have the Sun in the 1st house and will most likely have the same sign rising that the Sun is in.

RULERSHIPS

Each sign of the zodiac has a ruling planet; these are as follows:

♈	**Aries** is ruled by **Mars**	♂
♉	**Taurus** is ruled by **Venus**	♀
♊	**Gemini** is ruled by **Mercury**	☿
♋	**Cancer** is ruled by the **Moon**	☽
♌	**Leo** is ruled by the **Sun**	☉
♍	**Virgo** is ruled by **Mercury**	☿
♎	**Libra** is ruled by **Venus**	♀
♏	**Scorpio** is ruled by **Pluto** and **Mars**	♇ and ♂
♐	**Sagittarius** is ruled by **Jupiter**	♃
♑	**Capricorn** is ruled by **Saturn**	♄
♒	**Aquarius** is ruled by **Uranus**	♅
♓	**Pisces** is ruled by **Neptune**	♆

References in the text to the ruling planet correspond to the above list. Of course, any planet can appear in any of the twelve signs or twelve houses, so there is an infinite variety of placements possible for personal expression. It would be impossible to consider, in print, all of the various combinations.

ELEMENTS

The twelve signs of the zodiac are divided into four groups which each have common characteristics. This division is by elements. The Fire signs are Aries, Leo and Sagittarius. As a group, they are initiating, enthusiastic and outgoing. The Earth signs are Taurus, Virgo and Capricorn which are somewhat practical, steady and conservative. The Air signs, Gemini, Libra and Aquarius are generally communicative, people-oriented and mental. The Water signs, Cancer, Scorpio and Pisces are the feeling signs, receptive and deep.

DECANATES

Each sign is divided into three decanates, corresponding to the element of that sign. For example: Virgo — the first 10 degrees relate entirely to the sign of Virgo and would be wholly ruled by Mercury, the ruler of Virgo. The second 10 degrees are related to Capricorn and Saturn would be considered as an important key. The last 10 degrees have a Taurus overlay and Venus, the ruler of Taurus, should be considered

DECANATE TABLE

SIGN		1st Decanate 0°- 9° 59′		2nd Decanate 10°- 19° 59′		3rd Decanate 20°- 29° 59′
Aries Date	♈	Aries 3/21-3/30	♌	Leo 3/31-4/9	♐	Sagittarius 4/10-4/20
Taurus Date	♉	Taurus 4/20-4/30	♍	Virgo 5/1-5/10	♑	Capricorn 5/11-5/20
Gemini Date	♊	Gemini 5/20-5/31	♎	Libra 6/1-6/10	♒	Aquarius 6/11-6/21
Cancer Date	♋	Cancer 6/22-7/1	♏	Scorpio 7/2-7/12	♓	Pisces 7/13-7/23
Leo Date	♌	Leo 7/23-8/2	♐	Sagittarius 8/3-8/12	♈	Aries 8/13-8/23
Virgo Date	♍	Virgo 8/23-9/1	♑	Capricorn 9/2-9/12	♉	Taurus 9/13-9/23
Libra Date	♎	Libra 9/23-10/3	♒	Aquarius 10/4-10/13	♊	Gemini 10/14-10/24
Scorpio Date	♏	Scorpio 10/24-11/2	♓	Pisces 11/3-11/12	♋	Cancer 11/13-11/23
Sagittarius Date	♐	Sagittarius 11/23-12/1	♈	Aries 12/2-12/11	♌	Leo 12/12-12/22
Capricorn Date	♑	Capricorn 12/22-12/31	♉	Taurus 1/1-1/10	♍	Virgo 1/11-1/21
Aquarius Date	♒	Aquarius 1/21-1/30	♊	Gemini 1/31-2/9	♎	Libra 2/10-2/20
Pisces Date	♓	Pisces 2/20-3/1	♋	Cancer 3/1-3/10	♏	Scorpio 3/11-3/21

in reading this segment. In other words, each decanate is ruled by the planets associated with the other two signs of the triplicity (element). In this case, the Earth sign triplicity is Taurus, Virgo and Capricorn.

The Table of Decanates on page 282 lists general dates for the Sun in each decanate. You must realize that the dates given at the beginning of each combination are only approximate. The Sun does not enter each sign on the same day every year. One year, for instance, the Sun will enter Cancer on July 22nd and the next year, it will enter Cancer on July 23rd. but its entry into each sign is around the same day.

HOUSES

It is important for the reader to have a frame of reference for the houses of the horoscope. The affairs of the house that the Sun is in assume great importance in the life. Several astrology books have been written just on the subject of houses, but you only need a few keywords for each house.

1st house: This is the house of self-projection, your early childhood experiences, your appearance and personality.

2nd house: This is the area of the chart that indicates finances, possessions, self-worth and values.

3rd house: Here we find brothers, sisters, neighbors, early schooling, short trips and how you communicate.

4th house: This is home and family, real estate, heredity and background.

5th house: Creative ability shows here as well as romance, children, sports and speculation.

6th house: This is the house of health, how you perform your work, habits, pets, tenants and wardrobe.

7th house: Face-to-face relationships show here, also partnerships; how you relate to the public and your attitudes toward marriage.

8th house: This is the house of other people's support, their values, sex, tax matters, transformation.

9th house: Long distance travel, higher education, religion and philosophy and legal matters are all the province of this house.

10th house: This house represents your honor, ambition, career, business and one of the parents.

11th house: Long range goals, social activities, income from business and career, as well as friends and outside circumstances show here.

12th house: Behind the scenes activity, faith, inspiration, places of confinement, research and public welfare are found here.

The field of astrology is fascinating and extensive. Readers who wish to study more intensively are referred to the list of publications found in this work, especially *The Only Way To... Learn Astrology* series.

APPENDIX 2
HOROSCOPES BY ASCENDANT
ARIES ASCENDANT

Cale Yarborough
Barbra Streisand
Dean Martin
John D. Rockefeller
Princess Margaret Rose
Jack Valenti

Eddie Rickenbacker
Joseph McCarthy
Bette Midler
John DeLorean
Douglas MacArthur
Jim Backus

TAURUS ASCENDANT

Pearl Bailey
William Randolph Hearst
F. Lee Bailey
Gerald Ford
Amelia Earhart
Taylor Caldwell

Suzanne Somers
Robert Kennedy
Ludwig von Beethoven
Martin Luther King, Jr.
Angela Davis
Liza Minelli

GEMINI ASCENDANT

Gregory Peck
Tom Snyder
Henry Kissinger
Phyllis Diller
Julia Child
Cass Elliott

Guiseppe Verdi
George Patton
James Doolittle
Johannes Kepler
John Barrymore
Harry Belafonte

CANCER ASCENDANT

William Backhaus
Cher
Burl Ives
Henry Cabot Lodge
Lucille Ball
Lily Tomlin

Truman Capote
Ed Davis
Cathy Rigby
Alexander Woollcott
Bishop James Pike
Nicolai Rimsky-Korsakov

LEO ASCENDANT

Anita Bryant
Robert Peary
Marilyn Monroe
Olivia deHavilland
Alex Haley
Lyndon Baines Johnson

Eugene O'Neill
Pablo Picasso
Jane Fonda
Muhammad Ali
Jackie Robinson
Rudolf Nureyev

VIRGO ASCENDANT

Henrik Ibsen
Charlotte Bronte
Thomas Mann
Ernest Hemingway
Rosalynn Carter
Peter Sellers

Montgomery Clift
Dick Cavett
Emily Dickinson
Richard Nixon
Carol Channing
Patty Hearst

LIBRA ASCENDANT

Kareem Abdul Jabbar
Adolph Hitler
Jacques Cousteau
Nelson Rockefeller
Ethel Barrymore
Theodore Dreiser

John Lennon
Princess Grace
Uri Geller
David Bowie
Max Baer
Elizabeth Taylor

SCORPIO ASCENDANT

Gloria Steinem
Glen Campbell
Sylvia Porter
Clifford Odets
Benito Mussolini
Johann von Goethe

Mohandas Gandhi
Billy Sunday
Mark Twain
Dr. Tom Dooley
Ronald Reagan
Victor Hugo

SAGITTARIUS ASCENDANT

Marlon Brando
Robert Browning
Frank Lloyd Wright
Mary Baker Eddy
Bernard Baruch
Jackie Cooper

Eleanor Roosevelt
Bob Mathias
Jimi Hendrix
Conrad Hilton
Charles Lindbergh
Jackie Gleason

CAPRICORN ASCENDANT

Arturo Toscanini
Queen Elizabeth II
Robert Schumann
George Steinbrenner
Dustin Hoffman
Sophia Loren

Maury Wills
Erwin Rommel
J. Paul Getty
J. Edgar Hoover
Alan Alda
Adelle Davis

AQUARIUS ASCENDANT

Thomas Jefferson
Walter Slezak
Errol Flynn
George Sand
Jill St. John
H.G. Wells

F. Scott Fitzgerald
Robert Louis Stevenson
Helen Gahagan Douglas
Billy Mitchell
James Hoffa
Shelley Berman

PISCES ASCENDANT

Leopold Stokowski
Rudolf Valentino
Paul McCartney
Nelson Eddy
Robert Redford
Hamilton Jordan

Carole Lombard
Jack Haley, Jr.
Bruno Hauptmann
Gwen Verdon
Carroll Righter
Lawrence Welk

INDEX OF HOROSCOPES — ALPHABETICAL

All chart sources are indicated and classified according to Lois Rodden's system:

A = Accurate Data
B = Biographies or Autobiography
C = Caution, no source of origin
D = Dirty Data, more than one time/date/place

INDEX

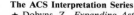

We calculate... You delineate!